Haight-Ashbury, Psychedelics, and the Birth of Acid Rock

Haight-Ashbury, Psychedelics, and the Birth of Acid Rock

ROBERT J. CAMPBELL

Revised and Edited by
David P. Szatmary

**EXCELSIOR
EDITIONS**

Cover photo: Common People - May 29, 2016: Scottish singer Bobby Gillespie lead singer of Primal Scream performing live on stage at Common People Southampton Festival, Southampton, May 29, 2016, in Hampshire, UK. Shutterstock

Published by State University of New York Press, Albany

Excelsior Editions is an imprint of State University of New York Press

For information, contact State University of New York Press, Albany, NY
www.sunypress.edu

Library of Congress Cataloging-in-Publication Data

Names: Campbell, Robert J., 1950–2016, author. | Szatmary, David P., 1951– editor.
Title: Haight-Ashbury, psychedelics, and the birth of acid rock / Robert J. Campbell ; revised and edited by David P. Szatmary.
Description: Albany : State University of New York Press, 2023. | Series: Excelsior editions | Includes bibliographical references and index.
Identifiers: LCCN 2022041860 | ISBN 9781438493367 (pbk. : alk. paper) | ISBN 9781438493350 (ebook)
Subjects: LCSH: Rock music—Social aspects—California—San Francisco—History—20th century. | Psychedelic rock music—History and criticism. | Rock music—1961–1970—History and criticism. | Hallucinogenic drugs—Social aspects—United States—History—20th century. | Hippies—California—San Francisco—History—20th century. | Merry Pranksters. | Haight-Ashbury (San Francisco, Calif.)—History.
Classification: LCC ML3917.U6 C34 2023 | DDC 306.4/8426097946109046—dc23/eng/20230113
LC record available at https://lccn.loc.gov/2022041860

10 9 8 7 6 5 4 3 2 1

Contents

Illustrations

Preface

This book has an interesting history.

Bob Campbell—I called him Wildman—was born and raised in Colorado and became a talented pianist at an early age, a fact I learned after his premature death from pancreatic cancer in late 2016. I met Bob in graduate school at Rutgers University in 1973. When we first met, we immediately became friendly as kindred spirits. We both had similar backgrounds and ways of looking at the world. He studied English and wrote a dissertation about Jack Kerouac, eventually meeting many of the Beats such as Allen Ginsberg, Gregory Corso, and William Burroughs. Unfortunately, Kerouac passed away in 1969, and Bob never met him. Bob and I formed a very short-lived band called the Fabulous Fleshtones for one of Bob's legendary parties, at which he invited all the people living in New Brunswick, New Jersey, including the street people, who hung around the train station, where he posted notices for the party.

Not only an amazing person, Bob was one of the most humble, understated, and surprising human beings that I ever met. One day, Bob mentioned that he ran around the neighborhood for some exercise. I asked him, "Bob, do you run much?" He said, "Yeah." "How far did you run?" I asked. "Oh, I don't know, maybe twenty miles," he replied. Being a non-runner, I asked Bob if he was any good. "Sure," Bob mumbled, "I won first place in the state track meet and got a full track scholarship to the University of Colorado." I looked at him in wonderment. "How did you do in college?" I continued. "Oh, OK, I guess, our team took fifth place nationally, and I ran against Steve Prefontaine."

A few years later, Bob took the bus to New York City to run in the New York Marathon. He partied the night before the race and woke up on someone's lawn. Late for the race, Bob ran several miles to the starting line and then finished the marathon in respectable time. In later life, Bob ran at least two miles, sometimes many more, for fourteen straight years without missing a day, including times, when he left the hospital to run later in the day.

Bob's breathtaking feats didn't end there. When I once asked him about his involvement in the '60 protests, he shrugged and said, "I belonged to SDS at the university and once took over a radio station to protest the Vietnam War. Under the Freedom of Information Act, I wrote to the FBI, but couldn't afford the Xeroxing costs because my file was so large."

Like most of the Haight residents, Bob was always curious and exploring new ideas, avenues, and possibilities. When Bob, I, and my wife Mary C. Wright were walking down the street in New York City one day in 1974, Bob noticed an ad for a band called Richard Hell and the Voidoids. Despite my reluctance, Bob insisted that we go to the Bowery. We made it to CBGB's and all became lifelong punk fans, going to see a legendary concert on New Year's Eve with Patti Smith and others.

After graduate school, Bob and I moved from the East Coast yet kept in touch with each other. We exchanged tapes, usually at Christmas, of some of the most amazing and awful music ever produced. In addition to such favorites as Wild Man Fischer, Furious Pig, and the Bonzo Dog Band, we discovered some crooners, who couldn't sing and, of course, William Shatner warbling his rendition of "Lucy in the Sky with Diamonds." Bob also sent me staggeringly brilliant letters sprinkled with quotes from everyone from T. S. Eliot to Rabelais.

To make a living, Bob worked at various jobs including as a contributor to and editor of the *Colorado Springs Independent* and, for sixteen years, as a teacher at Colorado Springs' Palmer Night School, an alternative school for at-risk youth.

About a dozen years ago, Bob sent me a manuscript about the '60s and asked me to read it. Though I had published a book about rock and roll, I didn't have many connections in publishing and couldn't really point him in the direction of a publisher. I didn't think anything else about the manuscript until three years ago, when Richard Carlin, a former editor of some of my books, who had been very helpful, became acquisitions editor at SUNY Press and asked if I had any ideas about manuscripts that he might find interesting. I asked him about Bob's acid-infused Haight-Ashbury material, and he indicated that he had at least a preliminary interest. Unfortunately, Bob had passed away a few years before and his partner, Terry Gretsky, and his daughter, Chantry, couldn't find it. They mentioned that Bob's records, thousands of books, posters, and papers had been put in storage after his death, and water had seeped into the storage locker, ruining much of it.

A year passed, when I received an email from Terry and Chantry saying that they had found what they thought was the manuscript and asked if I still wanted it. They sent it to me, slightly stained from the flooded storage bin. I sent it to Richard, he liked it, and it was approved by SUNY Press. Well, the result is in your hands with a little editing and revising from yours truly. In the true spirit of '60 Haight-Ashbury, I hope you have as much fun reading this book as I did, and may it change your way of looking at reality.

—Dave Szatmary

1

Setting the Stage

For the modes of music are never disturbed without unsettling of the most fundamental political and social conventions.

—Plato, *The Republic*, Book 4

Louis Armstrong once said, "You have to love to play," which can be taken in three ways. To perform jazz well, you have to: (1) be able to love, whether it be music or another person; (2) have a sense of play; and (3) take pleasure in performing. One of two key factors driving the Haight-Ashbury counterculture phenomenon—at least with the individuals who contributed most to its rise and fostered the instances of creativity that remain of interest over a half century later—was altered consciousness put into "play." Haight-Ashbury evolved out of a desire to see anew, to experiment with new perceptual styles, to expand consciousness—and then put it all into communal play. The entire Haight-Ashbury scene could not have developed as it did, however, if consciousness-changing psychedelics weren't an explosively catalytic factor in the mix.

Early on, Haight-Ashbury culture was an experiment in and celebration of a playful, gentle mode of liberated counterconsciousness. Those exercising it believed that it would lead to a new mode of being and, hence, a new society—if not a new world. Consciousness-altering drugs, marijuana included, were perceived as a tool toward *that* end.

The demise of Haight-Ashbury demonstrates with crystal clarity that mere drug use produces nothing. In fact, the Haight-Ashbury scene deteriorated in almost direct proportion to the extent that drugs became the point. The meaning of psychedelics is linked directly to the quality of the consciousness: the creativity, keen intelligence, and psychological vitality of the user. The counterculture lost its vitality and direction the more getting high became a substitute for creative input and imaginative endeavor.

Once drugs began to be treated as an end instead of a means, the sense of play giving rise to and animating the counterculture—"play" as in playing baseball, music, or chess—gave way to spacing out and mere hedonistic, self-indulgent, and self-glorifying excess. Meaningful contribution receded into imitative role-playing; exploratory pioneering lapsed into cosmic tourism; and exercise of interesting intelligence dissipated into airheaded non-entity, wowie-zowie deadweight.

While the creators of the Haight-Ashbury scene envisioned psychedelic drugs as a kind of software program by which to enhance one's own creativity and originality, increasing numbers of adherents used drugs in the manner of playing video games: something done for its own sake, with no point or purpose beyond the game itself. Timothy Leary—himself alternately a heavy hitter and an airhead (and you're never quite sure which is which)—put it succinctly in *The Politics of Ecstasy:* "Dropping out is the hardest yoga of all." All too many dropped out in an in an adolescent, dysfunctional avoidance of anything hard.

This difference of mindset constituted the crucial difference between Haight-Ashbury as it existed in the fall of 1965, when it was coalescing and gathering momentum, and Haight-Ashbury as it existed by 1968, when, ironically, its zenith of popularity brought about its rapid decline.

Drugs like LSD, mescaline, and psilocybin were a crucial catalyst of the counterculture, not its cause or its goal. Experimenting with psychedelics was but one factor in the vast array of wheel-within-wheel conjunctions, cross-currents, and generative overlappings that brought Haight-Ashbury into almost accidental being. And what was most joyful and life-giving about it was that it resided in splashing about in those giddy eddies and swirls.

Alternative consciousness, however, is not something one simply puts on like a shirt purchased at the identity boutique. It's a shirt one makes through exercise of attention, creativity, and craftsmanship in the creation of something pleasing, rewarding, and worthwhile. What the "flower child" never understood is that Haight-Ashbury was not a place you simply moved into. Haight-Ashbury in its full array of interrelated social, cultural, spiritual, political, musical, and artistic permutations was the fruit of a relatively small group of intelligent, creative people—most of them college age or older— striving to fashion "scenes" by which to live their lives in as interesting a fashion as possible. It was the fruit of their efforts to *create* these scenes that gave rise to Haight-Ashbury and evolved into "the '60s."

Haight-Ashbury was the product not of any movement or apocalyptic agenda, but rather of a number of separate scenes—some of them (as with Ken Kesey and the Merry Pranksters) already years in the making—coming into generative interaction in the summer and fall of 1965. It was at its vital best when, to quote Dylan, it was "busy being born": the period *before* it was discovered and played to the hilt by the media; *before* it was inundated by the wannabe hordes. Haight-Ashbury was at its peak when it was still local and small, a loose array of semi-interrelated convergences and semi-independent propensities that would interweave and reinforce one another to become something far larger than the sum of its parts. It was that early-on, still-in-the-making Haight-Ashbury, not the Summer of Love version that released a torrent of pent-up creativity, which eclipsed the all-dressed-up-with-nowhere-to-go quandary of the previous decade.

It is impossible to understand that time-and-place convergence, however, without an understanding of the general history of LSD in the twenty years leading up to the '60s.

The Trip Begins: The First Time

In life all finding is not the thing we sought, but something else.

—Ralph Waldo Emerson, *Journals* (April 11, 1863)

LSD was first synthesized in 1938 as part of a research project totally unrelated to "psychedelics." Sandoz Pharmaceuticals of Basel, Switzerland, was conducting research on rye fungus (ergot) in hopes of discovering a medicinal circulatory stimulant. Dr. Albert Hofmann was in charge of the project. By April 1943—eight years into the project—Hofmann had synthesized dozens of compounds from ergot without discovering the circulatory stimulant he was after. Acting on a nagging hunch, he went back to the twenty-fifth compound—LSD-25—to take another look. On Friday, April 16, he synthesized a new batch of the compound. In the course of preparing it, he absorbed a tiny amount through his fingertips, an accidental "dosing," which would snowball monumentally over the next twenty years. Describing the ensuing experience in his book, *LSD: My Problem Child,* Hofmann reported that he was "seized by a peculiar restlessness associated with a sensation of mild dizziness . . . I lay down and sank into a kind of drunkenness, which was not unpleasant and which was characterized by extreme activity of the imagination. As I lay in a dazed condition with my eyes closed . . . there surged upon me an uninterrupted stream of fantastic images of extraordinary plasticity and vividness, accompanied by an intense kaleidoscope-like play of colors" (Campbell 1971, 66).

Hofmann's experience—a three-hour, kaleidoscopic, perceptual experience of "striking reality and depth"—is key to understanding the Haight-Ashbury counterculture, from psychedelic music to the posters, light shows, tie-dyed, "freaky" apparel, and the desire to "freak freely" in a festively communal, mutually supportive fashion. It is no coincidence that Hofmann's account of his LSD experience—the "uninterrupted stream of fantastic images of extraordinary plasticity and vividness, accompanied by an intense kaleidoscopic-like play of colors"—perfectly describes a light show during a psychedelic dance concert at the Avalon Ballroom or the Fillmore Auditorium.

As would be the case with so many after him, Hofmann was sufficiently impressed by this experience that three days later he decided to explore further. He ingested 250 micrograms of LSD-25 and, forty minutes later, began experiencing dizziness, unrest, difficulty in concentrating, and a compulsion to laugh at nothing in particular and everything in general. He rode his bicycle home, soaring on acid. The scientist described this "trip":

> Everything seemed to sway and the proportions were distorted like reflections in the surface of moving water. Moreover, all the objects appeared in unpleasant, constantly changing colors, the predominant shades being sickly green and blue. When I closed my eyes, an unending series of colorful, very realistic and fantastic images surged in on me. A remarkable feature was the manner in which all acoustic perceptions (e.g. the noise of a passing car) were transformed into optical effects, every sound evoking a corresponding colored hallucination constantly changing in shape and color like pictures in a kaleidoscope. (Winter 2019, 125)

Hofmann was impressed, perplexed, and curious. Sandoz persisted (as would be the case with psychedelic acolytes in subsequent decades) in exploring LSD for potential medicinal applications. This research piqued the interest of the scientific community, and LSD began to be explored for possible applications in a number of areas, including psychological disorders, mental illness, and alcoholism.

One of the first people outside Sandoz to enter this research realm was Walter Stoll, a Zurich psychiatrist who was the son of Hofmann's supervisor at Sandoz. Stoll was the first person to experiment with LSD on people, and he published his findings in 1947. His report caused a sensation in the field of psychology, stimulating a flood of new research and scientific papers. Sensing potentially astronomical profits, the worldwide pharmaceutical industry began experimenting with and synthesizing mind drugs for use in psychological research and therapy—research that would produce such drugs as Thorazine, Valium, and Librium. Sandoz, meanwhile, began making LSD available to psychologists, psychiatrists, and lab scientists doing research on mental disorders.

There was a huge surge in the fields of psychology and psychoanalysis in the years following World War II. In 1940, less than three thousand psychiatrists practiced in the United States, a number that more than doubled a decade later. By 1956, more than fifteen thousand psychiatrists held membership in the American Psychological Association.

As this field boomed, it split off into a number of different camps, each having its theory as to the nature of the brain and/or consciousness. To cite but a few examples, the Freudians saw the mind in layered fashion as the id (the unconscious,), the ego (the waking, workaday mind), and the superego (the policeman enforcing social conditioning and norms), with the id being the wild card in behavior and therapy. The behaviorists, meanwhile, perceived the mind mechanistically and dismissed the unconscious as a myth. Extrapolating from data derived from tests on pigeons and mice, they described the human mind—hence, consciousness and behavior—as the function of a complex of stimulus-response influences. Still other researchers envisioned the brain in chemical terms, viewing mental disorder as a function of disrupted chemical balances that could be adjusted and manipulated through external intervention via drugs.

Within this context during the 1950s, research involving LSD, mescaline, peyote, and the like occurred. Most often, these drugs were used as psychometrics—that is, mimickers of madness. They were administered to patients to simulate schizophrenic-like episodes (and other mental dysfunctions) for study and treatment.

LSD and the Exploration of the Mind

I know who I was when I got up this morning, but I must have changed several times since then.

—Lewis Carroll, *Alice in Wonderland* (1865)

The 1950s witnessed a growing interdisciplinary interest between psychology, philosophy, linguistics, literature, and art about the nature of reality—or, to put it another way, the question of whether there *is* such a thing as an objective, fixed reality. If so, what is it? Can it be named, described, articulated, or pointed to? Exactly what would one be pointing to? Where do we look to locate and explore it: inside one's head; in language; the laws of physics; religion; ideology; emotions; pure positivistic fact? To put this question another way, is reality merely a reflection—the assumption that there is a corresponding, nuts-and-bolts referent for certain absolute actions we take for granted—as, for example, with such terminology as soul, God, the id/ego/superego, nature/human nature?

These questions go to the very heart of society and social order and our picture of reality. Is what we call reality nothing more than a learned and enforced social convention that changes with time, place, circumstance, and context? Is it merely an intellectual construct, a function of the linguistic structure into which one is born, what poet Wallace Stevens calls a "necessary fiction"?

Earlier in the century, intellectual figures like Canadian psychologist Richard Bucke, French philosopher Henri Bergson, American philosopher/psychologist William James, and Polish-American semanticist Alfred Korzybski proposed theories that—to facilitate both functional efficiency and physical survival—the physical brain filters out the vast majority of data available to perception at any given moment. There is a vast array of things going on and available to perceive that, in the act of perceptual apprehension, are filtered out, ignored, or reduced into insignificance. This filtered data, however, is every bit as much a part of reality as the edited, constructed, and arranged data the perceiver typically acts upon. Our normal, workaday reality is, in this view, a fiction: a convenient construct we agree to accept and act upon as reality.

These theorists argued, however, that in the "real world"—that is, the world as it exists separate from any act of human intervention and interpretation—there is no such thing as a dollar, a mile, a week, a pound, a quart, a degree of Fahrenheit (or centigrade), or a boundary line between Canada and the U.S. (or North and South Carolina, or the Indian and Pacific Oceans). These constructs are mere conventions, convenient abstractions, and necessary fictions. They exist solely in the mind, but we make them real by behaving *as though* they are real (which sounds like the teachings of a Freudian therapist or Zen master).

But it's even more complicated and problematic. One's apprehension—one's arrangement and interpretation—of reality (the totality of what is transpiring "out there" at any given moment) is a function of a vast array of personal factors: mood (optimistic or depressed, stressed or relaxed, happy or sad); physical state (fatigue, illness, sexuality); age; prior experience; intelligence; attentiveness; and a host of other needs, preferences, and priorities of the moment. The process of perceptual apprehension—the process of making the outside inside—transforms, deforms, reduces, contours, interprets, constructs, and construes reality. Any two people presented with the same poem, symphony, speech, sermon, fiscal forecast, movie, painting, or potential sexual partner will internally register and respond to very different things. In fact, any single person apprehends differently at different times. Which version—which act of apprehension—is real? Can there be said to be an ultimately true, correct, real version, or is everything a version? It goes without saying that the Stalinist, Cold Warrior, Muslim fundamentalist, and born-again Christian holds that there is an ultimate, highest reality.

How would consciousness be transformed if a chemical means were found to circumvent or shut off this filtering, distortive, reductive mechanism? Would that constitute a doorway to madness or to divinity? Would it be the avenue *to* truth/reality or a holiday *from* it?[1] Richard Bucke—a friend of Walt Whitman (who journeyed to Canada to visit him) and an influence on William James—argued in *Cosmic Consciousness* (1901) that culture-altering giants like Buddha, Jesus, Plotinus, William Blake, Honoré Balzac, and Walt Whitman experienced a massive, life-altering illumination because they found a way to step outside received, officially sanctioned consciousness and thereby gained access to a new, more comprehensive way of seeing and responding. By breaking through to a new reality—by seeing in a new way—they were able to tap into and activate a fuller range of the brain's registering capacity. It is precisely *because of* their breakthrough into ab/normal, non-workaday, non-business-as-usual modes of apprehension that we revere, read, discuss, and emulate them.

Literature has a long tradition of groundbreaking, society-changing writers, who used drugs (not the least of which was alcohol) as a tool for triggering a change in perception and thereby widen the range of consciousness available for use. Writers Samuel Coleridge and Thomas de Quincey were opium addicts. From 1844 to 1849, writers Charles Baudelaire, Gerard de Nerval, Victor Hugo, Alexandre Dumas, and Théophile Gautier gathered regularly at Le Club des Hashischins to smoke hash and marijuana. Edgar

Allan Poe experimented with the opium-based laudanum. Physician and social reformer Henry Havelock Ellis took peyote in 1887 and wrote about the experience in "Mescal: A New Artificial Paradise" (Ellis 1898). Writing in this article about a "silent and sudden illumination of all things around, where a moment before I had seen nothing uncommon," Ellis argued that "for a healthy person to be once or twice admitted to the rites of mescal is not only an unforgettable delight, but an educational influence of no mean value." He subsequently provided peyote to William Butler Yeats who, in reporting his experience, noted: "It seems as if a series of dissolving views were carried swiftly before me, all going from right to left, none corresponding with any seen reality. For instance, I saw the most delightful dragons, puffing out their breath straight in front of them like rigid lines of steam, and balancing white balls on the end of their breath" (Stevens 1987, 7).

William James—brother of novelist Henry James and venerated Harvard professor—experimented with nitrous oxide (laughing gas) and peyote (he threw up). Sigmund Freud experimented with cocaine, at one point becoming addicted. In *Uber Coca* (1884), he advocated its medicinal use. In 1924, German doctor Louis Lewin cataloged most of the world's known mind-altering plants in *Phantastica: A Classic Survey on the Use and Abuse of Mind-Altering Plants* (1924), and novelist Aldous Huxley reviewed it in the Chicago *Herald Examiner*.

Expanded Consciousness and the Layers of Reality

The eye altering, alters all.

—William Blake, "The Mental Traveler" (1863)

A man's mind is stretched to a new idea or sensation, and never shrinks back to its former dimensions.

—Oliver Wendell Holmes Sr., *The Autocrat at the Breakfast Table* (1858)

The use of mind-expanding drugs discovered by Huxley and others showed that psychedelics allowed us to remove at least some of the filters that we impose on our version of reality. In the course of going about our everyday, utilitarian lives, we constantly monitor our environment for information, which we are evaluating, narrating, arranging, and categorizing in accordance with whatever needs-of-the-moment are at the fore of attention. That processed, filtered reality—what we are really responding to from moment to moment *as* reality—is further contoured, edited, and modified by virtue of our cultural conditioning, value assumptions, experiential histories, ideological, religious, and philosophical beliefs, ingrained habits, and perceptual styles. Linguist Benjamin Whorf contended that *what* we see is largely a product of *how* we see, and *how* we see is largely a product of the language into which we are born, each language being a vehicle that arranges, categorizes, and perceives nature for its user in largely fixed and predetermined ways. Freud argued that the *what* and *how* of perception—and what we respond to *as reality*—is largely a process determined by social conditioning, parental intervention in early life, and past experience as an adult. Whatever our perceptual framework, mode, or style, what we take to be and respond to as reality at any given moment is a highly filtered (reduced, abstracted), arranged, and modified construction—this being essentially what Huxley means by the "screens" and "filters" that produce the consciousness that pervades daily life and culture.

One of the themes that resurfaces in countercultural history is that the experience of using psychedelic drugs forever changes the user's understanding of, and assumptions about, reality. Whoever passes through that door, Huxley insists, is forever a different person. As recounted by many observers, psychedelic drugs—LSD, peyote, mescaline, psilocybin—undermine our usual experience of reality by suppressing the mind's tendency to discriminate: to differentiate and categorize, filter and select, arrange and organize. Temporarily liberated from the preconceptions, value assumptions, ingrained criteria, and habits of categorizing that typically contour and shape our understanding, the perceptual faculties are freer to play, and the consequent perceptual experience is freer to unfold wherever the generative impetus leads. As writer and philosopher Alan Watts puts it, psychedelics serve to "suspend certain inhibitory or selective processes in the nervous impressions that is usual" (Watts 1962, 15). Judicious use of psychedelic drugs can help one see—apprehend, perceive, experience, feel—in profoundly different ways than before.

In my days teaching at Rutgers, I took my classes through an exercise meant to demonstrate the intimate connection between prose style and perceptual style. Giving them ten minutes for each step, the students were asked to describe the front of the room as though they were (a) writing the opening paragraph of a horror story; (b) writing an article for *Better Homes and Gardens;* (c) writing an article for *Mechanics Illustrated;* and (d) writing an article for *Rolling Stone.* Each step of the way, students were asked to articulate the kinds of things they selected for notice, what things were in the foreground and the background, and how they were described and narrated. Typically, the students readily understood that each of their articulations employed different usages—choices—of diction, syntax, and phrasing, and it subsequently dawned on them how each mode of articulation also required, if not dictated, a certain perceptual style. Each mode predisposed the apprehender not only to notice different things about the front of the room, but to evaluate, arrange, and describe those things differently in each case. It was always gratifying to watch the light—and/or confusion—come in their eyes when I asked them to decide, given that each instance ostensibly described the exact same thing (the front of the room), which of the descriptions was *better,* or even most *correct* or *accurate.*

The lesson they took away from the exercise, of course, was that considerations of "fact" and/or "truth" were more complex than they normally thought. What we selected to notice, and how we arranged, composed, attended to, interpreted, and articulated/described/narrated it, was an inextricable function of the perceptual style employed. One mode/style may be more useful, interesting, or appropriate, according to the needs of the moment, and all have their elements of truth and accuracy, but all are provisional with nothing fixed and final. As any marriage counselor, psychoanalyst, lover, or jazz musician will attest, an emotional fact can be as true, important, and relevant as a positivistic fact.

Psychedelic experience fosters this understanding, as evidenced in Blake's dictum "the eye altering alters all." Used judiciously and intelligently, LSD, mescaline, psilocybin, and peyote can serve as tools for enlarging the repertoire and widening the range of perceptual response. In lieu of the workaday, survival mode of awareness, one acquires a style of perception wherein objects—and, equally, ideas, values, principles, concepts, and categories—are seen to interrelate less as a network or grid than as a dance. One *feels* the cross-generative, interrelationship between objects, ideas, and emotions to be as important and meaning-making as the objects, ideas and, emotions themselves. Watts evokes the so-called bead game in Hermann Hesse's *Magister Ludi* (1943) as an example of this mode of perception in his *The Joyous Cosmology: Adventures in the Chemistry of Consciousness* (1962): "The game consists in playing with the relationships between configurations in various fields. The players will elucidate a common theme and develop its application in numerous directions. No two games are the same, for not only do the elements differ, but also there is no thought of attempting to force a static and uniform order on the world" (21). This description of the world apprehended as play—playing with, performing, interplay, theater, gamesmanship—is an apt account of the perspective fostered by the psychedelic experience.

Psychedelics also tend to shift perceptual orientation from linear to open-ended and from chronological to evolutionary. Alan Watts notes, for example, that "the associative couplings of the brain seem to fit simultaneously instead of one at a time" (1962, 34), resulting in an all-over, multidimensional, panoramic simultaneity of "knowing," as opposed to sequential, linear associative progressions. One's sense of time also changes, becoming more experiential, less abstract and more biological, less mechanical. Time is *experienced* more as an ongoing event-in-the-making than *understood* as a utilitarian unit of measurement.

One feels time differently. Under the influence of psychedelics, time is the time of biological rhythm, not of the clock and the time, work, and discipline of the clock. There is no hurry. Our sense of time is notoriously subjective and thus dependent upon the quality of our attention, whether of interest or boredom, and upon the alignment of our behavior in terms of routines, goals, and deadlines. As Watts pointed out, "here the present is self-sufficient, but it is not a static present. It is a dancing present: the unfolding of a pattern which has no specific destination in the future but is simply its own point" (Watts 1962, 27).

When perceptual orientation shifts from the linear, cause-and-effect sequence of the everyday event, consciousness itself becomes an integral participant in the "what happens." Consequently, the past of one's private perceptual history is brought into generative play with the in-the-making moment to create a multidimensional, multitemporal dynamic far deeper and more complicated than workaday perception. The categories normally separating past and present, objective fact (the table is wooden) with subjective fact (the table is useful) blur, or even disappear. One sees and makes sense in atypical ways, which brings all heretofore unquestioned, sacrosanct orthodoxies into question. As Aldous Huxley put it as early as 1954 in *The Doors of Perception*, the person who, under the influence of psychedelics, goes through "the door" will come back to the world a different person. One ceases to apprehend the world as a preordained, fixed collection of givens, which become fictitious and provisional. This perceptual style largely accounts for the popularity in Haight-Ashbury of the *I Ching*, wherein reality is apprehended as a momentary, still-in-the-making situation linked to, rising out of, and relevant to a confluence of forces governing *that* moment only, as opposed to a linear, cause-and-effect reality immune to and above time and circumstance.

It is typical for the person who experiences this profound sense of ontological relativity to conclude that what we take as reality is an arbitrary construct, a sociocultural convention, not an unmediated manifestation of nature. Exalted and amped, the individual apprehends this insight as a door opening out onto the divine and yearns to spread the psychedelic gospel in the manner of a religious missionary, Marxist emissary, or Johnny Appleseed. A sensibility given to "play" embraces this newfound relativity as liberating, redemptive, transforming, and empowering. The sensibility that needs certain "truths" to hold and retain their position (and, hence, ours) in the divine order of things finds this sense of relativity to be subversive, unmooring, and threatening. Indeed, the combination of heightened perceptual intensity, conceptual loosening, and sense of awe produced by psychedelics tends to foster reevaluation of one's understanding of "self" and place in the big picture. In lieu of a self that is viewed as a static unit that negotiates its way through a world "out there," the self is experienced as an active participant in and product of a vast, complex, multidimensional dance of interrelations. The givens that have heretofore guided one's behavior, choices, aspirations, and assumptions dissolve. Like Alice having passed through the looking glass, one sees differently; one exists differently.

The psychedelic experience prompts one to understand (and apprehend) reality as more of an ongoing, still-in-the-making *dynamic* than as a fixed and final construct (James's "Reality with a Big R"). This relativistic understanding of reality is hardly new in American letters. It informs Ralph Waldo Emerson's essays. It prompted Henry David Thoreau to "drop out" of society in order to "tune in" to his own consciousness and see in a more firsthand, experiential manner. It animates Herman Melville's exploration of what underlies going to sea in quest of Moby Dick (profit? entrepreneurial zeal? career opportunity? plunder? spiritual quest?). It is the central question of William James's *Pragmatism* (1907) and a frequent topic in his *The Varieties of Religious Experience* (1929). It is the generative impetus behind the remarkable stylistic experiments of Jack Kerouac's *Visions of Cody* (written during 1951 and 1952; Kerouac 1972). And, of course, it is the central theme of Leary's various psychedelic pronouncements and exhortations.

The transformative experience integral to psychedelics tends to be more volcanic than this description implies. The psychedelic experience is not a cerebral reverie with the tinkling of wind chimes, plink of sitars, and thoughts of ancient Tibet serenely wafting about. It is not an innocent stroll among the daisies in May on the way to feeding baby ducks at the pond. It is not a good idea for everyone. It is not recommended for the individual needing to retain a stable, unchanging frame of reference.

The infamous bad acid trip transpires when the sense of assumed reality which one orients oneself within the cosmos disintegrates, and brings about a panicked loss of reference. For someone experienced in psychedelics, however, that decentering experience produces feelings of liberated expansiveness, of release into new and open-ended possibilities of seeing and being. That transition from stable fixity into open-ended play is central to psychedelic culture, including music, art, and dress.

When people speak of the LSD hallucination—something I rarely experienced, but found interesting and pleasurable when it occurred—I suspect them to be referring to this disintegration of conventional frames of reference. I have read accounts of walls melting, furniture crawling, of seeing bats, and looking in the mirror to see horse heads—exhibit A being Hunter Thompson's *Fear and Loathing in Las Vegas*—but I take all this to be personal projections precipitated by the boundaries of everyday perception blending, overlapping, bending, and melding. I suspect those most prone to hallucination are those whose sense of reality is most unquestioned, unexamined, and taken for granted. I have never seen a chair melt, visited an Egyptian temple, or turned into a dragonfly. For me, the LSD hallucination is less a vision of things that are not there than it is a decentered mode of apprehending a world utterly taken for granted, a world arranged and categorized according to preconceived assumptions. Change the *way* one sees—the perceptual style, the new form of awareness—and *what* one sees changes.

Huxley hits the mark in noting that psychedelics "appear to give an enormous impetus to creative intuition" and that one sees things under their influence "the way [these things] appear when certain inhibitory processes of the brain and senses are suspended. . . . Consciousness-changing drugs are popularly associated with the evocation of bizarre and fantastic images, but in my own experience this happens only with closed eyes. Otherwise, it is simply that the natural world is endowed with a richness of grace, color, significance, and, sometimes humor, for which our normal adjectives are insufficient" (1954, 22–24).

To become aware of the vast, powerful, unbounded range of consciousness itself outside the normal perceptual framework can be wondrous, hair-raising, confusing, exalting, harrowing, revelatory, playful, and *fun*—not to mention consciousness-altering and life-transforming—sometimes all within a single psychedelic experience.

Leary quotes a passage from William James's *The Varieties of Religious Experience* (1902) that is amazingly apt in describing postpsychedelic understanding:

> Our normal waking consciousness, rational consciousness as we call it, is but one special type of consciousness, whilst all about it, parted from it by the flimsiest of screens, there lie potential forms of consciousness entirely different. We may go through life without suspecting their existence, but apply the requisite stimulus, and at a touch they are there in all their completeness, definite types of mentality which probably somewhere have their field of application and adaptation. No account of the universe in its totality can be final which leaves these other forms of consciousness quite disregarded. (388)

The most significant difference between Haight-Ashbury in 1964 to early 1966 and Haight-Ashbury thereafter can be located in how and why psychedelic drugs were generally used. The early residents of Haight-Ashbury viewed psychedelics as a tool by which to enlarge one's perception, to increase the directions one can go in any given response to the in-the-making moment, and then put those new modes of seeing into creative, meaning-making play. As the huge influx of refugees, drop-outs, teeny-boppers, wannabes, and dysfunctionals of various stripe gradually transformed the neighborhood into a media-circus ghetto, drug use—psychedelics very much included—became increasingly recreational, a way to stay stoned and avoid the problems and demands of straight existence.

Those who laid the groundwork and created Haight-Ashbury used psychedelics as an immensely interesting—and ultimately useful—vehicle for exploring the nature of consciousness. The key realization—and it's crucial—is that psychedelics are a tool, not an end. As Watts repeatedly noted, consciousness-expanding drugs are a physical aid in the same manner as are "microscopes, telescopes, cameras, scales, computers, books, works of art, alphabets." "Mystical insight is no more in the chemical itself," he noted, "than biological knowledge is in the microscope" (1962, 5). These drugs do not impart wisdom at all, any more than the microscope alone gives knowledge. They provide the raw materials of and tools for wisdom and are useful to the extent that individuals can integrate what they reveal into the whole pattern of their behavior and the entire system of their knowledge. Watts came back to this notion repeatedly. "Drugs of this kind," he intoned toward the end of *The Joyous Cosmology*, "are in no sense bottled and predigested wisdom" (83).

Such was not the attitude toward psychedelics (and drugs in general) of latter-day Haight-Ashbury drop-outs and dysfunctionals, and of the counterculture at large, after being a "hippie" degenerated into a shallow cliché, a way of dressing, talking, and behaving that one adopted like an actor trying to become a character fashioned by some playwright or screenwriter. The Haight-Ashbury pioneers tended to be far better educated, more experienced, sophisticated, and older than their Summer of Love successors. The wannabes and fugitives from mom and dad tended to view psychedelics as a ticket to the funhouse offering unlimited rides on the freaky roller coaster: getting laid, nonstop entertainment, and no job. The demise of Haight-Ashbury (and the counterculture at large) demonstrates that there is no more point to getting high per se than there is to getting drunk. Getting high, or *being* high, does not create a higher self, and treating drug use in that manner creates nothing more than a psychedelic skid row—as Haight-Ashbury became after 1968.

As noted as early as 1954 by Huxley, the key dilemma of psychedelics—and especially the attempt to make use of them as a way of life—is that the workaday world awaits you at the conclusion of each stroll through Eden. No matter how revelatory, mind-expanding, and transformative the psychedelic experience, after the first few transformative romps with the ontological platypuses and wallabies, you're basically repeating the same experience over and over—which was the essential message of Kesey's "acid-test graduation." What began as a tool for mind expansion and psychological growth became recreational. Nothing is wrong with recreation. One is taking a temporary holiday from everyday life each time one drinks a beer, has wine with dinner, or ingests an eggnog at Christmas, but what was formerly a breakthrough into new growth can degenerate into mere repetition—and as I told my writing students at Rutgers, to repeat an idea is not to develop it.

Though the first dozen or so experiences with psychedelics can be revelatory and transformative, there comes a point where continued repetition produces neither insight nor change. One gets stuck in a rut—as happened with Leary at Millbrook, Kesey at La Honda, and legions of Haight-Ashbury "heads" circa 1968 and after. One's wheels may spin at a hundred miles per hour, shooting off sparks and a holy glow, but there's no progression into new discovery or revelation. What formerly provoked revolutions in consciousness became stylized habit and lapse into cliché. What had been a catalyst for magic and growth become pathetic stasis. What, then, to do? Anyone who has "seen like Adam" is loathe to relinquish that sense of wonder described by Huxley—that sense of the world unfolding into unguessed-at splendor, possibility, and potential—that opportunity for play, doors to enter, and Eden to wander.

Pass the Acid: LSD Comes to the U.S.

If a stone be cast, there is no foreknowledge of where it may land.

—Flann O'Brien, *The Poor Mouth:*
A Bad Story about the Hard Life (1941)

By mid-century there were a good dozen research projects throughout the U.S. investigating hallucinogens and their effect on consciousness, creativity, and behavior. LSD first came to the U.S. in 1949 by way of research psychiatrist Dr. Max Rinkel, who gave it to his associate, Dr. Robert Hyde—making Hyde the first person to "trip" on these shores. Rinkel and Hyde went on to conduct an LSD study in a Harvard-affiliated mental clinic at the Boston Psychopathic Institute, testing the drug on 100 volunteers in 1949 and 1950.[2]

One of those whose interest was piqued by the possibilities of mescaline and its pharmacological cousins as a tool for researching schizophrenia was an English psychiatrist named Humphrey Osmond, who had moved to Canada in 1952 to take a position in a mental hospital in Saskatchewan.

Like almost all researchers at the time, Osmond viewed mescaline as a medical tool for inducing psychosis-like states in patients who could then be studied. Testing the drug on himself, Osmond took 400 milligrams and carefully monitored its effect on his awareness and interpretation of his surroundings. The experience convinced him that researchers misunderstood schizophrenia. Given that an ingested chemical could so utterly transform what he assumed to be reality, Osmond concluded that schizophrenics aren't deluded; they accurately report the reality of what they see and feel. Their dysfunction is not mental but chemical.

Osmond also concluded that, given how profoundly mescaline altered "normal" consciousness, the drug might prove to be a tool for gaining access to a more comprehensive—nonfiltered, nonreductive—reality. The study and exploration of this new reality might reveal volumes about the way consciousness functions in the process of making the outside inside.

Also in 1952, Osmond and his colleague John Smythies published a paper entitled "A New Approach to Schizophrenia" in which they theorized that the body under stress conditions produces a hallucinogen (in this case, metamorphosed adrenaline) that caused a change in perception that induced the individual to "turn off" reality as a maneuver for self-preservation—this being the schizophrenic state. Osmond and Smythies set out to find this hallucinogen. Osmond held in a subsequent paper, again coauthored with Smythies and published in *Hibbert Journal,* that no one can properly study schizophrenia without experiencing the state firsthand and that this state (or something very close to it) can be experienced by taking mescaline. He also argued that ingestion of mescaline provides access to the unconscious and that it behooves anyone interested in that subject to take it.

Osmond subsequently received a letter in praise of this essay from an unlikely source: novelist Aldous Huxley. Huxley invited Osmond to visit him in Los Angeles, offering himself as a guinea pig for Osmond's mescaline research. Huxley had the social pedigree, professional résumé, and intellectual credentials to make him a contact to be taken seriously. He was the grandson of T. H. Huxley, the nineteenth-century champion of Darwinism, and his mother was the niece of poet Matthew Arnold and the granddaughter of Dr. Thomas Arnold, legendary nineteenth-century headmaster of Rugby boarding school. Huxley was author of *Chrome Yellow* (1921), *Antic Hay* (1923), *Point Counter Point* (1928), and *Brave New World* (1932), an anti-utopian novel delineating a government that controls society through the dispensation and regulation of the drug "soma."

Though born and raised in England, Huxley moved to Los Angeles in 1938. He was interested in "the esoteric" as an avenue to higher states of consciousness, toward which end he studied Russian philosopher Pyotr Ouspensky and then Vedantic Hinduism under Beverly Hills guru Swami Prabhavananda. Another member of this circle was a youthful Alan Watts.

Huxley's move to the U.S. coincided with a more philosophic turn to his writing. He attempted in books like *Ends and Means* (1937) and *The Perennial Philosophy* (1945) to distill what he termed "the essence of wisdom," and it was in this context that he wrote Osmond in 1953 to praise his mescaline research and note his desire to explore its effects on his own consciousness.

In his letter, Huxley sounded remarkably like a "head" circa 1965 Haight-Ashbury, expressing his weariness with what he called "Sears & Roebuck" culture. He complained that growing up in such a culture, "the vast majority of individuals lose . . . all the openness to inspiration, all the capacity to be aware of other things than those enumerated in the Sears-Roebuck catalogue." It might be, he surmised, "that mescaline or some other chemical substance may . . . make it possible for young people to 'taste and see' what they have learned at second hand, or directly but at a lower level of intensity, in the writings of the religious, or the works of poets, painters and musicians" (Stevens 1987, 45).

In early May 1953, Osmond flew to Los Angeles to attend an American Psychological Association convention. Being in the neighborhood, Osmond paid Huxley a visit, bringing some mescaline with him. On May 4, Huxley was initiated into mescaline at age fifty-eight, finally experiencing for himself the state of "cosmic consciousness" he had spent the past twenty years exploring, reading, and writing about. He was absolutely floored by the experience, reporting that he felt himself pass through a screen—apparently that much-hypothesized filter—to enter a wondrous state wherein he was in firsthand touch with "eternity," "infinity," "the Absolute." Concluding that mescaline offers "the most extraordinary and significant experience this side of the beatific vision," Huxley wrote an essay about his experience that evolved into *The Doors of Perception* (1954), which would become a kind of bible of psychedelia. (The band, the Doors, took their name from this text.) Reading this work is central to understanding the subsequent psychedelic culture (Stevens 1987, 45).

Figure 1. Aldous Huxley, author of *The Doors of Perception*. Photo: Henri Manuel, 1925. *Source*: Wikimedia Commons, public domain. https://commons.wikimedia. org/wiki/File:Aldous_Huxley_-_photo_Henri_Manuel.jpg

Huxley derived the title from the William Blake passage, "If the doors of perception were cleansed everything would appear to man as it is, Infinite." Huxley reiterated the hypothesis of Bucke, Bergson, and William James that the brain filters out the vast majority of reality by "shutting out most of what we should otherwise perceive or remember at any moment and leaving only a very small and special selection which is likely to be practically useful," and that "most people, most of the time, know only what comes through the reducing valve" (1954, 23–24). In relaxing and/or circumventing this "reducing valve," mescaline opens the perceptual doors to a splendid panorama of data and sensation—a world of "visionary beauty"—otherwise unavailable to perceptual experience.

Huxley perceived mescaline to be a tool—a technology, if you will—by which to profoundly alter our understanding and apprehension of life. It is by means of this altered consciousness and understanding that we could proceed from (as Huxley put it to Osmond) Sears & Roebuck land into the "antipodes of the mind" inhabited by the "psychological equivalent of kangaroos, wallabies, and duck-billed platypuses—a whole host of extremely improbably animals, which nevertheless exist and can be observed." (1954, 24)

It suddenly occurred to Huxley an hour and a half into his trip that his perceptual faculties were profoundly and wondrously transformed. With his mind "perceiving in terms of intensity of existence, profundity of existence," he attained a "sacramental vision of reality" that ushered him into a state of "grace." He found himself existing in "a perpetual present made up of one continually changing apocalypse" (1954, 20, 22).

A significantly high percentage of authors who have written about their experiences taking LSD, mescaline, psilocybin, or peyote report experiencing this profoundly religious sensibility both while under influence of the drug and in the days, weeks, even months following. As Alan Watts put it in *The Joyous Cosmology*, "in this state of consciousness everything is the doing of the dogs" (1962, 58).

Amping out, Huxley was "seeing what Adam had seen on the morning of his creation—the miracle, moment by moment, of naked existence." Describing this mode of seeing, Huxley reports three flowers in a vase were "shining with their own inner light and all but quivering under the pressure of the significance with which they were charged" (1954, 17). Watts reported an experience nearly identical to Huxley's, noting: "Going indoors I find that all the household furniture is alive. Everything gestures. Tables are tabling, pots are potting, walls are walling, fixtures are fixturing—a world of events instead of things" (1962, 69). It is this mode of radiant, profoundly amplified intensity of perception—a truly transformative experience, described by Huxley as "a repeated flow from beauty to heightened beauty, from deeper to ever deeper meaning" (1954, 17–18)—that one sees described over and over in near identical fashion in accounts of the psychedelic experience.

Shifting his gaze from the flowers to the books lining the walls of his study did nothing to abate the glory. "Like the flowers," Huxley wrote, the books "glowed, when I looked at them, with brighter colors, a profounder significance." The books appeared "so intense, so intrinsically meaningful," he said, "that they seemed to be on the point of leaving the shelves to thrust themselves more insistently on my attention" (1954, 19). "This," he murmured with awe, "is how one ought to see."

Even while reveling in the glory, though, Huxley touched on an aspect of this experience that would figure profoundly in the evolution—and eventual collapse—of Haight-Ashbury in particular and the counterculture in general. Being privy via participating with mescaline to "the glory and wonder of pure existence," in "the manifest glory of things," one's conceptual map is reconfigured. In the face of all this rapture, the considerations of everyday life recede into irrelevance. Were one always "to see like this," Huxley noted, "one would never want to do anything else" (1954, 42).

"The contemplative whose perception has been cleansed"—by which Huxley means the person who has had the psychedelic experience (he sounds strikingly similar to the Diggers and the Haight-Ashbury acid mystics ten years down the line):

> does not have to stay in his room. He can go about his business, so completely satisfied to see and be part of the divine Order of Things. When we feel ourselves to be sole heirs of the universe, when the sea flows in our veins . . . and the stars are our jewels, when all things are perceived as infinite and holy, what motive can we have for covetousness and self-assertion, for the pursuit of power or the drearier forms of pleasure?"(1954, 43)

"How," he asked, rhetorically posing the counterculture stumper, "could one reconcile this timeless bliss of seeing as one ought to see with the temporal duties of doing what one ought to do and feelings one ought to feel?" (1954, 345). Mescaline "gives access to contemplation—but to a contemplation that is incompatible with action and even with the will to action, the very thought of action" (41). Bearing witness to the power and the glory, "the mescaline taker sees no reason for doing anything in particular and finds most of the causes for which, at ordinary times, he was prepared to act and suffer, profoundly uninteresting" (25). His perceptual map redrawn, caught between two "worlds," the initiate is given to reevaluating: "the world of selves, of time, of moral judgments and utilitarian considerations, the world (and it was this aspect of human life which I wished, above all else, to forget) of self-assertion, of cocksureness, of overvalued words and idolatrously worshiped notions" (46).

The conceptual remapping and value reconfiguration described by Huxley will play large in figures like Ken Kesey and Timothy Leary—both of whom abandoned promising careers in order to pursue the nonutilitarian "wonder of pure existence."

The problem, as Huxley put it, is that in "the inner world"—the world of "visionary beauty" accessed by mescaline—"there is neither work nor monotony." "The outer world," however, which is rife with work and monotony, "is what we wake up to every morning of our lives," and it is in "the outer world" that, "willy-nilly we must try to make our living" (1954, 46).

The danger of psychedelic experience, ironically, resides in the very quality making it so potentially valuable and profoundly wondrous. In opening perception to the miracle of sheer existence—a highly desirable, possibly even divine condition—a remapping takes place of a psyche that has been tooled, via years and years of social conditioning, for purposes of negotiating the outer world. Much of what in one's unenlightened state was deemed valuable recedes in one's enlightened state into comparative unimportance.

Born again with psychedelics, one is less willing to conform to or to aspire after the Old World, to credit what heretofore was given, to go by the old maps. The outer world, though, remains and awaits with all its work and monotony, and one blows it off as an illusion or as a "drag" at one's own peril. The psychedelic experience is, in consequence, equally a blessing and a curse, a gift and a danger, a door to grace (à la Haight-Ashbury circa the fall of 1965) and a door to boobish absurdity (à la Haight-Ashbury after 1968).

Much depends on whether the psychedelic experience is perceived to be a useful tool to supplement one's own thought, creativity, and imaginative participation in life, or whether it is pursued as an end in itself to escape from work and monotony. The psychedelic experience is less an answer than it is a posing of difficult (but fascinating) questions, and its use is not devoid of risk. Used intelligently, however, it can be a profoundly beneficial tool. As Huxley puts it in the closing paragraph of *The Doors of*

Perception: "The man who comes back through the Door in the Wall will never be quite the same as the man who went out. He will be wiser but less cocksure, happier but less self-satisfied, humbler in acknowledging his ignorance yet better equipped to understand the relationship of words to things, of systematic reasoning to the unfathomable Mystery which it tries, forever vainly, to comprehend" (1954, 79).

As would so many after him, Huxley heard the psychedelic call. On the basis of what he experienced that day on May 4, 1953, he cast his lot with "the glory and wonder of pure existence." Like Leary and Kesey after him, Huxley predicted that mescaline (and its pharmaceutical cousins) would give rise to a host of "biomedical discoveries that will make it possible for large numbers of men and women to achieve a radical self-transcendence and a deeper understanding of the nature of things." Convinced that mescaline can put mankind on a path to higher consciousness, he made it his mission to help people onto that path (1954, 79).

This pattern that would be repeated during the next ten to fifteen years: initiated by way of mescaline, psilocybin, LSD, or peyote into cosmic consciousness, an individual perceives the world in new, wondrous ways and, exalted by that discovery, goes out into the world to spread the psychedelic gospel and thereby save mankind.

Exactly like the newly psychedelicized Leary, Ginsberg, and Kesey would do ten years later, Huxley and Osmond went to a number of foundations proposing a project to give mescaline to a hundred of the world's foremost scientists, artists, philosophers, and intellectuals to explore how (and whether) mescaline frees the mind from habitual patterns and expands its range of possibilities. During the mid-1950s Eisenhower era, not a single foundation entertained their proposals.

Having issued his psychedelic manifesto via *The Doors of Perception,* Huxley found himself being contacted by and interacting with a plethora of individuals—some of them charming wackos and colorful crackpots, some of them truly heavy hitters—who, it turned out, had been exploring similar paths. This would prove to be an enduring propensity of psychedelics: to foster community by bringing together otherwise disparate people and scenes. Those initiated into the intense, revelatory psychedelic experience waxed enthusiastic and shared the transformative wonder of psychedelics with others. Friends are "turned on." "Heads" find each other. Contacts are made and circles formed, all of it very upbeat and communal in the promotion of something considered valuable and worthwhile, if not outright redemptive.

Two Heads Are Better Than One

I was an experiment on the part of nature, a gamble within the unknown, perhaps for a new purpose, perhaps for nothing, and my only task was to allow this game on the part of the primeval depths to take its course, to feel its will within me and make it wholly mine.

—Herman Hesse, *Demian* (1919)

It was at this contextual juncture in 1953 that Osmond was invited to lunch at the Royal Vancouver Yacht Club in Vancouver, British Columbia, in Canada, by someone who, by then, had been an acid apostle for years. The invitation came from Captain Alfred "Al" Hubbard, a figure cloaked in rumors, stories, speculation, money, networks of power, and connection.

In 1919, Hubbard invented a radioactive battery, which he sold to the Radium Corporation of Pittsburgh for $75,000, and a few years later during Prohibition, he landed in prison for eighteen months for assisting bootleggers run liquor past the United States and Canadian coast guards. At Prohibition's end, he became the number-two guy in charge of security at the mob-controlled Tropicana Hotel in Las Vegas.

During World War II, Hubbard served as an intelligence operative for the Office of Strategic Services (OSS), the precursor to the Central Intelligence Agency, and near the end of the war secretly and illegally smuggled heavy armaments from San Diego to Canada for eventual shipment to England by steering lightless ships at night up the coast to Canada and flying planes to the U.S./Canadian border, where he disassembled them and pirated them into Canada for illegal exportation to Britain. Reprimanded by the United States government, he moved to Vancouver and became a Canadian citizen. Though never directly associated with the CIA, the Captain subsequently claimed to have been involved with a shadow government, which held the real power in the United States.

After the war, Hubbard founded and successfully operated Marine Manufacturing, a charter-boat business, which allowed him to buy a Rolls Royce, a private airplane, and a twenty-four-acre home on Daymen Island off the coast of Vancouver Bay, equipped with an airplane hangar and a slip for his one-hundred-foot yacht. At the time of his June date with Osmond, Hubbard was scientific director of the Uranium Corporation of Vancouver and had friends and connections in very high places in industry and politics—and, apparently, in the Vatican. Charismatic, bon homme, high-energy, pragmatic, and can-do, on the chubby side and sporting a flat-top haircut, Hubbard would have fit right in at any American Legion, Rotary Club, or Knights of Columbus gathering. However, he moved in highly adventurous circles.

Later, Hubbard did undercover work for the Federal Narcotics Bureau and for the Food and Drug Administration. In the mid-'60s, he worked for Teledyne, a major defense subcontractor, and subsequently for the navy and NASA as director of human factors research, part of which involved testing psychochemical effects on helicopter avionics pilots.

Hubbard was also an ardent Catholic with a deep interest in mysticism, which inspired him to take LSD in 1951 at age forty-nine, when he chanced upon an article about LSD and rats by British psychiatrist Dr. Ronald Sandison, the first therapist to operate a public clinic utilizing LSD as a psychoanalytic tool. Hubbard's response followed the typical pattern. Hailing LSD as a deep, mystical experience, he was convinced the experience opened doors to the divine. As would Huxley, Kesey, Leary, and an array of initiates following him, Hubbard became a psychedelic missionary on a quest to save the world by exposing as many people as possible to this transformative experience. He unsuccessfully attempted to form a blue-ribbon commission to explore the possible uses of mescaline (and its cousins) in the areas of religion, philosophy, art, scientific invention, and parapsychology.

Hubbard never let official recalcitrance hold him down. Putting his money, clout, and connections to work, he contacted Sandoz and ordered forty-three *cases* of LSD-25. So armed, he set out to conduct as many psychedelic "sessions" as possible with leaders in business, industry, politics, science, religion, and the arts to foment a mass revolution in consciousness. Hubbard was profoundly committed to the cause. He flew all over the country and the world on acid missions, taking with him his leather bag filled with drugs, drug doodads, and mystic accessories, everything from consciousness-raising gases and acid to pictures of Jesus that he would brandish to his tripping companions. He reputedly tried to turn on Herbert Hoover, whom he liked and admired, but Hoover demurred. By 1959, he claimed to have personally conducted over 1,700 acid sessions.

Wherever in the world that research involving psychedelic substances was transpiring, Hubbard was sure to show up—hence his contacting Osmond after his article on mescaline was published and Huxley following the appearance of *The Doors of Perception*. It was Hubbard who guided Huxley through his second mescaline session in 1955. A few days before Christmas later that same year, he guided Huxley through his first LSD experience, causing Huxley to see "love as the primary and fundamental cosmic fact" (1954, 45). Many an acid-amped Haight-Ashburian would "see" that same "fact" ten years later.

Overwhelmed and exalted, Huxley concluded that LSD far surpassed even mescaline in its capacity to open the perceptual doors. Like Hubbard, he began musing on the possibility of exposing the world's best and brightest to LSD, envisioning a shift from a traditional culture to a psychedelic one.

Putting their heads together, Osmond and Hubbard developed high-dosage liquid LSD therapy as a way to facilitate a quasi-mystical breakthrough experience. With this therapeutic model, the perceptual chains of the subjects became suspended. First tested on Canadian alcoholics with stunning results, they applied the high-dosage concept to a number of other groups including juvenile delinquents and neurotics. It allowed people who experienced emotional blockages to shed their issues and undergo significant personality changes. Most patients praised LSD as a treatment and considered it much better than psychotherapy. Overall, the acid pioneers achieved a recovery rate between 60 and 70 percent.

Hubbard and Osmond introduced psychedelics to several important world leaders. They conducted LSD sessions variously with a prime minister, assorted assistant heads of state, United Nations representatives, and members of British parliament.

In 1957, Hubbard collaborated with Ross MacLean, administrator of Hollywood Hospital in New Westminster, Canada, to set up a private clinic focused on the use of LSD as a therapeutic tool for alcoholics. Hubbard, who used a cheesy diploma mill to get his doctorate, became the clinic's chief therapist with a hospital wing for his sessions. Later, Hubbard became friends with Timothy Leary while the latter was conducting psilocybin projects at Harvard. They had a falling out, however, when Leary disregarded Hubbard's warnings that he was too intemperate and freewheeling about his research in and the application of psychedelics.

Hubbard's activities during the '60s and '70s highlighted what an unusual blend he was of LSD missionary and establishment straight. Hubbard was the prime mover behind the late '50s foundation of the International Federation for Advanced Studies (IFAF), whose mission was to explore the therapeutic and problem-solving potential of LSD. When an avalanche of adverse LSD publicity forced closure of IFAF in 1965, its director—Willis

Harmon (who had been initiated into LSD by Hubbard)—accepted an offer to head up the Educational Policy Research Center at the Stanford Research Institute (SRI).

In 1968, Harmon invited Hubbard (by then semiretired) to join SRI as a special investigative agent in the Alternative Futures Project to spread LSD to political and intellectual leaders, especially the heads of Fortune 500 companies. He also investigated whether the New Left student leadership was being manipulated by the psychedelic subculture by gathering data about student unrest, radical politics, and drug use. Taking himself seriously enough to begin wearing—totally of his own volition, not as an SRI requirement—a khaki uniform, gold-plated badge, ammunition belt, and shoulder-holster pistol, Hubbard led raids on underground LSD labs. His motive was not to suppress acid; he himself was distributing it on a worldwide scale, free of charge, to turn on as many people as he could. Rather, he believed many of these labs operated with Mafia financing—a belief which turned out to be at least partly justified—and that they were producing adulterated acid for purely profit motives. By 1974, Hubbard lost his contract with SRI and moved into semi-retirement but continued his mission as an apostle for LSD until his death eight years later.

2

The Circle Widens

. . . Earth is Heaven
Whether Heaven is Heaven or not

—Emily Dickinson, "The Fact that Earth is Heaven"

An indication as to how widespread the interest in psychedelics was becoming by the mid-'50s is that the first international symposium on LSD took place in 1956. At this juncture, Osmond coined the term *psychedelic*, meaning "mind-opening," in a correspondence with Huxley. He introduced the term to the psychiatric establishment in an address to the New York Academy of Sciences in 1957.

It was also in the mid-'50s that an LSD "scene" evolved in Los Angeles. This was a kind of insider fraternity for the hip, a precursor to what would happen six to seven years down the line with Kesey and his circle at Perry Lane and La Honda, and with Leary and his circle at Harvard and Millbrook. Participants in the mid-'50s L.A. acid scene included Huxley, Alan Watts, writer Anaïs Nin, and novelist Christopher Isherwood (who had also studied Vedanta Hinduism with Huxley 1948). In conjunction with this scene, several Beverly Hills psychiatrists—most notably Oscar Janiger (a cousin of Allen Ginsberg), Sidney Cohen, Arthur Chandler, and Mortimer Hartman—began organizing LSD sessions (at $100 a pop) that became very chic. Some of their patients in turn began sharing LSD with friends, and several scenes evolved, some of them quite wild, involving everything from astral projection to telepathy and past-life exploration.

Participants in these maverick L.A. LSD sessions included musician Andre Previn, actors Jack Nicholson and James Coburn, and gadfly Lord Buckley. Buckley, in particular, was no acid novice. As early as the 1940s, he founded a mescaline club called the Church of the Living Swing, under which aegis he hosted mescaline parties on a rented yacht in the San Francisco Bay with live jazz by saxophonist Ben Webster and Johnny Puleo, with the Harmonicats. Actor Cary Grant also participated in these sessions. While living on the Key West Naval Base during filming of *Operation Petticoat* in the spring of 1958, Grant told two journalists (one of whom was Joe Hyams of the *New York Herald Tribune*) that he'd done over sixty LSD sessions over the past two years under the supervision of two Hollywood psychiatrists (probably Arthur Chandler and Mortimer Hartman). Sounding nearly identical to Leary four years later, Grant contended that his LSD experiences made him realize what a hypocritical, role-playing fraud he was. Thanks to his experiences with LSD, he said, he had been reborn.

As news of the psychedelic glad tidings spread through hip word of mouth and the likes of Huxley's book, the L.A. acid scene, and Grant's testimonial, one of the people who got wind of it was none other than Henry Luce, president of Time-Life and one of the frontline cold warriors of the Eisenhower era, and his wife, Clare Boothe Luce. Raised in China as the son of missionary parents, Henry Luce was a bastion of mid-century right-wing ideology, who willingly lent his publishing empire to CIA propaganda and boosterism of what he termed the "American Century." Right thinker or no, in 1958 Luce made a request to Sidney Cohen—one of the psyche-delic shrinks in the Huxley circle—to fly down to Arizona and guide him through a session (LSD was not illegal until October 1966). The experience affected him in the same way it affected most initiates: he became an acid enthusiast. In the late '50s and early '60s, Luce did at least a half-dozen sessions, with Huxley and Isherwood among his tripping partners. He even reported an acid-inspired vision of God on the golf links.

"Oh sure, we all took acid," Clare Boothe Luce once blurted on the *Dick Cavett Show*. "It was a creative group—my husband and I and Huxley and Isherwood." By all accounts, she was a leader of postwar American politics and later served as a member of President Ronald Reagan's Foreign Intelligence Advisory Board, which oversaw covert operations conducted by the CIA. She approved of acid sessions for highly placed politicians, and business leaders. " 'We wouldn't want everyone doing too much of a good thing,' she sniffed" (Lee and Shlain 1985, 71).

Henry Luce, meanwhile, was sufficiently impressed by LSD to give psychedelics favorable press in his Time-Life publications empire, including a seventeen-page piece on "magic mushrooms" by R. Gordon Wasson in the May 17, 1957, issue of *Life*. In that article, Wasson described years of searching for the fabled magic mushroom which ultimately led him to the jungles of Mayan Mexico. There, he finally got to ingest one of these mushroom in a midnight ceremony. In Wasson's description of this trip in his *Life* article, one all but hears the tinkle of sitars at Millbrook, feels the heat of black lights, and rides with Jefferson Airplane on a feedback soar against the backdrop of a light show at the Avalon Ballroom. Keep in mind, in an ultra-mainstream family magazine at the height of the Cold War, McCarthyism, and the Eisenhower administration, the article explained that:

> We were never more awake, and the visions came whether our eyes were opened or closed . . . They began with art motifs, angular such as might decorate carpets or textiles or wallpaper or the drawing board of an architect. They evolved into palaces with courts, arcades, gardens—resplendent palaces all laid over with semi-precious stones . . . Later it was as though the walls of our house had dissolved, and my spirit had flown forth, and I was suspended in mid-air viewing landscapes of mountains, with camel caravans advancing slowly across the slopes, the mountains rising tier above tier to the very heavens. (Wasson 1957, 108)

"For the first time," Wasson added, "the word ecstasy took on real meaning."

Luce would change his stance drastically in the mid-'60s, when the CIA and the federal government went on an all-out campaign to suppress LSD, including all research on it. He printed a series of highly sensationalized articles in *Life* about the destructive horrors of LSD—a position totally contrary to his personal experiences with the drug.

The story of Gordon Wasson affords yet another of those convergences so typical of the psychedelic revolution. After graduating from Harvard, Wasson reported as a financial correspondent for the *New York Herald Tribune* during the '20s. In 1928, he became a securities specialist for Morgan Guaranty and eventually rose to the rank of vice president. His pediatrician wife, Valentina, was Russian-born and a dedicated connoisseur of wild mushrooms. She set out to educate and interest her husband in her hobby, and the couple began researching the social and cultural lore of mushrooms. Together, they formulated a theory that the development of religion in Indo-European cultures was catalyzed by the ingestion of hallucinogenic mushrooms—the fly amanita being the most likely candidate. Europe, they hypothesized, can be divided into two historic camps: those who loved and used mushrooms, and those who didn't. The mushroom-loving peoples included the Slavic countries and regions of Austria, Germany, Italy, France, and Spain.

The Wassons took their theory seriously enough to learn several languages in search of linguistic clues and to devote vacations to traipsing through European and Slavic countrysides to interview peasants about mushroom legend and lore. When, in 1952, archaeological excavations in Mexico and Guatemala unearthed mushroom artifacts, the Wassons suspected them to be part of a pre-Columbian mushroom cult. Flying there to investigate, they learned of sixteenth-century Spanish texts, which mentioned ceremonial native use of a mushroom called "God's flesh" that reputedly induced visions. They also learned of an anthropological team that had witnessed a mushroom ceremony in a remote jungle village twenty years earlier.

The Wassons spent the next three years exploring, seeking contacts, following up leads, and delving into rumors and local legends. Their efforts culminated in a midnight ritual in the tiny village of Huautla de Jimenez on June 29, 1955, wherein Wasson finally got to eat "God's flesh" himself. His imagination "unhinged," he experienced visions of "beautiful form and color," and felt himself ushered into the presence of a "higher reality" (Wasson 1957, 108).

In the course of relating this experience one day to a lunch companion at the swank, private Century Club in Manhattan, Wasson was approached by an editor from Time-Life who had overheard his tale. The editor offered Wasson a chance to write-up his story for *Life*—hence the seventeen-page article in 1957. A young psychologist named Frank Barron read the article with great interest and hurriedly told his best friend Timothy Leary (they had been graduate students together at Berkeley) about it and urged him to read it.

At the time, Leary headed clinical research at the Kaiser Foundation Hospital in Oakland, California. His book *The Interpersonal Diagnosis of Personality* (1957) had been hailed by the *Annual Review of Psychology* as "the most important book on psychotherapy of the year" (Leary 2000, 24). He had a bit of a wild streak, though. He was a former West Pointer, who was forced out after being labeled a disciplinary problem (a problem that would define his entire life), he had been expelled from the University of

Alabama after he was caught spending the night in a girl's dorm room, his first wife had committed suicide on his birthday, and he divorced his second wife after a year.

At this juncture, Leary was bored, restless, and growing increasingly disenchanted with the prospect of a life devoted to psychological research. Recent research into the effectiveness of psychotherapy had yielded data he found disturbing: regardless of the slant or technique employed, one third of the patients, who underwent psychotherapy improved, one third showed little or no change, and one third regressed—and the same percentage of improvement applied to patients, who hadn't undergone psychotherapy. Conventional psychotherapy, he felt, was a dead end. Wasson's *Life* article piqued the interest of Barron and Leary in a way nearly identical to how Osmond's article had caught Huxley's eye four years earlier. Barron was intrigued enough to hunt up a few of these "divine" mushrooms as part of his ongoing research into the psychology of creativity.

In the years from 1957 to 1960, Leary summered at a villa in Cuernavaca, Mexico—something the "beautiful people" of academia were given to doing, what with the villas, swimming pools, and servants paid for by research grants. During his fourth summer at the villa in 1960, the year following his first academic year at Harvard, one of Leary's frequent guests (there was lots of partying)—an anthropology professor at the National University in Mexico City, who was a friend of Barron—told him about references in Aztec texts to "teonanacatl," the "God's flesh" of Wasson's article. When this professor found an Indian connection, who could supply him with a quantity of these mushrooms, Leary joined several other people on the Saturday afternoon of August 9 to gulp down six mushrooms with the aid of some beer. Leary went on to have the kind of experience that had been extolled to the high heavens by the likes of Osmond, Huxley, Isherwood, Hubbard, the Luces, and Wasson. Undergoing what he would later hold to be "the deepest religious experience of my life," Leary told of getting a ferocious, mind-bending "buzz" (literally) and then being ushered to "the center of Life," where "raw, rich, ever-changing panoramas" unfolded, revealing to him (à la Cary Grant and Huxley) the pomposity, "impudence," and "narrow arrogance" of academics like himself (Leary 1990, 31).

Whether an entertainer, academic, artist, or businessman, it seems strikingly common in accounts of initial encounters with psychedelic substances for the initiate to report seeing him/herself as a game-playing fraud. Alan Watts typically reported the following introspective progression and conclusion in *The Joyous Cosmology*: "I begin to see my whole life as a masterpiece of duplicity—the confused, helpless, hungry, and hideously sensitive little embryo at the root of me having learned, step by step, to comply, placate, bully, wheedle, flatter, bluff, and cheat my way into being taken for a person of competence and reliability. For when it really comes down to it, what do any of us know?" (1962, 37).

Leary claimed to have explored more of his mind in that four-hour session with mushrooms than he had done in the previous fifteen years as a professional psychologist and academic researcher. Experiencing the messianic reflex typical of psychedelic initiates, he became a true-believer convert. Like those before him, Leary was absolutely convinced that psilocybin was an invaluable tool for investigating consciousness and that the drug harbored profound implications for the future of mankind. Leary not only jumped on the bandwagon, which was already rolling and gathering steam; he hijacked it and drove it to Harvard Yard. Eventually, he began driving that bandwagon around the country, beeping his horn, and offering everyone rides (and photo opportunities). In yet another connection, Watts referred to Wasson's jungle adventure in *The Joyous Cosmology*, for which Leary wrote an introduction.

The CIA and Psychedelics

. . . there has been this feeling that perhaps the government is lying . . .

—Herbert Klein, director of communications for the executive
branch under Nixon (November 11, 1969)

It turns out that one of the people in Wasson's group, when he ventured into the Mexican jungles in quest of the magic mushroom, was a case officer in the CIA named James Moore. Moore had written Wasson the previous winter, passing himself off as a professor from the University of Delaware, who was interested in the chemistry of Mexican mushrooms. He asked if he could join Wasson in his explorations and sweetened the bait by mentioning that he had a contact in the Geschickter Fund for Medical Research, which might be willing to underwrite the expedition were he to go along. Wasson agreed. However, the Geschickter Fund was one of several funding fronts used by the CIA on behalf of massive, though secret, "national security" research into mind-altering drugs. The fund was keeping close tabs on Wasson's investigations. In fact, American intelligence agencies had been investigating, researching, experimenting with, using, and administering mind-altering drugs since the early '1940s: sometimes legally, often not; sometimes legitimately, but sometimes unethically; sometimes openly, but more often clandestinely.

The government's interest was first prompted by captured documents that revealed the medical arm of the Nazi Air Force had been giving mescaline to inmates at Dachau concentration camp as part of a program investigating drugs and techniques that could render a prisoner incapable of withholding information. In 1942, General William "Wild Bill" Donovan, head of the Office of Strategic Services (OSS) assembled a committee to oversee a top-secret research program that was trying to find a so-called truth drug that would render a person incapable of withholding information during interrogation. Donovan told this committee that finding such a drug was critical for U.S. national security. Over the next four to five years, this committee investigated everything from alcohol to barbiturates, caffeine, peyote, and marijuana, testing them on themselves, on each other, on U.S. military personnel, and then on civilians.

When the CIA was formed in 1947, the agency continued these studies, recruiting academics, psychiatrists, and personnel from police departments, criminology labs, and medical labs—even professional hypnotists—to be well-paid consultants in its "mind-control" projects. In one, from 1947 to 1953, mescaline was explored as a possible "truth serum" at the Naval Medical Research Institute in Bethesda, Maryland. To facilitate secrecy, these projects were eventually consolidated into a single project under the code name BLUEBIRD, with secret funding mechanisms set up. In August 1951, BLUEBIRD evolved into Project ARTICHOKE, with researchers given a free hand to pursue whatever leads they wished in whatever way they wished. When CIA interest in mescaline expanded in the early 1950's to include LSD and other hallucinogens for interrogation purposes, the search for consciousness-altering plants was expanded to include the entire globe: hence Moore's interest in accompanying Wasson in 1956.

In 1954, the CIA issued a directive ordering all domestic field offices to monitor LSD research being done within the U.S. Several CIA funding fronts were established to finance the monitoring program, including the Geschickter Fund for Medical Research, the Society for the Study of Human Ecology, and the Josia Macy, Jr., Foundation. When Osmond published his paper mentioning mescaline, CIA informants were sent to Weyburn Hospital in Saskatchewan to investigate; Osmond was contacted, without his knowing it, by CIA operatives throughout his career. Some "friends" he mentions in letters were, it turns out, CIA operatives. Osmond left Weyburn in 1963 for the Princeton Neuropsychiatric Institute, which was partly funded by the Society for the Study of Human Ecology, a group frequently used by the CIA. Osmond himself, though, never knowingly worked for or collaborated with the CIA.

When the agency began testing LSD on human subjects, it was initially administered to CIA-trained volunteers and then to CIA employees. Eventually, it was administered to prisoners, mental patients, heroin addicts, sexual deviants, and minorities: sometimes with their knowledge and consent, sometimes not, and with widely varying doses.

On April 13, 1953, Allen Dulles, the newly appointed director of the CIA, authorized Operation MK-ULTRA, a super-secret program run by Technical Services Staff (TSS). Originally, MK-ULTRA was a funding mechanism for ARTICHOKE, but it soon superseded its parent program. With LSD research a major component of this program, all TSS personnel took acid to gain firsthand experience. They subsequently began dosing each other without prior warning as a way to test its effects on behavior and decision-making. Eventually, they began dosing other agency personnel. One dosee, biological-warfare specialist Frank Olson, became so unhinged by his surprise dosing in a glass of cognac during a CIA symposium that he crashed to his death through a closed window on the twelfth floor of the Statler Hotel in New York City.

The MK-ULTRA program also opened a "safe house" in Greenwich Village under the supervision of George Hunter White, a former operative, who had overseen a project that administered marijuana to unwitting subjects and who had run a training school for American spies during World War II. As part of this project, White lured people to the safe house under various pretexts, surreptitiously dosed them, and then monitored the results. In 1955, the CIA transferred White to San Francisco, where as part of Operation Midnight Climax, he outfitted hotel rooms in New York City and San Francisco and paid addicted prostitutes $100 a pop to pick up johns, bring them back to the CIA pads, dose them, and then screw them as the acid kicked in—all of it watched by White from behind a two-way mirror. (Exactly what the spooks were hoping to learn from watching prostitutes screw tripping johns invites all manner of interesting speculation.) As it turns out, every now and then White and his associates let down their hair to do a little partying themselves: smoking a little grass, doing a little acid, whooping it up, and cavorting with the prostitutes. These CIA-monitored rooms remained in operation until 1963.

The CIA tried its best to recruit Al Hubbard in the 1950s, but he turned them down each time. He did, though, do undercover work for the Federal Narcotics Bureau. In 1953, the CIA unsuccessfully attempted to buy the world's entire supply of LSD from Sandoz. However, it did extract a promise from Sandoz to report all its sales of LSD to the CIA. By 1960, some 1,500 military personnel had served as guinea pigs in CIA-operated LSD experiments. Film footage still exists of soldiers marching in formation, driving jeeps, and reading radar screens while tripping.

In 1962, MK-ULTRA recruited students from Stanford University for their experiments. At Menlo Park Hospital, the CIA administered LSD, psilocybin, and mescaline to the unsuspecting undergraduates, which included future Grateful Dead lyricist Robert Hunter, who experienced "a shell of purple with foam crests of crystal drops soft nigh they fall unto a sea of morning creep-very-softly mist." In retrospect, chuckled Hunter, "the United States government was in a way responsible for creating the 'acid tests' and the Grateful Dead and thereby the whole psychedelic counterculture" (Genzlinger 2019, A23).

By the mid-'60s, CIA interest in LSD shifted to a hallucinogen called BZ, though some evidence exists that the agency tried to flood antiwar adherents with acid to immobilize their efforts. CIA enthusiasm over LSD dampened when they concluded that it does not lend itself to "control" purposes. It does break down inhibitions and alter behavior, but it makes perceptual experience—and behavior—unpredictable, unorthodox, *non-uniform*, and unscripted. As typified in Haight-Ashbury, LSD engendered an upbeat expansiveness, an awe of life, an inclination to explore, experiment, and play, a desire to share experience with like-minded others that the CIA hardly wanted to promote.

3

The Psychedelic (R)Evolution

Timothy Leary, Richard Alpert, and the Beat Generation

Fasten your seatbelts; this is going to be a bumpy ride.

—Bette Davis in *All About Eve* (1950)

Timothy Leary's sense of tapping into a divine wisdom upon ingesting psilocybin parallels the testimony of everyone who did psychedelics from Osmond to Cary Grant, from Huxley to Hubbard. Leary's profound experience transformed him into a psychedelic missionary devoted to saving the world by turning on as many people as possible. Leary had the drive, means, track record, connections, Harvard credentials, personality, charm, articulation, wiles, networking skills—and the high-octane combination of ambition and ego—to become a truly major missionary. His evangelism would give rise to and branch off into one of the two major divisions of the psychedelic revolution that would catalyze the '60s.

By 1959, Leary's academic stock was high enough that he was able to network his way into—literally *talk his* way into—a Harvard appointment. (Leary was reputed to wield a devastating combination of charm, wit, and articulated force, whether his subject be a bow-tied academic in a tweedy three-piece suit or a drop-dead gorgeous socialite in a slinky excuse-for-a-gown.) Initially, his career schtick was transactional psychology, an existential, humanistic approach to therapy wherein the experimenter, rather than remaining clinically aloof, functions as a participatory, collaborative facilitator to assist the troubled individual into achieving a transformative, behavior-altering "vitalizing transaction"—essentially, a moment, when everything clicks, which forever changes the patient.

Leary theorized—and this, recall, was prior to any ingestion of "God's flesh"—that our lives consist of an elaborate series of "games," each separate game having its own rules, expectations, codes, strategies, and fashions that we follow in the manner of an actor reading a script. To put it another way: the bus typically drives us, not we it. It was the mission of the transactional psychologist to put the individual back in the driver's seat and begin steering the bus to destinations of his or her choosing.

There was a lot more than academic conviction behind Leary's interest in this area of inquiry. He had some unresolved issues, hidden baggage, and contradictions of his own, for example the suicide of his first wife. He adored his role as Harvard professor (with all the requisite perks and prestige), even while absolutely and ferociously loathing to the deepest Howl-esque recesses of his potty-trained innermost being the entire concept of the middle-class ideal of the Organization Man, the Corporate Man, the Harvard Man, and the well-adjusted man. Like Kesey, he reveled in flouting the rules, testing the limits, and pranking the establishment. He was, in short, a kind of merry prankster, Harvard-style, East Coast branch. Leary, like Kesey, possessed a curiosity about the implications and ramifications of breaking cherished taboos. Upon arriving at Harvard, Leary was given a minuscule office (literally a hole-in-the-wall that just weeks before had been a coat closet) in the Center for Personality Research. In the summer following his first year at Harvard, Leary ate the fabled mushrooms. As an apostolic psychedelic convert—not to mention a flagrant opportunist, who saw in psychedelics a bandwagon for potential celebrity and fortune—Leary returned to Harvard in the fall of 1960. The mushroom experience had totally reinforced his theory about life as a complicated network of multifaceted gamesmanship. Enabled by the psychedelic experience to see what a phony and a fraud his whole identity had been, Leary considered it essential to discard the social conditioning, received abstractions, and conceptual machinery preventing him from being what Emerson (Harvard class of 1821) had variously called "Self-Reliant," "Man-Thinking," "living wholly within." Reborn, repentant, and revved-up, Leary was ready to journey to what he called "the uncharted margins" and go for the gold: to dive inward, using psilocybin as a tool, in quest of the Golden Fleece, the Golden Bough, the Holy Grail, and the Emerald City. He was amped, and he was in messianic, though giggly, dead earnest. He convinced his Harvard superiors to let him start a project to explore psilocybin as a transactional tool.

At the same time, Leary's old graduate school buddy, Frank Barron, finagled a year's appointment at Harvard for the 1960–1961 year, so the two—both having tasted "God's flesh"—joined hands as a psychedelic team. In their initial project, Leary and Barron administered psilocybin to 175 people, among whom were graduate students, psychologists, housewives, musicians, artists, and writers. They hoped to see what the ingestion of the drug enabled their subjects to learn about themselves. According to Leary, more than half of the psilocybin-takers felt that the drug had changed their lives, and 90 percent wanted to try it again.

Leary, meanwhile, ebulliently urged one and all of his Harvard colleagues—from senior faculty on down to teaching assistants—to give psilocybin a transformative whirl. He suggested to the curious that they read *The Doors of Perception*. More and more Harvardians—graduate students in particular—began dropping by and hanging around Leary's office. One of them was Ralph Metzner, a graduate of Oxford and a Ph.D. candidate in social relations. In the spring of 1961, he volunteered to participate in Leary's psilocybin project, which resulted in a collaboration that would radically change his life's course.

By pure chance, in the fall of 1960, Huxley took a residency in Boston as the Centennial Carnegie Visiting Professor in Humanities at the Massachusetts Institute of Technology (M.I.T.), lecturing to overflow audiences on "visionary experience." Leary—ever the master networker, ever one to bring in celebrities, stars, and people with money and connections as collaborators—talked Huxley into serving as an advisor to his psilocybin study. The two tripped together, and Huxley reiterated his theory, going all the way back to *The Doors of Perception,* that society could be profoundly changed by psychedelic experiences provided to the talented, the high born, and people in positions of influence, the kind of people, in other words, concentrated at Harvard. Huxley assured Leary that he was in an ideal position to advance the psychedelic cause—this being nothing less grandiose than the evolution of the species—but he needed to proceed shrewdly: keep everything low key, clinical, scientific, and scholarly. He warned Leary that the more successful and visible his project became, the more dead-serious opposition he would get. Leary, he suggested, was a tad too freewheeling, a bit too inclined toward the Gay-Paree, cocktail-party, dancing-girls, wake-up-with-a-tattoo approach.

Figure 2. Allen Ginsberg, Timothy Leary, and Ralph Metzner paying homage to Buddha, likely 1965. *Source*: Library of Congress Prints and Photographs Division, public domain. https://lccn.loc.gov/97519423

As was his unfailing wont wherever psychedelic studies surfaced, Hubbard soon materialized to check out Leary's research. He praised Leary's work and exhorted him onward. Osmond showed up that fall, too, coming to Boston to attend the annual conference of the Group for the Advancement of Psychiatry. Naturally, he and Huxley got together, Huxley taking Osmond to meet Leary. (For the record, Osmond considered Leary a tad "square.")

Leary was too much the live wire and loose cannon to limit his studies to clinical settings and scenarios. Part scientist, part huckster, part sincere seeker, part horny guy seeking greater opportunities for getting laid by pretty women, Leary began—somewhat akin to Hubbard and the Beverly Hills shrinks five years earlier in L.A.—holding dinner parties to "share" psilocybin with invited graduate students and people of "the arts." Rumors (not entirely unfounded) began circulating among the Harvard faculty about wild, orgiastic goings-on.

Leary took increasingly to dividing his weekends between New York City, where he did psilocybin with writers, musicians, and artists, and Newton, Massachusetts, where he hosted psilocybin weekends (with lots of sex) for socialites and jet-setters. By March 1961—five months into the psilocybin project—Leary had taken the drug a whopping fifty-two times and was getting sloppy. Increasingly, his idea of the evolution of the species included his notion of hedonic consciousness with pleasure as a way of life. Gradually, even Barron—senior advisor to the project and Leary's psychedelic collaborator—began to distance himself from Leary's party-hearty approach, and a split developed between them.

Moving in to take Barron's place was a well-heeled and well-to-do assistant professor of education and sociology named Richard Alpert. In yet another conjunction so common to psychedelic legend and lore, Alpert had been introduced to marijuana while he was working toward his Ph.D. at Stanford by way of a fellow psychology graduate student named Vic Lovell, who in 1960 hipped Kesey to the drug experiments in Menlo Park and went on to be a part of Kesey's Prankster circle

Alpert—the future Ram Dass—came from a background of enormous wealth which accoutrements included a 190-acre New Hampshire vacation farm—featuring a lake, a private golf course, and landing strip for the family's private plane—prep schools, Mercedes Benzes, and high-priced, sophisticated antique collecting. Alpert's wealth and connections were right down Leary's alley. On some weekends, Alpert and Leary would fly to Duke University in Alpert's Cessna to do psilocybin sessions at the J. B. Rhine Parapsychology Institute. But usually, the duo flew to New York City, where they psychedelicized wealthy patrons.

Leary's Circle Expands

They know how to eat of the best without ever having to work for it. And they eat whenever they feel hungry, drink when they are thirsty, at any hour of the day, without regard to the prescribed fasts, and they spend their time doing nothing and sleeping.

—Bishop Timothy complaining about the Messalians,
a fourth-century Gnostic sect

Leary's scheme to psychedelicize the world was aided and abetted by a coterie of eccentrics, visionaries, brilliant crackpots, and well-known enthusiasts.

While five to six years earlier Hubbard was a kind of acid guru to a Los Angeles circle that included the likes of Huxley, Osmond, and Watts, a similar, though less formidable, figure surfaced in 1962 around the Harvard environs in the person of Fred Swain. A World War II veteran and Air Force major, Swain became a Vedanta Hindu monk in 1948 and traveled to Mexico in 1961 to eat "magic mushrooms" in the mountains of Oaxaca. He had been living in an ashram outside Boston since 1960, when he began hanging out with Leary and his circle and introduced them to Hinduism as a religion more psychedelic than Christianity.

A second important figure was an Englishman named Michael Hollingshead, who arrived on the Leary scene shortly after writer William Burroughs's (*Naked Lunch*) disaffected departure and came with a mayonnaise jar filled with a gooey mixture of powdered sugar and distilled water laced with high-powered LSD. Hollingshead, though, was still a relative newcomer to LSD. His first experience left him exalted, but unmoored. His marriage was going down in flames, his sense of self turned inside-out and twisting in the breeze, so Hollingshead sought Aldous Huxley for advice. (As author of *The Doors of Perception*, Huxley was hounded by discombobulated psychedelic initiates seeking guidance.) Huxley counseled Hollingshead to consult Leary at Harvard. Leary duly provided Hollingshead a room in his attic and did a psilocybin session with him. Hollingshead reciprocated by offering Leary a taste of the goop in his mayonnaise jar. Leary initially declined, but he relented and took a taste after seeing how much fun Hollingshead and jazz trumpeter and big-band leader Maynard Ferguson were having on a trip. Off and running, Leary up-shifted to LSD as his cosmic vehicle, and Hollingshead went on to be a central figure of the Leary team. Four years later, Hollingshead, via his World Psychedelic Center in London, introduced Donovan, Keith Richards, and the members of the Yardbirds to LSD.

Leary described his introduction to psilocybin as a life-altering experience, but he was floored, exalted, stunned, and fundamentally changed by LSD. Acid transformed Leary into one of Kerouac's "fabulous yellow roman candles" that burn, burn, burn, and explode "like spiders across the stars and in the middle you see the blue center light pop and everybody goes 'Awww!'" (Kerouac 1957, 9). Leary felt that he was ushered by his initial LSD experience into "a burning, dazzling, throbbing, radiant core [of] pure pulsing, exulting light. It seemed like an endless flame that contained everything—sound, touch, cell, seed, sense, soul, sleep, glory, glorifying, God, the hard eye of God. Merged with this pulsing flame it was possible to look out and see and participate in the entire cosmic drama" (Leary 1968, 246).

The entire psilocybin research team was soon acid-amped, zonked, psychedelicized, their identities and perceptions retooled. Like Captain Ahab in search of Moby Dick, they threw the sextant overboard to rely on navigational dead reckoning. Like Huck Finn, they "lit out for the Territory," not about to let themselves be "sivilized" by Aunt Polly; they wouldn't be able to stand it. Like Dean Moriarty and Sal Paradise, they lit out for the open road. Like McMurphy in *One Flew Over the Cuckoo's Nest* (1962), they set out to undermine Big Nurse.

Figure 3. Poster for Richard Alpert's "A Discussion of LSD," 1965. *Source*: New York Public Library Digital Collections, public domain. https://digitalcollections. nypl.org/items/e8a14290-538b-0135-c361-0f7dfaf544cf

Leary's penchant for proselytizing and partying brought him into intimate contact with an array of personages, who figured large in bridging the gap between the Eisenhower, Cold War '50s, and the Haight-Ashbury '60s. He did an LSD session with Mary Pinchot, a painter and Washington socialite married to Cord Meyer, a high-level CIA official, who headed the Congress of Cultural Freedom in Europe. During one of her visits to Leary in Cambridge, Pinchot asked him to teach her how to guide LSD sessions so that she could turn on well-placed friends, who wanted to try it. She told Leary that one "very important man" in particular, whose identity she could not reveal, was interested in giving acid a try. Leary didn't know Pinchot was married to Meyer. Nor did he know that she was one of JFK's mistresses and that the two had smoked grass together *in* the White House. Subsequent to JFK's assassination, Pinchot herself was murdered, and her diary describing this period was taken from her home.

A genius at networking, Leary hosted and participated in socially chic psilocybin parties. Following one of these parties on the West Coast, Marilyn Monroe materialized in Leary's bedroom, asking him for some acid. At one of his frequent New York City parties, Leary met Peggy Hitchcock, a twenty-eight-year old, jet-setting, quasi-artsy (she liked "the arts") heir to both the Mellon and the Hitchcock fortunes. Her family owned a sixty-four-room mansion in Millbrook, New York—a two-hour, ninety-mile drive from New York City.

Meanwhile, Harvard—the mother ship and gravy train for Leary—was not altogether neglected. Leary and Alpert (and, increasingly, Metzger) forged on with ostensibly "clinical" psilocybin projects. They set up a pilot study in which psilocybin was administered to thirty-two inmates at the maximum-security Massachusetts Correctional Institute in Concord to explore whether the psychedelic experience could change the prisoners' behavior enough to lower the recidivism rate.

In spring 1962, Walter Pahnke, one of Leary's teaching assistants and a Ph.D. candidate in religion and society, conducted the now-famous "Good Friday Experiment" in Marsh Chapel at Boston University. He sought to explore the possible relationship between the psychedelic experience and the more traditional religious experience. The project—which lacked the official blessing of Harvard—brought together twenty theology students from a local divinity school to scrutinize the potential of hallucinogens to facilitate interaction with the Divine. Ten of the subjects were given psilocybin, and ten a placebo that merely made the face flush. All twenty participated in a religious service involving organ music, vocal solos, scripture readings, accounts of the visionary experiences of various mystics and saints, prayers, and an interval of silent meditation.

This "experiment" and its results became the subject of Pahnke's Ph.D. dissertation, wherein he related that nine of the ten subjects given psilocybin reported intense religious experiences, and only one of the ten given placebos reported having one. The psychedelicized celebrants reported feelings of joy, blessedness, peace, love, transcendence of time and place, and firsthand interaction with the sacred. They felt that their chemically induced state of consciousness linked them to the Divine as they knew it. Pahnke concluded that their psychedelic-fueled experiences were indistinguishable from, if not identical with" traditional mystical experience. As we have seen, individuals constantly refer to the connection between the chemically induced visionary experience and the traditional religious experience, which would figure prominently in countercultural developments. As one of numerous possible examples, Alan Watts—an ordained Episcopal priest—wrote in *The Joyous Cosmology* that: "I can find no essential difference between the experiences induced, under favorable conditions, by these chemicals [mescaline, psilocybin, LSD] and the state of 'cosmic consciousness' recorded by investigators of mysticism" (1962, 17).

As had happened many times previously, and as would happen repeatedly in the next two to three years, the ten divinity school students ingesting psilocybin resorted to quasi-religious language, terminology, metaphors, and phraseology to describe their experiences. They believed that psilocybin opened a door to the Divine. In 1991, most of the ten reported in a follow-up study that their experiences prompted positive changes in behavior and thinking that persisted throughout their lives. Within two years of the experiment, near-identical reports came out of Haight-Ashbury, where acid mystics and amped-out scenesters attempted to fashion a culture designed to foster, lend support, and give vent to that expansive, quasi-religious experience of love, joy, and contact with the Divine: though with a far more secular, less cosmically high-brow bent.

The Leary circle increasingly eschewed "square" academic texts for those more in line with Huxley's *The Doors of Perception*, Watts's *The Joyous Cosmology*, Robert Heinlein's science-fiction classic *Stranger in a Strange Land* (1961), Hermann Hesse's *Journey to the East*, various Buddhist and Taoist works, along with authors more hip to the wild blue yonder like Swedish evangelist Emanuel Swedenborg, poet William Blake, the French surrealists, and *The Tibetan Book of the Dead.*

Convinced they were on the inside track to godhood, Leary and his crowd became reckless, messianically overconfident, groovier-than-thou, brash, and pains-in-the-ass—a cycle apparently endemic to LSD "scenes"—witness Kesey, the Red Dog, and much of Haight-Ashbury, when on its downward spiral. Rumors began circulating about off-campus sessions that used drugs recreationally. Even Hubbard, the LSD missionary par excellence, warned Leary to tone down his act and stop rocking the Harvard boat. The party, though, continued unabated with the psychic noisemakers, streamers, and confetti flying away.

The bow-tie wing of academia was not amused. They began putting Leary on a leash, reining him in. He was attacked (not without justification) at faculty meetings for his loose methodology. He was accused (not without justification) of being too ready to characterize an amped-out sexual rout or an LSD dinner party as a religious experience. When, in the spring of 1962, the press got wind of strange doings at Harvard and began playing up the controversy, Harvard told Leary that all future psilocybin projects would have to be conducted in the presence of a licensed doctor. Leary and Alpert were ordered to turn over their supply of psilocybin to Harvard's custody, and a faculty committee was appointed to oversee future experiments. By year's end, the psilocybin projects were officially terminated. In May 1963, Harvard fired Alpert—the first time in the twentieth century that a Harvard faculty member was fired—and Leary's contract was not renewed. Leary, having read the handwriting on the wall, had already announced he wouldn't be coming back.

Leary responded by publicly thumbing his nose at the establishment and all its mean-spirited, short-sighted, square proclivities: an essentially adolescent, nyah-nyah-nyah mindset that colored his enterprise, often unnecessarily and self-destructively, from that point on. No longer saddled with the stodgy, beside-the-point constraints of academia, Leary and Alpert moved the party off campus and up a couple of notches. Styling himself a martyr to the cause, Leary adopted the mantle of psychedelic high priest, going so far as to giving this title to one of his books, with its cover bearing his psychedelicized visage. Leary eventually took his high priest identity seriously enough to begin wearing a white robe and golden headband.

With Harvard tightening the screws and the denouement to this soap opera obvious to anyone able to give it an objective eye, in January 1963 Leary cashed in on his jet-setter, socialite connections—the people he and Alpert had been turning on at weekend parties—to set up a "nonprofit" called the International Federation for Internal Freedom (IFIF) with offices in Boston, New York, and Los Angeles. Leary was president, Alpert director, and Metzger, Watts, and religious scholar Huston Smith served on the board of directors. IFIF promoted the principle that everyone should have unlimited freedom to use mind-altering chemicals as a tool for enhancing inner growth without government regulation or intervention.

Leary and company rented two large houses in suburban Boston and established two "colonies," or "transpersonative communities" (Leary's terms), whose purpose was to foster experiments in "transcendent living" ostensibly modeled on the psychedelic utopia described by Huxley in his final novel, *Island* (1962). Put in less grandiose terms, these communities were hippie, New Age communes. They prefigured the "scene" that would surface in the coming months at Millbrook with stereos blaring Thelonious Monk records,

Figure 4. Timothy Leary, high priest of LSD, October 23, 1970. *Source*: Author's collection.

rooms decorated with collages, and a meditation room overpowered by incense. Later that spring and the next year, IFIF set up camp in the twenty-room Hotel Catalina Beach Resort in Zihuatanejo, a remote, lush, tropical area along the Pacific coast of Mexico, with a plan to conduct month-long seminars in transpersonative community and transcendent living to teach the participants how to guide LSD sessions. (The LSD used in these seminars came through the good offices of Al Hubbard.) Leary renamed the site the Freedom Center and selected participants from five thousand applicants. As with the IFIF colonies back in Boston, this experiment in transcendence was rife with partying, boozing, and freewheeling sex. The psychedelic seminarians included psychologists and social scientists, a few artists and idle rich, a businessman, authors, and other assorted experimenters. Both Osmond and Huxley, significantly, turned down Leary's offer to join this "experiment," saying they disapproved of his publicity mongering. As an index to how airheaded Leary and company had become by this juncture, the community set up a tower on the beach and decreed that it be manned at all times by someone tripping on LSD, with solemn changing-of-the-guard ceremonies every sunrise and sunset.

This group, obviously, was not your low-rent, coupon-cutting crowd struggling to keep the utilities on and remain abreast of the kids' school lunch payments. Only those who could pay $200 a month and enjoyed job-free leisure could undertake this experiment in transcendent living. Nightly, all-night sexual orgies were reputedly the norm. "I remember a kind of loosening of sexual bounds," recalled one of the experimenters. "It was like a love fest" (Burleigh 2022, B5). By the second year of the psychedelic retreat after Leary read a paper at the Mexican Institute of Biomedical Research, the government considered Leary "absurd, confused, valueless" and expelled the group from the country. This pattern—indiscreet, in-your-face, high-profile, damn-the-neighbors revelry—would be repeated to similarly disastrous effects with Kesey at La Honda and the Red Dog Saloon in Virginia City.

The IFIF-ers, however, were not inclined to rough it, tone down their act, or take Saint Francis of Assisi as their model for transcendent living. They were far more akin to television evangelist Reverend Ike in a spiritual pig-out at the vortex of a high-priced hookers convention during the closing days of Mardi Gras. They continued consorting and partying with some of the wealthiest jet-setters of the time, a defining proclivity of Leary throughout his career.

Peggy Hitchcock, one of the true-believer jewels in Leary's beautiful-people crown, became the director of IFIF's New York branch.[1] With the IFIFers all dressed up and nowhere to go, Hitchcock mentioned that her family owned an ancestral estate in upstate New York—Millbrook—that might serve their purpose. Millbrook was co-owned by her twin brothers, Tommy and Billy Hitchcock, the latter a Lehman Brothers stockbroker, also in his twenties, who had spent his recent years working in London. The social and genetic pedigree of Peggy, Tommy, and Billy Hitchcock matched the wealthiest, high-born status of nearly anyone in the world. Their father, Tommy, who had been a polo phenomenon known as the "Babe Ruth of Polo," died test-piloting a P-51 in 1944. Their mother was the daughter of William Larimer Mellon, founder of Gulf Oil. Mom's family had also founded Alcoa Aluminum and the Mellon Bank. In the mid-'60s, the Hitchcock clan was worth a reputed $5 billion. The Hitchcock siblings each enjoyed trust fund incomes of $15,000 a week and $7 million a year.

Leary tuned in, turned on, and cashed in on the Hitchcock largesse. Peggy introduced Billy to Leary, and Leary, naturally, promptly did an LSD session with Billy, whereupon Billy, who fancied himself a bit of an outlaw, put the family mansion at the disposal of Leary and his followers for the token rent of $500 per month. Millbrook was an Addams Family–style edifice with an extravaganza of turrets, porches, fretted woodwork, nooks and crannies, rich (though genteelly fraying) red carpeting, a panoply of mandalas and occult signalia, and a labyrinthine sixty-four-room interior. One entered the five square miles of estate through a gatehouse and reached the house by means of a mile-long, tree-lined driveway. The estate housed several "quarters," each luxurious in its own right. Situated amid polo fields, riding stables, tennis courts, an ornamental fountain, and acres of pines, streams, and ponds, it became a psychedelic paradise, just the thing for undisturbed experiments in transpersonative community.

The party was on. In September 1963, a core group of around thirty devotees, disciples, hangers-on, artists, musicians, and fellow seekers—plus your expedient sprinkling of celebrities and wealthy jet-setters—moved into Millbrook and set about exploring unfamiliar realities, sharing priapic ecstasies, doing a lot of LSD-centered partying (eerily paralleling Kesey at La Honda on the other side of the country), and founding a quasi-religious movement destined to retool mankind. Once again, we see that psychedelic-fueled compulsion to form groups ("tribes") in shared celebration of "The Experience."

Hollingshead described this scene extensively in *The Man Who Turned On the World* (1973). He detailed communal tripping and drug-fueled sex with an emphasis—in theory, at least—on "love" and "radiance" in an atmosphere of serenity and high-minded contemplation to achieve permanent spiritual transformation. The scene was part ashram, part research institute, part scholarly enterprise, and part sexual deer park.

Leary and company nevertheless persisted in viewing themselves as the priestly/scientific vanguard of a psychedelic revolution. They kept extensive records of the vagaries and evolution of their mental states, discussed their experiences and compared notes, and started a quasi-academic journal, the *Psychedelic Review.* Leary went so far as to devise—in dead seriousness!—the blueprint for mankind's next 500 years. Eventually, three "religious" sects sprouted up within the Millbrook complex: Leary and his League for Spiritual Discovery (LSD), the Neo-American Boohoo Church (headed by psychiatrist Art Kleps, who believed in tripping twenty-four hours a day), and a Hindu ashram.

Personages, who partook of sessions at Millbrook during this period, read like a who's who of the superstar '60s counterculture: everyone from NASA scientist Steve Groff to psychiatrist R. D. Laing; from Humphry Osmond to jazz musicians Charles Lloyd, Charles Mingus (he liked to work in the gardens), and Maynard Ferguson, who moved with his wife and kids into Millbrook; from Paul Krassner (editor of *The Realist*) to Andy Warhol star Viva Superstar. The local townspeople watched developments at Millbrook with as much rising concern as had those at Harvard and Zihuatanejo. The neighbors complained and demanded that the authorities *do something.* A team of deputies led by an assistant district attorney named G. Gordon Liddy—of the future Nixon administration and Watergate disgrace—staked out the mansion for months. Early one morning in April 1966, the team kicked in the front door and conducted a five-hour search of the joint that yielded nothing more than a small quantity of marijuana. Liddy, though, had failed to follow certain legal procedures, and the "bust" was subsequently thrown out of court. The Dutchess County constabulary responded by clamping down even harder, laying siege to Millbrook, blockading roads in and out of the estate, and conducting searches of all comers and goers.

The party, for all intents and purposes, was over. One cannot, after all, live "transcendentally" and properly blueprint the next 500 years of mankind's development under conditions that restrictive. When, in the spring of 1967, Billy Hitchcock decided to split for the West Coast—by then, all the best LSD action was found there—he gave everyone the boot and Leary a parting check of $14,000. Leary and company took the show back on the road and began looking—like the Pranksters in 1964—for a "cool place." Leary ended up on the West Coast in Southern California with the Brotherhood of Eternal Love, an ultra-idealistic (initially, at least) group that, in its devotion to spreading the acid brotherhood, developed into a worldwide drug distribution network. Leary would also end up in prison, and then variously associate himself with the Weather Underground and the Black Panthers via Eldridge Cleaver in Algeria, but that's beyond the scope of this story. (For a good rundown of Leary's post-Millbrook history and the evolution of the Brotherhood of Eternal Love, see chapter 9 in Lee and Shlain 1985.)

Seeds were being planted in a number of chic hothouse gardens that, in the next few years, resulted in a vast harvest of weird blooms. A number of separate-but-simpatico constellations were slowly converging to bring about an explosive conjunction of elements of '40s, '50s, and '60s culture.

The Beats and the '60s

I realized that these were all the snapshots which our children would look at someday with wonder, thinking their parents had lived smooth, well-ordered, stabilized-within-the-photo lives and got up in the morning to walk proudly on the sidewalks of life, never dreaming the raggedy madness and riot of our actual lives, our actual night, the hell of it, the senseless, nightmare road. All of it endless and beginningless emptiness.

—Jack Kerouac, *On the Road*

Hold back the edges of your gowns, Ladies, we are going through hell.

—W. C. Williams, Introduction to *Howl and Other Poems*

Much of what would become the '60s counterculture was a direct outgrowth of the literature and lore of the so-called Beat Generation circle of Jack Kerouac, Allen Ginsberg, William Burroughs, Gregory Corso, and Neal Cassady. Mid-'50s works like "Howl," *Naked Lunch,* and *On the Road* rocked literary America and became the scripts from which '60s counterculturists riffed. The entire beatnik culture was an offshoot of the Beats, who served as a kind of transitional bridge between the '50s and the '60s.

Almost every counterculture frontrunner—from Yippie Abby Hoffman to Bob Dylan, from Jerry Garcia of the Grateful Dead to Ed Sanders of the Fugs—cited their reading of Kerouac's *On the Road* as one of the chief formative influences of their lives. The Beats helped to prime the pump for the emergence of psychedelic culture on both sides of the Atlantic. British '60s participant Barry Miles noted, for example, that: "By general consensus, the era of British psychedelia began with the 'Poets of the World/Poets of Our Time' reading at the Royal Albert Hall . . . on Friday, June 11, 1965," that featured such poets as Ginsberg, Ferlinghetti, and Corso (Henke 1997, 17–18). Even Scottish-born psych-folkie Robin Williamson of the Incredible String Band cited Kerouac as one of the primary formative influences on his musical and intellectual development.

"As soon as *On the Road* came out," Jerry Garcia explained, "I read it and fell in love with it, the adventure, the romance of it, everything" (DeCurtis 1993, 45). Rock Scully, a frontline participant in the evolution of Haight-Ashbury and later manager of the Grateful Dead, has similarly noted of Garcia's formative years how much he was influenced by reading the Beats. Garcia, he observed "is well read. The beats are his guys: Jack Kerouac, Gregory Corso, William Burroughs, and Lawrence Ferlinghetti. Jerry was fifteen when *On the Road* came out, and it became his bible, one long be-bop wail to hedonism and transcendence" (Scully and Dalton 1996, 23). Scully also recalled that Grateful Dead bassist Phil Lesh, when he first met Garcia, "loved Allen Ginsberg's *Howl* so much that he was in the process of setting it to music" (25).

The relationship of the Beat subculture (by way of North Beach) to the '60s counterculture (by way of Haight-Ashbury) was, like all relationships, both provocative and problematic. There's a reductive stereotype at work in the use of categorical nomenclature like "the Beats," "the hippies," "the counterculture" and "the '60s," but it is nevertheless true that the Beats—and to a lesser extent the urban-underground beatnik scene that it in part prompted—were more literary, cerebral, idea-oriented, small-grouped, and ingrown-toenail existential than the hippies, who were more given to communal, mass-participatory, jubilant bacchanals, festivals, and be-ins. While the beatnik worshipped the be-shaded, goateed hipster bop musician letting loose a complicated improvisational run in a smoky, darkened, gin-joint, jazz dive, the hippie worshipped the long-haired, freakily clad rock guitarist on a psychedelic feedback soar, performing with a backdrop of blobbing, swirling psychedelic lights in a massive tribal gathering at sites like the Avalon and the Fillmore.

Kerouac used to say in the years of his post–*On the Road* slide into alcoholism, "I'm King of the Beats, but I'm not a beatnik" (Charters 2015, 279). He generally loathed hippies, believing them to be shallow, lightweight fakes, who failed to earn their hipster affectations. In his single linkup with the Merry Pranksters, he asked them—in rhetorical, not information-seeking fashion—whether they were Communists. As Scully remembered:

> When the Grateful Dead began, San Francisco was still in that transitional period from Beat to Hip. We aspired to the bohemian, outlaw code of the Beats. They smoked grass, ate magic mushrooms, grew beards, and wore Levi's and plaid flannel shirts. They were into jazz, Zen, and existentialism. . . .
>
> But it is not exactly a mutual admiration society. The Beats from North Beach look askance at us hippies. We are on a different wavelength. This has to do with musical tempo and electronics and the changing of an era. Of course, there is one other little factor: the mind-bending drugs. . . . You can't read a book when you're on acid. (Scully and Dalton 1996, 22)

It makes for an interesting evening's conversation over beers to speculate on the extent to which the Haight-Ashbury counterculture would have evolved without Beat texts like *On the Road*, "Howl," and *Naked Lunch*, and without Beat figures like Kerouac, Ginsberg, Burroughs, and Cassady as precursors and models off which to riff. The fact remains, however, that Neal Cassady, Kerouac's best friend and model for Dean Moriarty in *On the Road* and for Cody in *Visions of Cody*, became a key figure in the Ken Kesey/Merry Prankster circle and drive the Prankster bus; and that Allen Ginsberg became a central cog in the entire Haight-Ashbury, '60s counterculture scene, surfacing everywhere from India to the Lower East Side, from Millbrook to La Honda, from Liverpool to the Gathering of the Tribes.

The overlappings, connections, and interconnections between the Beats and the '60s counterculture were considerable. Burroughs, Ginsberg, Kerouac, and Cassady experimented extensively with consciousness-altering drugs from the '40s on, utilizing everything from marijuana to cocaine, Dexedrine, morphine, heroin, and peyote (the latter easily procured from a store on the corner of Tenth Street and Second Avenue in the Bowery). Kerouac used speed so much at one point in the mid-'40s that his hair began falling out and he wore pancake makeup to hide skin problems.

Burroughs went so far as to deliberately addict himself to morphine and then heroin. Five years or so older than most of the others in the Beat circle, Burroughs functioned as a kind of worldly mentor to the others in terms of the literary and intellectual netherworld, the hip underworld, and experimental drug use. In 1953, Burroughs ventured alone into Amazonian South America for the specific purpose of exploring the hallucinatory properties of the drug yage (ayahuasca—which, by the way, has the same psychoactive property as the hallucinogen DMT—N-dimethyltryptamine).

In the late '50s and early '60s, Ginsberg became all but obsessed with the idea of using drugs as a tool of visionary experience and consciousness expansion, and as a vehicle for creative breakthrough and stylistic retooling. He viewed this quest almost as a moral obligation, and he pursued it less in pleasure—many of his experiences were horrific and painful—than as an escape from real-world responsibility and work. Toward that end, he experimented with every drug (and combination of drugs) from marijuana, to peyote, cocaine, amphetamines, mescaline, yage, heroin, morphine, and nitrous oxide (laughing gas). Meanwhile, he read widely on the effects of hallucinogens on the mind.

Ginsberg's quest took him far and wide, bringing him into contact with an amazing array of the cultural elite. In the late spring of 1959, he was invited by social scientist and linguist Gregory Bateson to participate in research experiments on LSD being conducted at Stanford University. Having read *The Doors of Perception* and *Heaven and Hell* (Huxley's later book on LSD), Ginsberg jumped at Bateson's invitation. "It was astonishing," he reported of his acid experience. "I lay back, listening to music, and went into a sort of trance state (somewhat similar to the high state of Laughing Gas) and in a fantasy much like a Coleridge world of Kubla Khan saw a vision of that part of my consciousness which deemed to be permanent and transcendent and identical with the origin of the universe—a sort of identity common with everything—but a clear and coherent sight of it" (Schumacher 1992, 311).

In a follow-up to (and in imitation of) Burroughs, Ginsberg toured South America in 1960 in quest of yage. He took several varieties of it in varying doses on a number of occasions in several locations. Some of the experiences were horrific and left permanent scars on his psyche, but Ginsberg was dead serious about his experiments and followed them through doggedly, learning whatever they could teach him about consciousness. (His correspondence with Burroughs about his experiences appear in Burroughs and Ginsberg 1963.) He brought a gallon jug of yage back with him to New York that he shared with poet Peter Orlovsky and Kerouac.

Ginsberg's activities and pronouncements on behalf of marijuana legalization attracted the attention of the Group for the Advancement of Psychiatry (GAP), an academic body that gathered annually to study a particular subculture and/or sector of society. The focus of the group's 1960 convention, held in Boston, was the Beat Generation, and Ginsberg was invited to address the assemblage. Ginsberg chose for his topic the relation between creativity and altered states of consciousness. In the course of discussing what his experiments in altered states of consciousness had taught him, Ginsberg read several of his drug-related poems, including "Laughing Gas," "Mescaline," and "Lysergic Acid." This same conference brought Osmond to Boston, during which Huxley took him to meet Leary. Osmond buttonholed Ginsberg following his address to tell him about Leary. Upon returning to New York, Ginsberg duly contacted Leary, and within a week Leary was at Ginsberg's Lower East Side sixth-floor walk-up apartment door in hopes of recruiting him as a knight errant for his psychedelic roundtable.

Leary ironically proved to be a babe in the woods compared to Ginsberg as to his knowledge of and firsthand experience with drugs in general and psychedelics in particular. Leary was such a novice, in fact, that he smoked marijuana for the first time during this initial meeting with Ginsberg. Ginsberg's first impression of Leary was the same as Osmond's: he considered him well-meaning, enthusiastic, and naive. As Ginsberg later said of Leary and his suburban Boston lifestyle at that time:

> [Leary] had no idea that every poet in San Francisco had . . . taken peyote and mescaline long ago. Or that everybody was smoking pot. He'd never smoked pot . . . Leary had this big beautiful house, and everybody there was wandering around like it was some happy cocktail party, which was a little shocking to me at first because I still thought of myself as a big, serious religious mediator. And they were all so cheerful and optimistic and convinced that their kind of experiment would be welcomed as a polite, scholarly, socially acceptable, perfectly reasonable pursuit and would spread through the university and be automatically part of the curriculum. Like Leary couldn't conceive of meeting any academic opposition, I kept saying, "You have no idea what you're going to meet, what you're up against." (Stevens 1987, 146)

On November 26, 1960, Ginsberg traveled to Boston to do a psilocybin session with Leary in his Newton home. After taking a dose, he took albums by Beethoven and Wagner to an upstairs bedroom, stripped naked, and waited for the angel choirs. As the drug kicked in, he began feeling that someone—namely, Allen Ginsberg—needed "to take on the responsibility of being the creative God and seize power over the universe" (Hartogsohn 2020, 53). Heeding the cosmic summons, Ginsberg proclaimed himself "the Messiah"—yet another instance of the messianic complex so typical of and endemic to psychedelics.

This incident has become a staple of psychedelic lore. As the psilocybin kicked in, Ginsberg and Orlovsky traipsed downstairs naked—streaming waves of psychedelic glory in their wake—and attempted to telephone Burroughs in Paris, writer Norman Mailer in New York, President John Kennedy in the White House, and Premier Nikita Khrushchev in Moscow. But alas, the only person they managed to contact was Kerouac in Long Island. Ginsberg exhorted Kerouac to rush up to Newton and try LSD, but Kerouac protested that he couldn't leave his mother. (Kerouac did a psilocybin session with Leary in New York City on December 13 that is described in entertaining length in Leary's autobiography, *Flashbacks* [1990]. Leary reports that his experience tripping with Kerouac was a bummer. Kerouac was such a manic, boozy, overwhelming, and sometimes cynical tripping companion that it occasioned Leary's first negative acid experience.) That night, Leary wrote in his memoirs, he and Ginsberg "started planning the psychedelic revolution." Inflamed, exalted, expansive, they agreed to join forces in an avowed mission—strikingly similar to that of Hubbard and Huxley—to "turn on" as many people throughout the world as possible with the aim of provoking a mass revolution in consciousness.

Leary, Ginsberg, and a growing coterie of acolytes began promoting psilocybin (and later acid) in the same way a Marxist true believer pushes revolutionary consciousness on the proletarian masses, or a fundamentalist Christian pushes born-again Christianity on the unredeemed: proselytizing, seeking converts, attempting to contour society and petition the establishment with their "saving" vision and agenda. Ginsberg entertained millennial visions of psychedelics fostering a mass change in sensibility based on "a sense of wide-open, nonjudgmental, nonprejudicial inquisitiveness" (Whitmer 1987, 159), essentially the sensibility of Haight-Ashbury's founders.

With evangelic, man-on-a-mission fervor, Ginsberg proceeded to pass out psilocybin to poet Robert Lowell, Grove Press publisher Barney Rossett, artist Willem de Kooning, painter Franz Klein, trumpeter Dizzy Gillespie, and jazz innovator Thelonious Monk (at the Five Spot Café). Monk complained that the psilocybin had no effect on him (or his band) and asked Ginsberg if he had anything stronger. Gillespie, though, raved and wanted more, both for himself and for his band members. When Neal Cassady got wind of psilocybin via Ginsberg, he tore up to Harvard for a session and emerged from it every bit as enthusiastic as Ginsberg and Leary, proclaiming it "the Rolls Royce of dope, the ultimate high" (this being well before his encounter with Kesey and the Pranksters).

Having reeled in Ginsberg (and Cassady), Leary flew to Tangiers in hopes of talking Burroughs into coming back to Harvard (Burroughs's alma mater) to participate in his psilocybin project. At the time of Leary's arrival, Ginsberg and Corso were visiting Burroughs, and Leary turned on the entire assemblage: Corso, Ginsberg, Burroughs, and poet/playwright Allen Anson. Burroughs had a bad trip, complaining in classic Burroughs fashion about the "purple fire mushroom from the Pain Banks" and noting that "there are many hostile territories in the cerebral hemispheres" (Shumacher 1992, 359).

Despite his negative experience, in August 1961, Burroughs took Leary up on his offer and flew to Boston to participate in the Harvard experiments and address a panel on psychedelics at an American Psychological Association conference. In his presentation, "Points of Distinction among Psychoactive Drugs," Burroughs compared psychedelics to narcotics. A twenty-year veteran of serious drug use and experimentation, Burroughs was hoary with battle scars left by Odyssean trips through the nether regions. Leary, by comparison, was still a tail-wagging pup. Leary later acknowledged that Burroughs was way ahead of any Harvard researcher in this area, noting: "[Burroughs] saw me as a Notre Dame coach of consciousness, giving my players locker-room pep talks about inner freedom" (Schumacher 1992, 432).

Burroughs's approach to the Harvard study differed significantly from Leary's. Burroughs envisioned his participation as an opportunity to explore the mind by way of nonchemical avenues via computers, biofeedback, and neurological implants. He concluded—and not without some basis in fact—that Leary's primary motivation in bringing him to Harvard was to make him a spokesman for psilocybin in a sort of worldwide infomercial. Burroughs denounced Leary and called his project "ill-intentioned," saying: "I hope never to set eyes on that horse's ass again. A real wrong number" (Whitmer 1987, 126).

In a few years, Leary expanded his operation to the West Coast with missionary zeal. From June 13 to 18, 1966, Leary and his followers staged an "LSD Conference" through the extension division of the University of California at Berkeley. He hoped to investigate "the continuing and widening controversy" over LSD in the "first comprehensive survey of the topic." The high priest of acid charged $1.50 to attendees. Speakers featured Richard Alpert, Frank Barron, and several other academics and physicians. Tellingly, Leary did not invite Ken Kesey, who had already begun to promulgate his own approach to expanded consciousness through psychedelics.

LIFELONG LEARNING
UNIVERSITY OF CALIFORNIA EXTENSION | BERKELEY

The LSD Conference

June 13-18, 1966

Figures 5a, 5b, and 5c. Program for LSD Conference at UC Berkeley, 1966. *Source*: New York Public Library Digital Collections, public domain. https://digitalcollections.nypl.org/items/47255690-5382-0135-e794-59c113226593

SCHEDULE

MONDAY, JUNE 13

11 a.m.– 1:30 p.m.	Series registration only (for those not previously registered by mail) Wheeler Auditorium Admission to individual lectures will be sold only at the door before each lecture as space permits.
2:30 p.m.	*Stability and Change in Human Intelligence and Consciousness* FRANK BARRON Wheeler Auditorium
4–5 p.m.	Open Discussion*
8 p.m.	*LSD: Problems and Promise* SIDNEY COHEN Wheeler Auditorium

TUESDAY, JUNE 14

1 p.m.	*LSD: Implications for Law Enforcement* JOSEPH D. LOHMAN Wheeler Auditorium
2:30 p.m.	*The Role of Psychedelics in Shamanism, Witchcraft, and the Vision Quest* MICHAEL J. HARNER Wheeler Auditorium
4–5 p.m.	Open Discussion*
8 p.m.	*LSD and the Art of Conscious Living* RICHARD ALPERT Wheeler Auditorium

WEDNESDAY, JUNE 15

1 p.m.	*Chemistry and Pharmacology of Hallucinogenic Drugs* STERLING BUNNELL Wheeler Auditorium
2:30 p.m.	*Therapeutic Uses of Ibogaine* CLAUDIO NARANJO Wheeler Auditorium
4–5 p.m.	Open Discussion*
8 p.m.	*We Are All One* A multi-channel media-mix of film, tape, oscilloscope, stroboscope, kinetic and live images explored in six integrated movements, *We Are All One* has been described as a kind of non-chemical psychedelic theatre. It is presented by USCO, a group of artists, engineers, and filmmakers. Their media-mixes have been performed at MIT, the University of Rochester, Brandeis University, the University of Buffalo, the Rhode Island School of Design, the University of Wisconsin, the University of British Columbia's Vancouver Arts Festival, and the New York Filmmakers' Cinematheque. Pauley Ballroom

Figure 5b.

THURSDAY, JUNE 16

1 p.m.   *The Myth About Psychedelic Drugs*
              PAUL LEE
              Wheeler Auditorium

2:30 p.m.   *Indications and Contra-Indications for LSD Therapy of Alcoholism*
              ABRAHAM HOFFER
              Wheeler Auditorium

4–5 p.m.   Open Discussion*
              (USCO artists will be available to discuss media-mix techniques.)

8 p.m.   *The Molecular Revolution*
              TIMOTHY LEARY
              Wheeler Auditorium

9:45 p.m.   *We Are All One*
              (repeat performance if demand warrants)
              Pauley Ballroom

FRIDAY, JUNE 17

1 p.m.   *LSD and the Law*
              ALBERT BENDICH
              Wheeler Auditorium

2:30 p.m.   *Consciousness Politics in the Void*
              ALLEN GINSBERG
              Wheeler Auditorium

4–5 p.m.   Open Discussion*
              (Sidney Cohen will be available for discussion of Eric Kast's paper, "LSD
              and the Dying Patient." See note below.)

8 p.m.   Films, experimental and documentary, relating to the psychedelic drugs
              Wheeler Auditorium

SATURDAY, JUNE 18

1 p.m.   *A Descriptive Approach to the Psychedelic Experience*
              ROLF VON ECKARTSBERG
              Wheeler Auditorium

2:30 p.m.   *The Religious Significance of Artificially Induced Religious Experience*
              HUSTON SMITH
              Wheeler Auditorium

4–5 p.m.   Open Discussion*

8 p.m.   PANEL: *What Do We Not Know?*
              PAUL LEE (Moderator)   SIDNEY COHEN   HUSTON SMITH
              RICHARD ALPERT   ABRAHAM HOFFER
              Wheeler Auditorium

* Open discussion periods for speakers and participants will be held each day in Wheeler
  Auditorium or adjoining classrooms (no separate admission fee).

Figure 5c.

4

Moving to the West Coast

The Kesey Wing

"Lu ral lu ral lu" may be more impressively sung than very real wisdom talked.

　　　　　　　　—Henry David Thoreau, *Journals* (February 6, 1841)

In 1958—roughly the same time that the Beats became prominent and Timothy Leary moved from the Kaiser Foundation Hospital in Oakland to Harvard and discovered "God's flesh"—a recent graduate of the University of Oregon showed up at Stanford University by way of a Woodrow Wilson Fellowship designed to encourage graduate students to become college teachers. In the era of the Sputnik scare and space race between the United States and the Soviet Union, when the government poured money into disciplines like physics and engineering, liberals widely feared that unless counteractive steps were taken to shore up the humanities, the liberal arts would wither on the vine. In consequence, oodles and oodles of money—and tenured college teaching jobs—were being made available to graduate students in the humanities. This Woodrow Wilson fellow, Ken Kesey, had moved to Oregon from his birthplace of La Junta, Colorado—a largely Chicano farming community—when he was in third grade, after his father got a job on a dairy ranch in Oregon. The first person in his family to graduate from high school, Kesey married his high-school sweetheart during his junior year at the University of Oregon. After graduating, he worked for a while in his father's creamery.

At the University of Oregon, Kesey had been a scholarship varsity wrestler and a major in performing arts: an unheard-of jock/academic combination in those years. For his required graduation recital, he performed an imitation of hipster comedian Lord Buckley. At the time of his arrival at Stanford, he was in the process of writing a novel about football. He decided, accordingly, to apply for admission to the Stanford Writing Program; he was accepted. The following spring, he landed the Woodrow Wilson Fellowship, and he and his wife found living quarters on Perry Lane, a bohemian neighborhood in Stanford, site of the old Stanford farm, which formerly served as an army training camp during World War I. A dozen or so cabins—little more than shacks—were hastily erected as troop housing. In ensuing decades, that leafy, bucolic, run-down enclave evolved into a ghetto-of-choice for artsy hobos in search of cheap housing (rents in 1958 were $60 per month) in a rustic setting. Perry Lane developed a certain bohemian exclusivity; you had to know someone to get in.

Upon moving in to Perry Lane, Kesey went "coffeehouse." He grew a beard, began playing the guitar (after a fashion), and singing (so to speak) folk songs, smoked grass for the first time, and got drunk for the second time (the first was at his bachelor party). He set aside the football novel for a novel called *Zoo* about a rodeo rider's son, who moved to North Beach and began consorting with beatniks.

In 1959, Kesey heard from fellow Perry Laner Vic Lovell, a Ph.D. candidate in psychology, about a drug research program at Veterans Hospital in nearby Menlo Park that paid volunteers $20 a day to take drugs while researchers questioned, observed, and administered tests. It turns out that this program was sponsored by the CIA's MK-ULTRA program, and the data compiled went into CIA files. Acting on Lovell's tip, Kesey signed up. Among the drugs he ingested in the program were psilocybin, mescaline, LSD, and super-amphetamine IT-290. It was also about this time that Ginsberg was getting his initiation into LSD under the tutelage of Gregory Bateson at Stanford.

Like almost everyone, Kesey's initiation into consciousness-altering drugs produced a profound sea change—or, more exactly, reaffirmed and reinforced propensities already there but which had been held in check by social conditioning. One of the proclivities reaffirmed, apparently, was messianic: a desire à la Osmond, Huxley, Hubbard, and Leary to spread the psychedelic word. Kesey underwent the progression so typical of the psychedelic initiate: first, the desire to share the experience, and then the compulsion to "turn on" as many people as possible with the aim of provoking a mass revolution in consciousness. Within several months of becoming a volunteer, Kesey took a job in the same hospital as a psychiatric aid in the mental ward working a midnight-to-eight shift. Discovering that the cupboards where the drugs were stored weren't locked, Kesey helped himself. Back at Perry Lane, psychedelic drugs became one of the key ingredients in his famous venison stew. In short order, many Perry Laners started experimenting with LSD—at the time, as legal as beer or wine—along with peyote, psilocybin, and the like. Similarly to L.A. five years before, LSD catalyzed a "scene" that would prove consequential far beyond itself. In March 1963, Kesey and other Perry Laners such as Vic Lovell wrote to Leary and asked to form an International Federation for Internal Freedom (IFIF) research group to further explore LSD and other psychedelics. Many of Kesey's classmates in the writing program, his Perry Lane friends, and people who began frequenting the parties they threw would become the core of his Merry Prankster circle.

Figure 6. Ken Kesey, 1964, photo shoot for *Sometimes a Great Notion*. Photo: Hank Kranzler. *Source*: Special Collections & University Archives, University of Oregon Libraries. https://oregondigital.org/catalog/oregondigital:df73g9851

At this juncture in a ten-month span, Kesey wrote *One Flew over the Cuckoo's Nest,* at least partially inspired by his ongoing use of psychedelics. Significantly, Kesey dedicated the book to Vic Lovell, the Perry Laner, who told him about the Menlo Park drug experiments and who would become a Prankster in Kesey's circle.

In February 1962, the novel was published to widespread acclaim.[1] It is both the archetypal '60s novel and an index to how Kesey envisioned himself. In his role as Prankster ringleader, Kesey was a proto-Randle McMurphy: a heroic "disrupter" (half con man, half hero), who glories in giving rollicking hell to the life-negating, authority-enforcing Big Nurse, and in inciting the "loonies" to liberate the loony bin. Soon, royalties poured in, and the book was made into a Broadway play. At age twenty-six, less than three years out of the dairy farm, Kesey had made it big.

There were several Beat/'60s conjunctions on the Perry Lane scene, especially William Burroughs's novel *Naked Lunch,* which created a creative stir among the Perry Laners. Though blocked from publication in the United States until 1966, when the Massachusetts Supreme Court declared it obscene, *Naked Lunch* nevertheless circulated among the Perry Lane circle in its original 1959 French publication. The influence of *Naked Lunch* on the Perry Lane scene arose from Burroughs's prose style—particularly the way he evoked altered states of consciousness. It is less a novel than a nonlinear collection of what Burroughs calls "routines": a loosely related pastiche of characters and scenarios of a poetic and surrealistic nature. In the vein of Jean Genet's *Our Lady of the Flowers* (1943), *Naked Lunch* treats grotesque, taboo, bizarre (sometimes depraved, sadistic) nightmare incidents and subject matter with poetic and lyrical beauty. When Burroughs's *Naked Lunch* appeared on Perry Lane," Lovell noted, "it was incredibly influential to all of us in saying, 'There are new directions.' Especially Kesey. Ken read *Naked Lunch* a great deal. He was very much influenced by it" (Whitmer 1987, 201–2).

The growing scene at Perry Lane facilitated another element that would be seminal to the advent of Haight-Ashbury: the so-called Chateau located at 838 Santa Cruz Avenue in nearby Menlo Park. The Chateau was a large, run-down house in a weed-strewn yard set back from the street on a hill. It was owned by an artist named Frank Serretoni, who rented out rooms to various party animals and high rollers. It evolved into a quasi-beatnik, Animal House with parties sometimes lasting for three-to-four-day stretches. The Chateau scene flourished from 1961 to 1963, after which it became a Baptist church. Eventually, it was torn down and replaced by condos. At

Chateau parties, the members of the Grateful Dead first met—with the exception of Bob Weir, who was barely a teenager at the time. Neal Cassady—who, like Ginsberg, seemed to pop up everywhere when something interesting surfaced—stayed at the Chateau on and off, as did Jerry Garcia, who lived in the pup house out back, and Robert Hunter, longtime "folkie," and future Dead lyricist. Hunter became Garcia's running buddy (they lived for a while in two cars parked side-by-side, eating meals out of tin cans).

Other Chateau frequenters included future Haight-Ashbury luminaries such as Rod Albin (brother of future Big Brother bassist Peter Albin), Jorma Kaukonen (future Jefferson Airplane lead guitarist, then a student at Santa Clara University, a private Jesuit school), Phil Lesh (future Grateful Dead bassist, then a college student composing classical music in the mode of Paul Hindemith, Walter Piston, and Karlheinz Stockhausen), Roy Seburn and Page Browning (both future Pranksters), and Mimi and Richard Farina. (Mimi was Joan Baez's sister; Richard was the folk singer and author of the underground classic *I've Been Down So Long It Looks Like Up to Me*.) One of the now-fabled "happenings" at the Chateau was the so-called Groovy Conclave—an epochal, wall-to-wall party that began on November 18, 1962, and lasted for five days.

The Chateau and Perry Lane scenes overlapped with various habitués showing up at each other's parties. As Jerry Garcia remembered it, "Kesey used to live on Perry Lane, which is just down from Stanford, and we lived over at the Chateau, which was maybe two or three blocks away, and we would stumble over to their parties and some of them would spill over to our parties. But we really were different scenes because we were much younger . . . We were all just dropouts and they were college people" (Troy 1994, 68).

Neal Cassady probably became the most important connection between the Chateau and Perry Lane scenes and the evolution of the counterculture two to three years down the road. Cassady first materialized at Perry Lane by way of a January 1963 work-in-progress reading by several writing students. Many times, the Perry Laners had readings—high-art excuses for parties—wherein various writing students would read passages from their works in progress, the readings being, in effect, the literary equivalent of a musical jam session. One of the readers on this particular occasion was Larry McMurtry, then working on his second novel, *Leaving Cheyenne* (1962). As was customary, the reading was conducted in the living room of one of the Perry Laners. In the middle of the reading, jam-packed with people, a frenetic, hyperactive Neal Cassady appeared and proceeded to climb over everyone to get to the front, doing one of his nonstop free-associative mono-logues all the while. His radar uncannily attuned to potentially significant "scenes," Cassady had read *One Flew over the Cuckoo's Nest* and wanted to check out Kesey. He began showing up at Perry Lane parties and readings.

At the time, Cassady was an ex-con on probation. He had been arrested on April 8, 1958, for offering joints to two undercover agents in return for giving him a ride while hitchhiking. He got sentenced to a prison term in San Quentin of five years to life, but secured an early release for good behavior on July 4, 1960. Subsequently, Cassady was in and out of jail frequently, usually because of his unending stream of traffic violations. As the prototype for Dean Moriarty in Kerouac's *On the Road,* Cassady was enthusiastically embraced and celebrated by the Perry Laners. He would go on to become a key cog in the Kesey scene, eventually driving the Kesey bus and earning the moniker "Speed Limit" for his extreme use of amphet-amines, his driving habits, and his approach to life.

On February 8, 1926, Neal Cassady was born in a homemade trailer hitched to the back of a Model-A while his quasi-Oakie parents were passing through Salt Lake City en route to California. By the time Neal was seven, his father was a full-fledged wino, and Neal grew up with his father in flophouses on Denver's skid row. He became a prolific car thief, reputedly stealing over 500 cars, and did time in reform school. Despite his skid-row upbringing, Cassady frequented the public library and avidly read both philosophy and literature. He pulled off the improbable feat of hooking up with a small core of Ivy Leaguers—Jack Kerouac, Allen Ginsberg, William Burroughs chief among them—who would be the prime movers and formulators of the still-to-be-formed Beat Generation.

Cassady's link with the Beats came about largely by way of a Columbia University alumnus and the supposedly Denver civic pillar named Justin Brierly. Bespectacled and mustachioed, an attorney and realtor, Brierly was a director of the Central City Opera House Association.[2] He was also a committee member of the Ivy League Scholarship Board in Denver and had enough influence at Columbia to appear at campus groundbreakings along-side former president Dwight D. Eisenhower, then Columbia University's president (Amburn 1998, 153). Brierly also did counseling and teaching at East High School, which Cassady attended (without graduating) during the mid-'40s. A pedophile, he adopted certain students (always males) as protégés and works in progress, making some of them objects of sexual attention. Recognizing a raw, untutored brilliance in Cassady—who by now had a rap sheet (six convictions) and had spent a year in jail—Brierly became a kind of mentor, trying to steer the obviously intelligent youth toward a more academically serious direction. His efforts were not altogether altruistic; he also seduced Cassady, ushering the adolescent into his first homosexual experience (Turner 1996, 79).

A previous East High Brierly protégé, Hal Chase, had gone on to Columbia. There, he became friends with Allen Ginsberg and his circle of friends, which included Kerouac, Burroughs, and Lucien Carr, who later became editor of United Press International. Chase lived with Kerouac (who, by then, was a Columbia dropout) throughout his junior year at Columbia (1946–1947) in an apartment he shared with Edie Parker (Kerouac's then girlfriend and later wife) and Joan Vollmer (who would marry Burroughs, have a child by him, and be shot in the head by him in a William Tell stunt in Mexico). It was a drug-saturated, decadent scene of brilliant, all-night talks and consortings with a steady influx of petty criminals, drug users, pushers and addicts, and Times Square hipsters. During visits home, Chase told the latest batch of Brierly protégés—Cassady and Ed White—about the scene at Columbia, and Kerouac wrote letters to Chase over the summer, which Chase in turn showed to White and Cassady. White graduated with a degree in architecture at Columbia (he later designed Denver's Botanical Gardens). There, he became lifelong friends with Kerouac, the two going to jazz clubs and conducting serious discussions about literature and writing problems.

Cassady carefully listened to all the talk of this scene and soaked it in like a sponge. He yearned to go to Columbia, but his checkered career, academic and otherwise, made that as likely as finding a vegetarian Eskimo. Chase, though, supported Cassady, going out of his way to convince several Columbia professors, writer Lionel Trilling among them, to give Cassady a shot at Columbia by way of an oral, rather than written, examination. Like so many who knew Cassady, Chase was convinced Cassady was intellectually brilliant. Cassady—as would be typical throughout his life—never showed up for the exam that Chase had taken such pains to set up.

Brierly paid a visit to his alma mater just prior to Christmas in 1946 to see how Chase was faring, only to find him immersed in a scene of hothouse decadence with Ginsberg (a Jewish homosexual aspiring poet), Burroughs (a well-born Harvard alum turned heroin addict, homosexual, and Times Square hipster), and Kerouac (a Columbia dropout, ex-jock, Merchant Marine, sexual switch-hitter, and aspiring novelist). The order of the day was drugs, petty crime, and steamy sex of multiple varieties, mixed with hip-but-cultivated talk and serious artistic pretensions.

Cassady chomped at the bit in eagerness to check out this Ivy-League coterie of poets, hipsters, jazz buffs, student swingers, and serious partiers. He vaguely hoped—despite having blown his previous chance—to somehow talk, finagle, bluff, or con his way into Columbia. He boarded a bus (his sixteen-year-old wife in tow) and took off for New York City, somewhat akin to the way he'd simply shown up at Perry Lane in 1963. There, Chase took Cassady on the rounds, in the course of which he met and became friends with Kerouac. Kerouac already knew of Cassady via Chase as "the jail kid" (see the opening pages of *On the Road*). They were mutually impressed, but for different reasons, and went on to become close friends, eventually making the series of cross-country trips that became the basis for *On the Road* and other novels by Kerouac, and which would at least partly inspire Kesey's 1964 cross-country bus trip with Cassady at the wheel.

Such was the scenario in 1962, five years after *On the Road* was published (Kerouac wrote it in 1951, but it was first published in 1957). Cassady profoundly influenced people who—psychologically, creatively, and spiritually—were all dressed up with nowhere to go (but raring to GO). He became a central figure in the Beat inner circle of the '40s, the model for the main character in *On the Road*, more or less the bible of '60s counterculture. Twenty years later and, on the opposite coast, he became a key cog, role model, and quasi-guru for the Kesey/Grateful Dead circle, one of the defining forces in the Haight-Ashbury evolution. Cassady had an amazing knack for zeroing in on culturally transformative scenes before they had fully germinated and come to the attention of the wider public.

Cassady's influence on Jerry Garcia provides a good example of his effect on nearly everyone whose path he crossed. On a number of occasions, Garcia described the importance of Cassady to him. He characterized Cassady as an authority on "subjects that haven't been identified yet" (Amburn 1998, 352) and noted how his mind was repeatedly "blown by how deep [Cassady] was, how much he could take into account in any given moment and be really in time with it. Neal represented a model to be of how far you could take it in the individual way" (Troy 1994, 80).

In 1963, Stanford sold the Perry Lane property to a developer who bulldozed it and constructed a shopping center. (The site is now the north parking lot of I. Magnin in the Stanford Shopping Center.) Kesey wanted to keep the party going. Taking advantage of his considerable *Cuckoo* royalties, he purchased a log cabin on six rural acres in the redwood hills of La Honda, situated on the peninsula between Palo Alto and the ocean, roughly fifty to sixty miles from San Francisco and fifteen miles east of Stanford, making it essentially the West Coast version of Millbrook. The Perry Lane hardcore—most of them highly intelligent, supremely educated, some of them serious writers, some of them merely scenesters par excellence—transferred their ongoing party from Perry Lane to La Honda, many of them living there in tents, Kesey providing the food, exhorting the troops, scripting, narrating, and orchestrating the "scene."

That fall, Ken Babbs returned to the Kesey fold following a stint in Vietnam as a Marine helicopter pilot. The tour of duty was necessitated by his ROTC scholarship back in his days at the University of Miami in Ohio, where he had majored in English and played basketball on college teams good enough to make it to the NCAA tournament twice. He had come to Palo Alto for the same reason as Kesey: the Stanford Writing Program.

By now, Kesey was close to completing his second novel, *Sometimes a Great Notion,* and word of the scene at La Honda was spreading: in no small measure because Kesey, similar to Leary, hoped to "turn on" and reel in as many celebrities, cultural heavy hitters, and big names as he could. The party began to escalate and expand at La Honda, with the likes of Cassady, writer Hunter Thompson, Ginsberg, writer and ecologist Stewart Brand, the Hells Angels, and even poet and editor Malcolm Cowley. Some of the party-goers staying for protracted periods. This was hardly a teenage crowd. Most of the originals were in their mid-twenties or older, with Thompson over thirty, Ginsberg in his mid-thirties, and Cassady in his late-thirties. "We weren't old enough to be beatniks, and we were too old to be hippies," quipped Kesey (Flanagan 2021, 3).

Other La Honda full-timers, regulars, and frequenters included Sandy "Dismount" Lehmann-Haupt (brother of Christopher Lehmann-Haupt, chief book reviewer at the *New York Times* for thirty years), George Walker (aka the "Psychedelic Courier," who attended Stanford Law School), Mike "Mal Function" Hagen (a frat brother of Kesey's at the University of Oregon), Ron "Hassler" Bevirt (just out of the army), Ed McClanahan (Stanford Writing Project product and author of several novels and nonfiction books), Gordon Lish (novelist, later an editor at Knopf), Gurney Norman (Stanford Writing Project graduate and novelist), Robert Stone (Stanford Writing Project product and author of *Dog Soldiers* [1974] and *Children of Light* [1986]), Peter Beagle (Stanford Writing Project graduate and novelist), artist Roy Seburn, and Ron Boise (a sculptor whose works became part of the acid parties and Trips Festival lore).

The Merry Pranksters, the Psychedelic Bus, and Acid Tests

> Life is a picnic, en costume: one must take a part, assume a character, stand ready in a sensible way to play the fool.
>
> —Herman Melville, *The Confidence-Man* (1857)

Nothing succeeds if prankishness has no part in it.

> —Frederick Nietzsche, *Twilight of the Idols:*
> *Or How to Philosophize with a Hammer* (1889)

And as we League brothers traveled throughout the world without motor-cars or ships, as we conquered the war-shattered world by our faith and transformed it into Paradise, we creatively brought the past, the future and the fictitious into the present moment.

> —Hermann Hesse, *The Journey to the East* (1932)

The crowd at La Honda, headed by their pilot Ken Kesey, started to plot a revolution of a decidedly apolitical bent. They were out to change consciousness (which counts more than anything political, they held) more than government—an approach and point of view closely akin to such "radicals" as Emerson, Thoreau, and Whitman a century or so earlier. In the words of Ken Babbs, they wanted to become "astronauts of inner space" (Greenfield 1997, 73). Kesey and his group wanted everyone to question everything by "pranking" them. "I'm a troublemaker," Kesey asserted at the time. "I try to stir things up wherever I go, in whatever I do. That's what the whole hippie movement is all about; to do outrageous things that cause people to ask questions. Whatever else comes of it, if nothing else comes of it the hippie movement will have had great value" (Burton Wolfe 1968, 196).

On June 17, 1964, fourteen of the psychedelic conspirators populating La Honda embarked on a vacation adventure. Their number included Kesey, his wife and two kids, his brother Chuck, his cousin, Dale, Ken Babbs, his brother John, Ken's girlfriend Paula "Gretchen Fetchin' the Slime Queen" Sundsten, Neal Cassady, his neighbor and former Stanford classmate and fledgling philosophy professor, Jane Burton, Steve "Zonker" Lambrecht, Sandy "Dismount" Lehmann-Haupt, George "Hardly Visible" Walker, Mike "Mal Function" Hagen, Ron "Hassler" Bevirt, and aspiring actress Kathy "Stark Naked" Casano. This crew of Merry Pranksters, as they named themselves, set out on a cross-country trip in a 1939 International Harvester school bus purchased by Kesey for $1,250. The bus's previous owner had adapted it for the use of his twelve kids by installing bunks, benches, and a sink, so it was ideal for Kesey's group, who also spray painted the bus in crude, quasi-psychedelic designs and colors and equipped it with a network of sound and video equipment. They also installed a turret by welding on an old dryer drum to it, added a ladder, and enclosed it with a windshield. The Pranksters named the colorful bus "Further."

Figure 7. The Merry Prankster psychedelic bus "Further." Photo: Joe Rosenthal. *Source*: Special Collections & University Archives, University of Oregon Libraries. https://oregondigital.org/catalog/oregondigital:df73g987k

The Pranksters took the trip to ostensibly make a film starring Cassady called *Intrepid Travelers* and to visit the World's Fair in Queens, New York, part of New York City's 300th anniversary celebration, where they would attend the party for Kesey's second published novel, *Sometimes a Great Notion*. Several participants joined in as a way to get to New York, where they intended to remain to work or stay with friends. But most of all, Kesey and his band of Merry Pranksters wanted to lighten the mood of the country with psychedelics. In November 1963, upon returning to California from the opening of the Broadway play for *One Flew over the Cuckoo's Nest*, in the wake of the assassination of President John Kennedy, Kesey noticed "a grief—everyone in the United States felt it; not so much that we'd lost Kennedy, but we'd lost a chance at a real different, better, hipper, gentler world. So we decided to do the most American thing we could do—travel across the country" and dispense bags of psychedelic goodies to the masses (Vila 2018, 3). This trip would become a mythic, almost religious element of '60s countercultural lore, but beatification was an after-the-fact bestowal, partly in consequence of Tom Wolfe's novelization of the event in *The Electric Kool-Aid Acid Test*. The actual trip was hardly the stuff of myth or cultural apocalypse. The bus roared, vibrated fiercely, and broke down frequently. Conditions were cramped, sleep was fitful and difficult, there were long stretches of tedium and boredom (with the occasional tiff or two), and it took place in the heat of the sweltering summer. As participant Ron Bevirt remembered: "You have to realize that this was an unpleasant trip. It was noisy and chaotic on the bus. Some people wanted to be left alone and others wanted to keep sticking a camera in everyone's face. On top of that, it was hot. This was summer and we were going through the South. We couldn't get cool. We couldn't stop sweating. At times we couldn't hear anything but the noise of the bus" (Anthony 2004, 35).

In the course of this trip, Kesey shelled out over $70,000 on food, forty-five to fifty hours of 16-millimeter film, and gas—this in 1964 dollars, when gas cost between twenty to twenty-five cents a gallon.[3] Footage of the trip reveals little or no outward sign of anything apocalyptic, mythological, or of near-holy import. Take away the psychedelic paint job and freaky costumes, and what one sees is as mundane as most family vacation videos.

As elaborated by Wolfe in *The Electric Kool-Aid Acid Test*, trip highlights included: a group acid experience at Wikieup, Arizona; a stopover at Larry McMurtry's house in Houston;[4] a layover at Lake Pontchartrain near New Orleans; a stopover in New York City, where the Pranksters met Jack Kerouac (who openly rejected them); an overnight and daylong visit to Millbrook (Leary avoided and all but ignored them); a stopover on the way back home at the Calgary Stampede in Alberta, Canada; and a pit stop at the Esalen Institute at Big Sur. Hardly the stuff of serious third-eye terrain.

It is important to keep in mind how pre–Haight-Ashbury all this was. At this juncture, Barry Goldwater was the GOP presidential nominee (while driving through Arizona, the bus sported a banner reading "A vote for Barry is a vote for fun"); the Freedom Summer was transpiring in Mississippi, but segregation still afflicted most of the U.S., with Lester Maddox and George Wallace militantly pro-segregation governors; Beatlemania had just begun in the United States; and few Americans could locate Vietnam on a map. The word *hippie* didn't yet exist. One has to smile at the thought of how the Pranksters and their bus must have affected locals as they traveled, Cassady at the wheel, through hamlets and small towns in the Bible-Belt South: Kesey and his crew savoring and milking the "goof-the-squares" prank, painting their faces and dressing in American flag motifs, their expensive stereo system blaring full-bore, and their video camera at the ready.

The group returned to La Honda eager to continue their scene with even higher-octane aspirations, ready to draw the entire Bay Area underground into their "movie." Post-trip additions to the scene at La Honda included acid guru and magnate Augustus Owsley Stanley III, the Grateful Dead (still known as the Warlocks), teenager Carolyn "Mountain Girl" Adams, light-show operator John Page Browning, Paul Foster (an early computer genius-nerd, likely the artist for the first acid-test poster, and famous for the sign he wore atop his mummy costume at acid tests that read, "You're the Pepsi Generation and I'm a pimply freak"), "June the Goon" (so dubbed for her interminable discourse about psychological hang-ups and one of Cassady's innumerable girlfriends), Lee Quarnstrom (who quit his job as reporter for the *San Mateo Times* to become a Prankster and subsequently a reporter and columnist for the *San Jose Mercury News*), and Denise "Mary Microgram" Kaufman (also a member of the all-girl rock band, the Ace of Cups). Joined by increasing numbers of Bay area "heads" and countercultural front-runners, Kesey and his group commenced all-out experimentation with a perceptual style centered on the psychedelic experience. La Honda became a hub for acid parties featuring freakily costumed heads, light shows, Day-Glo, underground music, electronic hyperstimulation, and experimental exercises in massive cognitive dissonance. Kesey and his crew wired trees in his six-acre spread with loudspeakers and microphones, painted the trees Day-Glo colors, and hung them with a variety of weird collages, signs, and bizarre sculptures (a number of them by Ron Boise, famous for his series of sculptures depicting sexual positions from the *Kama Sutra*).

Hunter Thompson, a struggling, still-unknown, oft-fired fire-snorter of a journalist who had been living in San Francisco and Big Sur off and on for several years, was just then writing a piece about Kesey and the Pranksters for *The Nation*. Checking out the La Honda scene, Thompson was partly intrigued, partly unimpressed. He offered his impression of what would appear to be a kind of acid test rehearsal in a May 2, 1965, letter to *The Nation* editor Don Cooke:

> I was down at Kesey's house in La Honda last night, bearing witness to one of the strangest scenes in all Christendom—a wild clanging on tin instruments in a redwood hillside, loons playing flutes in the darkness, mikes and speakers planted all over, mad flashing films on a giant trampoline screen; in all it was pretty depressing—that a man with such a high white sound should be so hung up in this strange campy kind of showbiz.

He MC'd the whole bit, testing mikes and tuning flutes here and there as if one slip in any direction might send us all over the cliff in darkness. Like a kid's home circus, a Peter Pan kind of thing, but with sad music somewhere up in the trees above the kiddie carols. I drank twenty beers and left sadly sober. (Thompson 1997, 512)

Meanwhile, La Honda's neighbors—whose tastes, interests, sympathies, and backgrounds were hardly of the Perry Lane bent—began complaining, and the police started showing up, sniffing around, watching, and compiling dossiers. La Honda was raided by eighteen cops on April 24, 1965. Kesey and twelve others were busted for marijuana possession. The bust had been brewing for a long time, and Kesey had been all but inviting it for even longer, unwilling to rein in his outrageous flamboyance or refrain from thumbing his nose and making faces at Big Nurse. Like McMurphy in *Cuckoo's Nest,* Kesey ended up getting nailed by Big Nurse. The April 24 bust, combined with a subsequent, even stupider bust (on Kesey's part), would be the beginning of the end of the Kesey movie in the Bay Area.

Eventually, the La Honda scene got so crazy, chaotic, and carnivalesque that the Prankster regulars decided to stage revelries for the public. They took their acid parties on the road—they would come to be known as acid tests—holding them at a variety of houses, clubs, locales, and venues— including the Fillmore Ballroom in San Francisco—as a way to provide a psychedelic experience in surroundings replete with live rock music (LSD was still legal at this time), light shows, Cassady raps, Kesey monologues, freaky clothing, dancing, and general high weirdness, but out in the open among throngs of enthusiastically participating, sympathetic, and contributive like-minded freaks.

The Pranksters fashioned and sponsored these acid parties as a kind of unscripted, improvisatory, prank-driven theater designed to provoke participants into questioning the conventions and norms, which previously they had taken for granted as reality. They tended to be chaotic, hyper-sensory, and somewhat edgy affairs, the goal being to radically transform consciousness in as many participants as possible by provoking them into abandoning the traditional script. Ontology, not ideology, was the target. The uncontrolled, unpredictable, and unexpected were courted and fostered. Essentially, the first Trips Festival—the event that largely galvanized and launched the countercultural scene on a mass scale—was a direct extension and imitation of these acid tests, which in turn were modeled after the parties that had been taking place at La Honda and earlier (though on a smaller scale) at Perry Lane.

The recently formed Warlocks—soon to be renamed the Grateful Dead—became the house band for these parties in a fortuitous development. On December 4, the Warlocks first performed at the San Jose Acid Test (the fourth to date, but the first specifically called an "acid test"), the same night as a Rolling Stones concert at the Cow Palace. In hopes of drawing in new recruits (and maybe, miraculously, the Stones), the Pranksters drove their bus to the Cow Palace to pass out thousands of handbills announcing that night's party and cryptically asking the readers if they could "pass the acid test." Some 400 people showed up for the party. Earlier in the day, Page Browning, a Prankster who had come to La Honda by way of the Chateau, telephoned Jerry Garcia to talk him into bringing his band to play at that night's party. The band showed up and played, becoming an acid-test fixture thereafter. An index of the changing times, only months before, the Warlocks had been named Mother McCree's Uptown Jug Band, and in a few more short months they would be the very psychedelicized Grateful Dead.

The proto-Dead's experience playing at this party would have cultural repercussions impossible to foresee. At this point, the Warlocks were essentially a struggling bar band playing covers of Sam the Sham and the Pharaohs' "Wooly Bully," the Lovin' Spoonful's "Do You Believe in Magic?," and revamped bluegrass numbers in taverns and strip joints in Redwood City, the East Bay, and in San Francisco on Broadway and in North Beach. Garcia claimed that his experiences playing at the acid tests profoundly changed his approach not only to music, but to life in general. "The Acid Test," he would later remark, "was the prototype for our whole basic trip. We were lucky to have a little moment in history when LSD was still legal and we could experiment with drugs like we were experimenting with music" (Troy 1994, 72). Garcia would eventually marry one of the Pranksters: "Mountain Girl," Kesey's erstwhile girlfriend, who had a baby by Kesey at age eighteen. (The fact that he was already married with two kids was apparently an obstacle to neither. She continued to live near Kesey in Oregon until his death in 2005.)

The psychedelic counterculture evolved on two fronts—one centered in the Northeast by way of Leary, the other located in Northern California by way of Kesey—but the two camps were different in temperament, practice, and aim. Leary, through the *Psychedelic Review,* came on like an ultra-hip priest aiming to change the world through the sacramental use of consciousness-altering psychedelic drugs. He emphasized "set" and "setting," discoursing on the advisability of a serene, contemplative environment (paisley cushions, incense, robes, sitars wafting in the meditative distance) and freedom from distraction to foster a spiritual experience leading to inner discovery and expansion of mind.

Kesey, on the other hand, favored a more freewheeling, prankish approach that treated the acid[5] experience as a carnivalesque experiment in transactional interaction in which the outrageous and the unexpected were cultivated, not avoided. Envisioning themselves as psychedelic provocateurs, playing Monty Python to Leary's Yogananda, they "pranked" people via their out-front outrageousness, costumes, and antics into responding, thereby drawing them into their "movie" and making them co-participants. Instead of serene, sacramental contemplation, they set up communal, interactive acid tests employing all manner of electronic, visual, and aural stimuli. In lieu of sitars and wind chimes, they brought in the hairiest, scariest-looking rock band they could scrounge up, cranked up the music to ear-splitting volume, and exhorted everyone to be abnormal and "freak freely."

Ginsberg, who took part in both the Kesey and the Leary scenes, found that "Millbrook was much more sedate and expansive, not half as rough and ready and wild and American, and as gung-ho as La Honda. It was another generation. [La Honda] was more like a psychedelic circus than a psychedelic community, though [both La Honda and Millbrook] had strong central family relationships with kids and wives" (Whitmer 1987, 161).

The Beatles imitated both approaches. They reflected the Leary schtick by way of their semi-worshipful, beautiful people linkup with the Maharishi Mahesh Yogi. Their song "Tomorrow Never Knows" quotes directly from Leary's *Psychedelic Prayers* and was written by Lennon in the wake of his first truly profound acid trip in December 1965. (The song, Lennon would later reveal, was meant to evoke the sound of "a thousand chanting Tibetan monks"; Lennon took LSD almost daily thereafter [Derogatis 2003, 24].) The Beatles also used the Kesey bus trip as inspiration for the *Magical Mystery Tour* concept and film project.

As different as they were in temperament and approach, Leary and Kesey shared a tendency for self-promotion that sometimes bordered on the shameless. Both sought out publicity, fame, and celebrities; both saw themselves as leaders of and spokesmen for a "movement"; both used their positions to get laid; and both hoped—despite all the high-minded rhetoric—to make a whole lot of money. (To this day, I read Leary, in particular, with a combination of fascinated respect and utter loathing. There is something Beverly Hills chic about him: an aura of swimming pools, car phones, BMW convertibles, beautiful people, villas and estates, jet-setting celebrities, and stunning blondes eager to "star fuck.") Both were an equal mixture of genuine sincerity and shameless bullshit, of trailblazing heroism and thoroughgoing hucksterism. Both pursued famous or infamous celebrities: Leary catered to socialites, Kesey to Hells Angels.

Whatever else they were, though, Kesey had the chops to write an era-defining novel in *One Flew over the Cuckoo's Nest,* and Leary wrote the most acclaimed psychology treatise of 1957, taught at Harvard, and wrote some era-shaping texts. Both had an era-altering impact on American—if not world—culture. Both became a significant part of twentieth-century lore. They defined and galvanized much of what would become "the '60s" by these two very different but related scenes.

Of course, innumerable offshoots, variations, and permutations of these two main groups took shape during the 1960s. In addition to the LSD acolytes and missionaries as exemplified by the League for Spiritual Discovery à la Leary and Millbrook and the psychedelic anarchists as exemplified by the Merry Pranksters, the politicos coalesced around California college campuses, as exemplified by the Free Speech movement and man-the-barricaders at Berkeley. The apolitical, dropout hippies as exemplified by Haight-Ashbury and the thousands of communes scattered throughout rural America formed yet another version of both the Kesey and Leary camps. There was some overlapping, and there was a good deal of mutual sympathy, but there was also occasional friction among (and within) the various camps. The politicos wanted to confront and change society to make it more just and free and to end the Vietnam war. The Pranksters wanted to confront and change society to make it more interesting, freaky, and fun. The Learyites wanted to confront and change society to make it more enlightened, cosmic, and mellow—and, hence, saved, healed, and cured. The hippies just wanted to drop out of the dominant culture to create an alternative life style with lots of laid-back drugs, sex, rock and roll, and righteous vibes. The dropouts considered the politicos frantic, obsessive-compulsive, and hung-up. The politicos considered the dropouts hedonistic, self-indulgent airheads. These competing outlooks essentially originated from the same fight both sides were carrying on against the values of their parents back in the suburbs.

Augustus Owsley Stanley III

In late April and early May of 1965, unprecedented quantities of LSD began being distributed in the Bay Area by a former Air Force radar technician, who called himself Owsley. He became known variously as "Merlin," "White

Rabbit," "Bear," and "the Acid King." It was largely this influx of LSD that made possible and drove the huge escalation of psychedelic culture that autumn, when the Haight-Ashbury became the center of the psychedelic counterculture.

Owsley's formal name—Augustus Owsley Stanley III—harbors bloodlines of a decidedly patrician tint of blue. His grandfather—Augustus Owsley Stanley I—was a U.S. senator from Kentucky, who fought fiercely against corporate monopolies. The Stanley Committee dismantled the U.S. Steel monopoly and changed the way business was conducted in the U.S. Stanley I also authored the Clayton Antitrust Act, which to this day remains the primary tool for combating monopolies (Whitmer 1987, 187).

Probably the most informative (and entertaining) profile of Owsley comes from Charles Perry, longtime writer for *Rolling Stone* and author of *Haight-Ashbury: A History.* When he attended Berkeley as a student during the early '60s, Perry lived in a rooming house with bohemian-minded roommates. Perry, though, wasn't your garden variety free spirit, haunting coffee houses with red-checker table cloths and folk music. One of the early LSD enthusiasts in the Bay Area, he introduced all his housemates to the drug. In 1964, an odd guy in his late twenties, who called himself Owsley showed up at Perry's rooming house, wanting a room. Separated from his second wife, Owsley had come from L.A. to go back to school. The more he talked, the more odd and intriguing he seemed to Perry, even by Berkeley nonconformist standards. Owsley claimed he had been booted out of prep school for smuggling booze into dorms as a freshman, had once been committed to St. Elizabeth's (the Washington, D.C. bughouse, where poet Ezra Pound had been incarcerated in lieu of prison), and had once studied Russian in preparation for going into the Russian Orthodox priesthood. A ballet enthusiast, he had his own ballet slippers; a beekeeper, he had his own beekeeping suit.

Owsley didn't converse—he expounded in the manner of an expert lecturing on his specialty, and he had viewpoints, opinions, and theories about everything, some of them brilliantly odd, some so baroquely wacko as to leave his conversant at a conversational loss. He ate only meat, for example, in the belief that vegetables poisoned the human digestive system. Longtime Grateful Dead manager Rock Scully remembered Owsley as "a perfect monomaniac," who believed himself "an expert on everything" with an opinion on "anything you can name" (Scully and Dalton 1996, 36). Perry reported that Owsley had smoked grass for the first time only a few weeks prior to showing up at the rooming house, but he was already obsessed with the subject of getting high. And it was Perry who, several weeks later, ushered Owsley into his first LSD experience.

Irony of ironies, Owsley wasn't all that impressed by his initiation into psychedelics. He liked speed far better—so much so that he became an insufferable speed freak. It got to the point where the house residents convened a secret meeting to discuss ways to get rid of Owsley. Their dilemma was solved when Owsley got evicted for offering speed to the rooming house's live-in Chinese landlord.

Early in the fall semester, Owsley dropped by the Biological Sciences building at Berkeley to reconnoiter the lab facilities. In one of the second floor labs, he spied a comely first-year graduate student with an off-the-charts IQ named Melissa Cargill. Owsley and Cargill began talking chemistry and then underground chemistry. They immediately hit it off, then paired off (she dumped her boyfriend three days later to take up with Owsley) and set about exploring the world of underground pharmaceuticals.

Owsley's sojourn at Berkeley was short-lived. He dropped out when he landed a job as a technician at a San Francisco TV station. Still enamored with speed, he and Cargill set up a methedrine lab in the bathroom of their rented house at 1647 Virginia Street in Berkeley. Profits from that venture financed Owsley's entry into LSD production, which, at the time, was still legal (LSD wasn't formally outlawed until October 1966). Meth, though, was illegal. The police raided the illicit lab on February 15, but Owsley beat the rap on a technicality. The batch under production at the time—nabbed by the police as evidence—was still a step or two shy of being methedrine, so he technically wasn't yet guilty of manufacturing it. In a move that speaks volumes about his personality, Owsley wasn't satisfied with the not-guilty verdict. He successfully sued the state to get his lab equipment back, a move that underlines the in-your-face, goof-the-squares tendency that all but guaranteed his eventual downfall.

Owsley decided to go into big-time LSD production. With things now a tad hot for him in the Bay Area, he decided to start an acid tabbing operation in L.A. Ever the flamboyant scenester, by now Owsley was also playing patron to an up-and-coming band called the Warlocks which had been cavorting in the Kesey acid-test scene. The group badly needed to woodshed somewhere to revamp and expand their repertoire, so they accompanied Owsley to L.A. to practice, write songs, and rehearse new material. Owsley rented a multi-roomed house next door to a gambling parlor on the edge of the Watts district, and the group practiced downstairs all day while he tabbed acid in the attic. (See chapter 4 of Scully and Dalton's

Living with the Dead for an immensely entertaining account of this period.) When they returned to San Francisco, Owsley and the band carried with them a huge batch of LSD.

Owsley prided himself on the quality of his acid—it was reputed to rival the drug produced by the Sandoz Laboratory in purity. Though LSD had been central to a growing number of "scenes" in L.A. and the Bay Area long before Owsley, he also made LSD widely available. He manufactured the acid that counterculture adherents gobbled up at the acid tests, the Trips Festival, the Human Be-In, and the Monterey Pop Festival. Owsley synthesized the acid that the Beatles took on their first trip. LSD cannot be taken if it's not available, and much of the Haight-Ashbury scene unfolded by way of LSD circulated by Owsley's messianic entrepreneurship. Without Owsley's wheeling and dealing, the psychedelic scene would have most likely remained far more localized and underground—the outside world largely oblivious to it. His acid reputedly turned on as many as ten million people.

When LSD first surfaced in underground circles circa 1962, it sold for $7 a pop in sugar cubes. By 1964, it cost $2.50 a hit. The price dropped even lower, when Owsley entered the picture. For a while, he insisted that his dealers sell it for no more than $2 a hit, and he schemed to lower it to 25 cents a tab, although he never realized his goal.

For much of Owsley's reign as LSD superstar, Robert "Tim" Scully and Melissa Cargill manufactured much of the LSD. By his own account, Tim Scully—not to be confused with Grateful Dead manager Rock Scully— grew up as a nerdy scientific whiz kid. He was runner-up in the Bay Area Science Fair as a junior in high school for developing a linear accelerator, which impressed his principal enough for him to arrange for Scully to skip his senior year and enter the University of California, Berkeley. Far from a conventional Berkeley undergraduate, Scully did electronic work on the side, and his technology skills became so in demand that after two years he took a leave of absence from the university. By age twenty, he made enough money to buy his own house.

In April 1965, Scully took acid and had the kind of transformative revelation that produces an LSD missionary. The ontological rug was jerked out from under him. Well-meaning and untainted by cynicism, street smarts, or worldly experience, Scully was convinced—à la Huxley, Hubbard, and Leary before him—that LSD could transform—and, hence, save—the world if enough people had their perceptual map redrawn and their psychic awareness retooled by taking it. He made it his life's mission to make that happen. Saving the world proved harder than good intentions.

A little research revealed that several key ingredients needed to synthesize LSD—lysergic acid monohydrate and ergotamine tartrate—were extremely expensive and all but impossible to obtain. Scully needed connections and partners in high places.

In the fall of 1965, Scully met Owsley. They talked electronics and philosophy, and Owsley held forth at raconteurial length about the Kesey scene. Owsley, though, didn't take Scully under his LSD wing at first. Instead, he recruited Scully's expertise in electronics to build sound equipment for the Dead. It wasn't until the spring of 1966 that Owsley, Cargill, and Scully finally set up a lab together in a rented house in the Point Richmond neighborhood near San Francisco. Owsley approached LSD with a religious fervor but also believed in raising his material wealth simultaneously and equally with his spiritual plane. With Scully in tow, Owsley flew to New York to consult with Leary about the psychedelic revolution and explore the East Coast market potential for LSD. While there, he discussed partnership possibilities with Billy Hitchcock.

Scully was an acid Saint Francis. Like Hubbard and Huxley, he never tried to make money off acid and never aspired for underground super-stardom. He genuinely believed that he toiled for the ultimate benefit of mankind in his role as an acid chemist. His idealism would end up getting him burned by compatriots, whose high-mindedness evaporated as convenience, expediency, and venality dictated.

Owsley, in contrast, combined a meticulously honed aura of cape-twirling mystery with cocksure flamboyance. He sported $400 hippie outfits, drove expensive sports cars, consorted with underground celebrities, showed up wherever the scenesters congregated, and patronized and gave out bags of free LSD to frontline musicians such as the Grateful Dead, the Jefferson Airplane, Moby Grape, and Blue Cheer (see his paean to Blue Cheer on the liner notes to their debut album, *Vincebus Eruptum*). His lawyer was the vice mayor of Berkeley.

Owsley did his superstar strutting while LSD was legal. When the drug was outlawed in the fall of 1966, the game changed dramatically. The police loved nothing better than to bust the acid guru, and they suddenly had far greater ability to do it. Trying to escape their clutches, Owsley cooled it for a while, become far less visible, and struck a decidedly lower profile.

Despite the change in the law, Scully retained his missionary zeal. He was Saint Paul among the Ephesians, Joan of Arc among the French peasantry, and Lenin among the Russian workers. He lobbied hard for Owsley to set him up in a lab somewhere outside California. Owsley finally relented, providing Scully a lab in Denver, in the neighborhood adjacent to City Park in the vicinity of East High School, which Neal Cassady had attended twenty years earlier. Owsley had access to only limited quantities of lysergic monohydrate, so Scully temporarily supplemented LSD production with 5,000 tabs of a new drug, an amphetamine called STP, which sent users on a three-day, soul-killing trip with no exit.

On December 21, 1967, the inevitable happened. The cops caught Owsley tableting the latest fruits of Scully's Denver lab in a house in Orinda, California. They confiscated 750,000 doses of LSD and STP worth $10 million on the street—which his lawyer argued in court to be entirely for Owsley's private use! At thirty-one years old, the King of Acid, caught red-handed, was looking at some serious jail time. He got off amazingly easy, though. Where Leary would be sentenced to thirty years in prison and fined $30,000, when customs officials found three ounces of grass in his car, Owsley was given a mere three-year sentence and a $3,000 fine: chump change for him. He served a year at Terminal Island in L.A. and two at Lompoc Prison near Santa Barbara. Owsley subsequently worked for the Grateful Dead building sound equipment and helping them with their recording studio. He eventually moved to southern Australia, where he lived making jewelry and painting psychedelic patterns on stones until his death in 2011.

With Owsley out of the picture, Scully turned to Hitchcock, who had moved to the Bay Area and linked up with a mysterious, quasi-mystical, legend-laden, ultra-entrepreneurial organization known as The Brotherhood of Eternal Love. Led by an ex-biker acid mystic named John Griggs, the Brotherhood started as a commune and became the International Federation for Internal Freedom (IFIF) of dope circles that authorities called the Hippie Mafia. They approached Hitchcock about going into partnership for massive dissemination of LSD, less for profit than for save-the-world aspirations. Eventually, the Brotherhood initially procured most of their LSD from a lab in Denver that Tim Scully had formed with several other chemists after a loan of $12,000 from Hitchcock.

When authorities raided and closed down the Denver lab, Hitchcock bankrolled Scully and Nick Sand to open another acid laboratory on property in rural Windsor, California, sixty miles north of San Francisco. The Brooklyn-born Sand had been the "alchemist" in Arthur Kleps's psychedelic-fueled Neo-American Boohoo Church in Millbrook and had followed Hitchcock to the Bay Area when the Millbrook crowd got the heave-ho. In the lab's six months of operation from December 1968 to June of 1969, the two chemists turned Hitchcock a $7 million profit. They transformed a 500-gram batch of lysergic acid monohydrate costing $20,000 into 3.6 million tabs of Orange Sunshine, which sold at two bucks a pop.

Hitchcock opened Swiss bank accounts and laundered the enormous LSD profits through Bahamian banks also used by the CIA and Bebe Rebozo, a somewhat shady Florida banker and confidant of Richard Nixon. A global wheeler-dealer, Hitchcock considered acid an underground thrill. He promptly squandered the better part of $67 million in Brotherhood and Owsley money via high-risk investments and was getting himself deeper and deeper into a tangled financial morass of global proportions.

Scully quit the acid business following the Windsor venture. However, he found himself busted, thanks to the backstabbing weaselness of Hitchcock. In major trouble with the federal government on a variety of counts with the noose tightening, in May 1973, Hitchcock turned himself in for income-tax evasion. In a bid to save himself, he offered to turn in evidence of his acid enterprises. The Feds agreed, and Hitchcock named names and identified the Bahamian and Swiss banks used to launder and sock away drug profits. He told the governments everything he knew about the Brotherhood of Eternal Love.

In April 1973, Sand and Scully, who made almost no money through their chemical wizardry, were indicted based on the testimony of Hitchcock, who claimed that he only served as a "financial advisor" to them. Scully was sentenced to twenty years, and Sand to fifteen. Hitchcock never did a day of jail time. He got a suspended sentence and a $20,000 fine—which he paid by sitting down and promptly writing a check. Sand skipped bail and went on the lam to Canada. Scully—the idealist and purist—did two years at the federal prison on McNeil Island in Washington State, getting early parole in 1979 as a model prisoner. While in prison, he worked on biofeedback and interface systems to help the nonvocal handicapped.

5

The '60s at Berkeley

Civil Rights and Free Speech

We like to think of everything as true or false, which fends off realms of experience that make us feel uneasy.

—Ronald Sukenick, founder/publisher of the *American Book Review*, author of *Down and In: Life in the Underground* (1988)

The answer is never the answer. What's really interesting is the mystery. If you seek the mystery instead of the answer, you'll always be seeking. I've never seen anybody really find the answer—they think they have, so they stop thinking. But the job is to seek mystery, evoke mystery, plant a garden in which strange plants grow and mysteries bloom. The need for mystery is greater than the need for an answer.

—Ken Kesey, interview in the *Paris Review*, no. 130 (Spring 1994)

By 1962—about the time Leary was orchestrating his psilocybin projects at Harvard—college students were becoming increasingly active in the fledgling but growing civil rights movement. In increasing numbers, they participated in marches, voter registration drives, freedom rides, and desegregation campaigns deep in the heart of Dixie itself. Only a few years before the blossoming of the psychedelic Haight-Ashbury, the Cold War was in full swing, Kennedy had only recently succeeded Eisenhower, a youthful and still-folkie Bob Dylan was just beginning to appear in Greenwich Village coffee houses, and an equally youthful Joan Baez in San Francisco folk clubs. Riots erupted that year on the campus of the University of Mississippi, when a young African American, James Meredith, attempted to enroll in the heretofore all-white school. As the civil-right movement gathered steam, media coverage made the nation witness to kneeling, singing African American (and white) demonstrators, women and children among them, being sprayed with fire hoses, clubbed by policemen, and mauled by police attack dogs while bug-eyed, fist-shaking, jeering (and sometimes club-wielding) townspeople hooted at the "niggers" and "nigger lovers." In June 1963, Kennedy responded to a national groundswell of revulsion by proposing civil rights legislation mandating universal voting rights, equal employment opportunities, and an end to segregation in all public places. Three months later, a massive March on Washington attracted 160,000 African Americans and 40,000 whites, including Bob Dylan and Joan Baez. With increasing frequency, widening sectors of society, and especially young Americans, evoked a grand countercultural vision that stood in stark contrast to the mindset, which propped up an establishment that was more and more seen as corrupt, unjust, and anachronistic.

Berkeley before the '60s

These developments had profound repercussions nationwide—even in a locale as far away as lily-white, traditionally conservative Berkeley, California. Throughout the '40s and '50s, the Berkeley city government, its business community, and the University of California, Berkeley, were bastions of conservative thought, value assumptions, and aspirations. Being next door to San Francisco and home to a cosmopolitan university, Berkeley practiced a certain tolerance of "deviance" (anything to the left of center), but conservatives traditionally held the power and drove the bus, both in the city and on the campus.

Until a dozen high-rise dorms were constructed in the '50s, there had been a dearth of campus housing at the university, making the Greek system the heart of campus social life. Though fraternities were not politically oriented, their politics were Eisenhower Republican, the look clean cut, button-down, and flat top, and the focus was on grades and careers amid a glut of drunken weekend partying. The Greeks dominated student government (Associated Students of the University of California) and the *Daily Cal,* the student newspaper. Berkeley reflected the American Century mindset evangelized by Henry Luce in *Life*. Until the mid-'60s the town of Berkeley had the lowest number of bars and the highest number of churches per capita of any US city with a population over 100,000. In the fall of 1964, tuition at Berkeley cost a mere $90 a semester. FBI director J. Edgar Hoover encapsulated the prevailing mentality of the conservative right at the time when, in his address to the 1960 Republican National Convention, he lambasted "communists, beatniks and eggheads" as "America's greatest enemies."

By the late '50s, however, a few pockets of change surfaced. Along the four-block length of Telegraph Avenue adjacent to campus, coffeehouses and bookstores catered to nonconformists, "folkies," and "lefties."

On campus, Clark Kerr, the Berkeley president, was a practicing Quaker and a Kennedy liberal, who believed in the march of progress. He envisioned the role of the university—he used the term *multiversity*—to educate students to be the managers and leaders of that march to progress. Cracks in the traditional conservatism were spider-webbing throughout the Berkeley edifice. As early as February 1958, liberal-leaning students formed a political organization called SLATE (referring to a slate of candidates) as a challenge to Greek hegemony. In effect, SLATE served as a vehicle for non-Greek students to run for student government and opened the elections to African Americans and Jews, who had been banned by the sororities and fraternities. SLATE's perennial causes included an end to compulsory ROTC service and establishment of a co-op bookstore. Nonetheless, in 1966, conservative traditionalists strong-armed the university into banning SLATE from campus—largely on a technicality.

Another serious flash of leftist political activism surfaced in the spring of 1960, when the House Un-American Activities Committee (HUAC) convened hearings in San Francisco's City Hall to expose alleged communist activity in the Bay Area. It targeted Bay Area labor leaders and school teachers, who were subpoenaed for official committee questioning. In those Cold War days, foreign policy—and, not infrequently, domestic policy—was crafted out of a belief that a ruthless, Moscow-centered international communist conspiracy was dedicated to toppling the US government. Every bush and potted plant concealed a commie conspirator. Everything from juvenile delinquency to modern art, from labor unrest to the civil rights movement and beatniks was the handiwork of communism. HUAC and Wisconsin Senator Joseph McCarthy desperately wanted to root out the "communists, beatniks and eggheads" who infested organized labor, college faculties, and the ranks of artists and actors. The Loyalty Act (1947), signed into law by President

Harry Truman, allowed anyone to be removed from government service who was deemed to be soft on communism or who demonstrated a history of alcoholism, "sexual deviation," mental illness—or even membership in a nudist colony. HUAC summoned people for questioning not only for their purported activities, but for suspected beliefs and/or sympathies. Anyone deemed insufficiently zealous in their anti-communism—who, for example, demonstrated too much tolerance for commies or commie sympathizers, or who failed to report communists—was subject to a HUAC subpoena.

The San Francisco hearings provoked a barrage of fallout. On May 13, 1960, hundreds of Berkeley students joined the throng, which attempted to attend the start of hearings. But the committee had anticipated this possibility by stacking the hearings with pro-HUAC attendees by issuing HUAC supporters white cards that gave them preferred admittance. Only a handful of seats were left for non-cardholders. Those denied admittance—nearly everyone who opposed the hearings—conducted a quasi-sit-in in the rotunda, from where they clapped, chanted, and sang "God Bless America" in an attempt to drown out the proceedings from which they had been excluded. The protesters were serenaded by a nineteen-year-old folkie who had come up from Palo Alto named Joan Baez.

Eventually, the mayor ordered fire hoses to be turned on the protesters, washing them down the marble stairs of the vestibule. Of the sixty-four protesters arrested, thirty-one were Berkeley students. A documentary called *Berkeley in the Sixties* contains footage of this scene, as well as the now famous outburst during HUAC questioning, when Soviet expert William Mandel declared, "If you think I am going to cooperate with this collection of Judases, of men who sit there in violation of the United States Constitution . . . you are insane!" (*Spider Magazine*, 1960). A crowd of nearly 5,000 protesters and picketers showed up every day of the hearings. Even months afterward, dissidents could be seen marching about the city carrying placards that denounced the HUAC hearings as a "witch hunt."

Bay Area Bohemia

In the meantime, a vaguely political underground was fermenting in Bay Area coffeehouses and bohemian enclaves. During these years, a folk circuit materialized, in venues such as the Cabal and Jabberwock in Berkeley; Vesuvio's, the hungry i, the Gas Haven, and Coffee and Confusion in North Beach;

the Offstage in San Jose; the Van Damme in Sausalito; and the Tangent, St. Michael's Alley, the Boar's Head, and Kepler's Bookstore in Palo Alto. Established in the summer of 1961, the Boar's Head was started by Rod and Peter Albin, the latter being the future bass player for Big Brother and the Holding Company. Located in the loft above a bookstore, the Boar's Head opened on Friday and Saturday nights and featured an open-mic policy. This circuit proved to be fertile ground for performers, who would figure large in the '60s counterculture such as Mimi and Richard Fariña, Joan Baez, comedian/social commentator Lenny Bruce, Lord Buckley, and the folk group the Limeliters, one of whom was Lou Gottlieb, later the thoroughly psychedelicized owner of the Morningside Ranch commune.

The folk coffeehouse scene circa 1960 attracted the hip-inclined, downwardly mobile, nonconformist crowd, and avant-garde communards, artist-intellectuals, connoisseurs of coffee and chess moves, and beatniks and bohemians of every stripe. Kesey took to growing a beard, playing the guitar, and singing folk songs upon moving into Perry Lane, signaling his identification with the emerging discontents. Many of the soon-to-be psychedelic rock luminaries—including Janis Joplin, Jefferson Airplane guitarists Jorma Kaukonen and Paul Kantner, Grateful Dead icon Jerry Garcia, and Quicksilver Messenger Service vocalist David Freiberg—cut their musical teeth in the Bay Area folk coffeehouse circuit. In the early '60s, Garcia looked like a typical coffeehouse folkie with slicked back hair and a buttoned-down shirt.

North Beach in San Francisco was home to City Lights, a bookstore sympathetic to the progressives, who bridged the Beat and Haight-Ashbury eras. Located on Columbus Avenue, it opened in 1953 largely as a vehicle for publishing an avant-garde culture magazine called *City Lights*. Initially, the store sold Italian anarchist newspapers, but it soon evolved into the world's first all-paperback bookstore. Lawrence Ferlinghetti founded the store, and in 1955 bought out cofounder Peter Martin and began publishing local poets. It was City Lights that published Ginsberg's controversial and influential *Howl and Other Poems* in late 1956.

Bay Area bohemianism even predates the '50s. Ginsberg came to San Francisco in 1954 to find an already thriving avant-garde and progressive political scene presided over by Kenneth Rexroth, who hosted a Friday night salon and discussion group in his home. Frequenters included poet and novelist Kenneth Patchen, a surrealist poet known by Ginsberg during his Columbia days named Philip Lamantia, Berkeley poet/professor Thomas Parkinson, and poets Jack Spicer, Robert Duncan, and writer Michael

Figure 8. The ever-present Allen Ginsberg in action at a protest. *Source:* National Archives, public domain. https://catalog.archives.gov/id/7419629

McClure, who was fictionalized as Pat McLear in Kerouac's *Big Sur* (1962). As Ginsberg said of the Bay Area scene in 1954:

> It had a tradition of philosophical anarchism with the anarchist club that Rexroth belonged to, a tradition receptive to person rather than officialdom or officiousness. There already had been a sort of Berkeley Renaissance in 1948 with Jack Spicer poet, Robert Duncan poet, Robert Blaser poet, Timothy Leary psychologist [Leary came to the Bay Area in '48 for entirely academic reasons], Harry Smith, great underground filmmaker, one of the people who originated the mixed media light shows . . . [and] little magazines like *Circle* magazine . . . that didn't exist in the more *money-success-Time*-magazine-oriented New York scene. (Schumacher 1992, 184–185)

In the early '60s, the San Francisco Mime Troupe also began making a name for itself among the coffeehouse crowd by staging existentially subversive, quasi-Dadaistic "happenings." Stewart Brand—later a proto-Prankster, major player in the Trips Festival, and founder of *Whole Earth Catalog*—hung out with the Mime Troupe early on. The promoter and manager of the Mime Troupe was a streetwise cynic by the name of Bill Graham, who had fled Nazism as a youth, quit a lucrative corporate job, and later became the grand impresario of psychedelic rock. All this ferment and interconnection spilled over into and became a major factor in the political scene as it evolved at Berkeley. It was the sociocultural context out of which the Free Speech Movement unfolded.

Freedom Summer and Beyond

In the summer of 1964, thirty or so Berkeley students joined a thousand or so college kids in a major civil-rights campaign—Freedom Summer—on behalf of voter registration, free schooling, and the establishment of health and welfare programs in poor African-American communities in Mississippi. One of the Freedom Summer participants was San Francisco State University student Rock Scully, who, less than two years later, would become manager of the Grateful Dead. That fall, the Berkeley contingent returned to a San Francisco where white-collar jobs were as unavailable to African Americans as they were in Mississippi. This group of returning Berkeley students formed a local chapter of C.O.R.E. (Congress of Racial Equality) and set up tables in Sproul Plaza (and on the adjacent Bancroft strip) to distribute literature and recruit students for the burgeoning civil rights campaign.

The C.O.R.E. students began to apply locally the principles they had practiced in Mississippi, targeting local businesses and establishments that refused to hire minorities. Chief among them in Berkeley were Lucky Supermarkets and Mel's Drive-In, the arch-conservative *Oakland Tribune*, local auto dealers, and the swank Sheraton Palace Hotel in San Francisco. They conducted a particularly galvanizing three-day sit-in at the Sheraton that drew such liberal luminaries as Lawrence Ferlinghetti, Alan Watts, and writer Ralph Gleason, who later cofounded *Rolling Stone* magazine. The Sheraton eventually capitulated by signing an agreement to begin hiring African Americans.

C.O.R.E. activists also went after Lucky Supermarkets adjacent to the Berkeley campus on Telegraph Avenue. The activists heaped grocery carts

Figure 9. Joan Baez performing in front of Sproul Hall during the Free Speech Movement. *Source*: Joan Baez on Sproul Hall steps. Ira Sandperl on right, Free Speech Movement Photographs Collection, UARC PIC 24B:1:18, The Bancroft Library, University of California, Berkeley.

with food and other items, and then, after everything had been bagged and rung up on the cash register, slapped their foreheads and claimed they had forgotten to bring money. They practiced this strategy so often that the stores temporarily shut down to return the food to the shelves. The activists hinted to Lucky that they would remember to bring money with them if the store's hiring practices changed.

When SLATE published a letter in the *Daily Cal* calling for "an open, fierce and thorough-going rebellion on this campus," local businesses demanded that the Berkeley administration stop this disruptive rabble-rousing (Goines 1993, 149ff). On September 14, 1964, just prior to the start of classes, the administration banned any group with a political (i.e., nonacademic) orientation from setting up recruiting tables, distributing literature, or soliciting funds in Sproul Plaza or on the sidewalks fronting it—the traditional locale for doing so. Until then, the activists comprised only a handful of students, former students, and nonstudents. They immediately characterized the administration's ban as an attempt to squelch civil-rights activism. When the activists defied the ban and the administration used campus police to enforce it, the students got exactly the political theater for which they had hoped. Stepping up the pressure, they began holding regular noon-time rallies that steadily grew in size, eventually attracting as many as 5,000 students.

On October 1, Jack Weinberg—an activist in his mid-twenties, who until recently had been a graduate student in the Berkeley math department—set up a C.O.R.E. table and began collecting funds. When he was arrested (as he knew he would be), handcuffed, and led off to a police car, students spontaneously surrounded the car and sat down to prevent it from leaving, precipitating a thirty-two-hour standoff. They rigged a sound system, and student after student climbed atop the car—Weinberg inside all the while—to give speeches, quoting Plato, Thoreau, and Gandhi. The number of students surrounding the car vacillated over the thirty-two-hour period from several hundred in the wee hours of the night to three hundred in the afternoon. (Weinberg originated the '60's slogan, "Don't trust anyone over thirty.") Essentially, this thirty-two-hour standoff precipitated the Free Speech Movement (FSM) at Berkeley—an event that profoundly changed not only that campus, but nearly every other college campus in the US over the next six to seven years.[1]

During this stand-off, Mario Savio—a twenty-one-year old junior, philosophy major, and fiery orator who only weeks before had been a Freedom Summer participant—catapulted to prominence. Savio and Weinberg became the most prominent figures in the Free Speech Movement at Berkeley. When, over the course of the next month, the student versus administration conflict began bogging down, the FMS leadership planned a sit-in in Sproul Hall for December 2, 1964, and hoped that a mass arrest of students—they were expecting 1,000 to 2,000 arrests—would energize the entire Berkeley student body into action. At a pre-sit-in rally, Savio gave his legendary "stop the machine" speech, the best-known portion of which included:

> There is a time when the operation of the machine becomes so odious, makes you so sick at heart, that you can't take part; you can't even tacitly take part, and you've got to put your bodies upon the gears and upon the wheels, upon the levers, upon all the apparatus and you've got to make it stop. And you've got

to indicate to the people who run it, to the people who own it, that unless you're free, the machine will be prevented from working at all!

Joan Baez closed the rally in benedictory fashion by singing "The Times They Are A-Changin'" and "We Shall Overcome."

The subsequent FSM sit-in occupied all four floors of Sproul Hall. Some 367 police were called in, and they arrested and hauled off 773 sit-in participants—the largest mass arrest in the state to date—removing them one-by-one over the next two hours while a stunned campus looked on in shock. Nothing of this sort had ever happened before at any college campus anywhere in the U.S. It seemed particularly disturbing to a significant percentage of the Berkeley faculty, who were themselves refugees from such oppressive scenes in Europe, and what they saw unfolding had profoundly alarming associations.

Figure 10. Mario Savio addressing the crowd during the Free Speech Movement. *Source*: Mario Savio in the Greek Theatre, Free Speech Movement Photographs Collection, UARC PIC 24B:1:21, The Bancroft Library, University of California, Berkeley.

The sit-in and mass arrest had exactly the effect the FSM leadership had envisioned: galvanizing the faculty and student body alike in support of the protesters and in opposition to the administration. With the university in a state of palpable and growing crisis, Clark Kerr—essentially a mildly liberal "moderate," not the fascist tyrant the students painted him as being—called a university-wide meeting. After four hours of debate, the faculty voted 824–115 for a resolution to support FSM demands, after which the administration capitulated. The faculty exited the building to a quarter-mile-long, double row of students applauding them. It was Savio's twenty-second birthday.

To understand the sea change in sensibility that this event caused, keep in mind that until 1963, ROTC was *mandatory* for every male student at Berkeley. (The mind boggles at the vision of Mario Savio participating in ROTC drills and wearing an ROTC uniform to classes.) And only several months earlier that summer—simultaneous with the Freedom Summer—the Republican National Convention, held in San Francisco at the Cow Palace, had named Barry Goldwater its presidential candidate. Goldwater was an outspoken opponent of, and had voted against, the Civil Rights Act; he was particularly notorious with the student Left for the photoelectric flagpole at his Arizona home that automatically launched into an electronic rendition of "Stars and Stripes Forever" at the first light of the rising sun.

The FSM victory catalyzed student militancy new to the United States: a willingness to challenge the powers that be and a profound questioning of what, up to now, had been presumed to be "normal," desirable, moral, and "American." The emergent student Left contended—with justification—that the rhetoric of ultra-patriot conservatism à la Joe McCarthy, HUAC, Goldwater, and J. Edgar Hoover was being employed in defense of segregation, injustice, and inequality. In consequence, the heretofore sacrosanct values governing and driving the '50s and early '60s were inverted on college campuses. Where, up to then, a college education (or, more precisely, a college degree) represented a highly desirable entryway into corporate America acceptance, '60s students viewed a college education as a vehicle for escaping the "trap" of the establishment. They regarded conformity to mainstream values, ideals, and aspirations as a manifestation of robotic programming and moral failure, a kind of conformity-equals-success equation. On the other hand, students believed rebellion reflected a sign of moral vitality, in much the same sense as and in the same tradition of Emerson's "The American Scholar" and "The Divinity School Address," Thoreau's "On Civil Disobedience," and Martin Luther King Jr.'s "Letter from a Birmingham Jail."

The FSM constituted the first post-beatnik stirrings of what became the counterculture. In an oft-times way-too-simplistic, black-and-white fashion, this worldview deemed establishment culture to be corrupt, morally bankrupt, and increasingly irrelevant. Rejection or subversion of that culture was deemed heroic, life-affirming, and liberating—essentially the morality play enacted in Ken Kesey's *One Flew over the Cuckoo's Nest*. Openly rebellious and defiant youth presented themselves as the children of light, the champions of freedom and equality, and cast their conformist elders as obstructionist supporters and embodiments of darkness, injustice, and spiritual death. Dylan's anthem "The Times They Are A-Changin'" spoke directly to this worldview.

Within the next two to three years, the Berkeley style of student politics spread to almost every major campus—and innumerable smaller campuses—throughout the United States (with the possible exception of the Southern colleges), a development that was viewed with horror, disgust, anger, fear, and loathing by "mother and fathers throughout the land." In another instance of the incongruous phenomenon so prevalent in countercultural history, prosecution of the 800 or so Berkeley students arrested during the roughly two-month FSM protest was led by Deputy District Attorney Edwin Meese III, later a major player in the "family values" return-to-conservatism of the Reagan presidency.

A brief, highly ironic aside: The closest one can come in the period between the late '80s and 2005 to the revolutionary student left circa 1964–1970 can be found by attending an ultra-right militia meeting. Though the polar antitheses of the '60s in terms of ideology, the rhetoric heard at just about any militia meeting bore a striking similarity to any SDS meeting in the '60s: the urgent need to overthrow a corrupt, sinister, deceitful, tyrannical government; accusations of repression and eroding freedoms; evocation of wild and impossibly convoluted conspiracy theories; and a near-religious conviction that the group represented the truth and acted as a force for the light. Witness the readiness of both '60s liberals and '90s conservative radicals to blow up buildings. Note also how eerily close the arguments *for* guns and *against* gun control mesh vis-á-vis the conservative right in the '90s and the Black Panthers in the '60s and '70s. The apocalyptic religious group, the Branch Davidians, and the Panthers made near identical arguments in defense of their propensities to stockpile and use guns. Any number of parallels can be drawn between the rhetoric of the Weathermen of 1968, the Symbionese Liberation Army of the early '70s, the Branch Davidians of 1995, and the Montana Freemen circa 1998.

6

Precursors to the Haight

The Red Dog Saloon

To be called a good companion and fellow-boozer is to me pure honor
and glory.

—François Rabelais, Prologue to
Gargantua and Pantagruel (1534–1562)

The Red Dog Saloon opened for business in Virginia City, Nevada, on
June 29 in the summer of 1965, with the Charlatans as house band It
represented the first significant foray into and manifestation of psychedelic
culture outside of the Leary and Kesey circles. As such, it figured large in
the play of events that, in the coming fall, would launch the Haight-Ashbury
into spiraling prominence.

Many of the core participants in this venture lived in the Pine Street
neighborhood of San Francisco and would give birth to the Family Dog.
The initial idea for the Red Dog venture came from Don Works, who had
moved to Virginia City from San Francisco because he was a member of
the Native American Church (NAC), which used peyote as a sacrament.
He hoped to commune there with NAC co-religionists of the Washoe and
Paiute Indian tribes. Works lived in a two-room, cinder-block cabin fronting
two abandoned mines.

Virginia City is one of those "charming" remnants of the Wild West
that granola-macramé-Mercedes yuppies so love to discover and gentrify by

opening art galleries, wine bars, high-toned real-estate offices, and heliports. The town has a storied past, having figured large in a massive mid-nineteenth-century silver boom. From 1862 to 1864 Mark Twain lived there when he was a journalist for the *Territorial Enterprise*. By 1965, Virginia City had become a semi-ghost town harboring a colony of artist and mind-adventure types (Don Works being exhibit A), who lived in uneasy but mostly peaceful co-existence with the folks native to the area.

One weekend in early 1965, Works got a visit from two friends named Chandler Laughlin and Mark Unobsky. Unobsky was a trust fund kid originally from Memphis. An incorrigible problem child, totally unwilling to toe the line, Unobsky grew up attending private schools with intermittent side trips into mental wards. By 1965, he had turned folkie and become a gun collector. Laughlin had been a Berkeley politico and owner of a folk coffeehouse there. Most recently, he had been dealing marijuana. Sensing that the cops were closing in, Laughlin hid on Pine Street for several months to keep out of sight.

During the visit, a two-day blizzard roared in to keep the trio confined to Works's two-room cabin. In the course of that confinement, they began pipe-dreaming about opening a folk night spot in Virginia City. Their fantasy germinated and took root. With the help of a loan from the folks back home, Unobsky purchased the vacant, largely derelict Comstock House Hotel and began remodeling it for his nightclub. Drawing upon his personal tastes and the area's silver-boom history, Unobsky furnished his nascent club with a theme of elegant Wild West by way of whorehouse plush, with a whiff or two of marijuana and a small dose of Purple Haze acid. He painted the walls red and the trim black, installed an antique, mirror-backed bar, and hung gold-braided, red-and-turquoise velvet drapes purchased from a movie theater in San Francisco.

While on a supply run to San Francisco, Laughlin enthused about the Red Dog project to a Pine Street buddy and visual artist named Bill Ham and free-spirited artist/architect George Hunter, whom Ham introduced to Laughlin. This chance meeting proved momentous. Hunter had achieved a kind of bohemian notoriety in the neighborhood around San Francisco State University (SFSU) for his shoulder-length hair, Edwardian clothes, and elegantly freaky tastes. He had come to San Francisco with his girlfriend from L.A., where he had studied architecture and art. Some of Hunter's designs had been used to build houses, and he would later create the album cover to *Happy Trails* by Quicksilver Messenger Service, as well as the record jacket for the first, self-named *It's a Beautiful Day* album.

Though not a student at this point, Hunter hung out on the San Francisco State campus and put together a band—in theory, at least. Hunter himself couldn't play an instrument. He had been organizing the band by using criteria less musical than architectural. In effect, he designed the band according to standards of "hipness." For a pianist, he tabbed Mike Ferguson, who owned a store in the area called Magic Theatre for Madmen Only, a precursor to the head shop, selling antique clothes, knickknacks, art, hash pipes, rolling papers, and grass, on occasion. For lead guitarist, Hunter recruited former folkie Mike Wilhelm, who had learned guitar from acoustic bluesman Brownie McGhee. Hunter and Wilhelm had attended high school together in LA and had run into each other again by chance at the Blue Unicorn, Haight-Ashbury's first coffeehouse/hangout. The bass player was SFSU student Richie Olsen, who Hunter met though his girlfriend. Dan Hicks (later of Dan Hicks and His Hot Licks renown), the band's drummer, was a SFSU student majoring in radio and television broadcasting. Hicks, the most musically adept of the band members, had played in jazz dives and dance orchestras in his hometown of Santa Rosa, located in the North Bay area of San Francisco. Hunter met Hicks, when the latter showed up at Hunter's Downey Street apartment one day looking to buy some grass.

This ostensible band—the other member was Sam Linde—was comprised of the frontline proto-hippies of the SFSU area in early 1965, their credentials residing more in the "hip" than the musical line. Their association with Hunter came about more through mutual friends and chance meetings than any musical prowess. The band was formed primarily as an exercise in cool and display of hipness—an excuse to look groovy while holding a guitar. (Marty Balin would employ similar criteria in putting together Jefferson Airplane.) Appropriately, Hunter and his cohorts paraded at the San Francisco Airport and near downtown hotels with empty instrument cases under their arms. Most of the band members didn't even own instruments. They originally called themselves the Androids and then the Mainliners (in homage to William Burroughs) before becoming the Charlatans.

At the point Ham introduced Laughlin to Hunter, the Charlatans had yet to play a gig. They had, however, dozens of publicity photos taken of themselves variously decked out in Edwardian duds, cowboy outfits, letter sweaters, and even '20s rowing uniforms. Laughlin nevertheless invited Hunter to bring his group to Virginia City to audition for the Red Dog, which they did, disastrously stoned on acid (the management having dosed them). They still got the gig, their first paying job.

Bill Ham, meanwhile, managed two apartments on Pine Street, a three-block neighborhood, which had been evolving a scene that would play a large role in the coming months. Many of the figures central to Haight-Ashbury, Ham among them, came out of the Pine Street scene. Pine Street was situated just south of upscale, all-white Pacific Heights and just north of downscale, largely African American Fillmore. A good half-dozen Pine Street apartments were inhabited by types, who would later be known as hippies—musicians, marijuana dealers, artists, film students, theater types, intellectuals, wild weirdos, and various psychedelic front-runners—somewhat in the same mode as Perry Lane and the Chateau. The police semi-tolerated this scene because Pine Street served as a semi-acceptable buffer between the Fillmore African Americans and the affluent whites of Pacific Heights.

A shaggy-bearded Southerner, Ham managed rooming houses at 2111 and 1836 Pine Street, the latter known as the Dog House because nearly everyone living there had a dog. Ham, an expressionist painter, had been experimenting with a little-known phenomenon called "light shows" and presented them to live jazz accompaniment as evening entertainment for enthusiastically stoned and tripping Pine Streeters.

A significant number of Pine Streeters participated in the Red Dog enterprise that summer, including Ham, who did the lights. Another Pine Streeter was future poster artist great Alton Kelly, a former motorcycle racer and helicopter mechanic, who had come to San Francisco from Connecticut in 1964. At this juncture, Kelly was a collage artist experimenting with Day-Glo paint. He lived in the Dog House with his girlfriend, Ellen Harmon, who had been close friends with Janis Joplin during her first Frisco go-round in 1963. Kelly designed and constructed the sign hanging in front of the Red Dog, a stoned-looking dog with its tongue hanging out.

Because the entire Red Dog staff from management to the dishwashers took acid—on Monday nights, when the Red Dog was closed to the public, the staff held invitation-only acid parties as an opportunity to cultivate the outrageous. Drawing on the Wild West heritage of Virginia City, playing up the western/Edwardian look of the Charlatans, and picking up on Unobsky's interest in guns, everyone associated with the Red Dog carried antique rifles and hip-holstered pistols and generally gave themselves over to velveteen, red plush, high-whorehouse decadence and improvisatory high weirdness.

In June 1965, the Red Dog opened its doors to the public with Owsley on hand with one of his early batches of acid. The Red Dog bouncer, a 380-pound Washoe Indian, who wore a top hat and a sash, became the model for the image that became the Family Dog logo. The original plan called for the Charlatans to open the Red Dog with a two-week gig, but the engagement extended for the entire summer. In an attempt to distance themselves from the British Invasion then in vogue in the US, the band cultivated a combination of country, blues, and camp via numbers like the ragtime/blues song "Alabama Bound," the folk tune "Codine," bluesman Robert Johnson's "32-20," and Hicks's "How Can I Miss You When You Won't Go Away?"

Predictably, friction developed between the town merchants there for the long haul and the Red Dog crowd there to party. Brash, reckless, and high-spirited, the Red Doggers were openly into drugs, rowdiness, and debauchery. Shades of Kesey at La Honda and Leary at Harvard, they were unwilling to rein in the craziness enough to keep the neighbors from freaking out. The initially enthusiastic town people began to resent the crazies and wished them gone. One day, a tombstone was delivered to the Red Dog management with all their names on it. Originally sporting guns as theatrical props and fashion accessories, the Red Doggers began "packing" weapons for self-protection.

Word spread among the still small acid circles in Frisco about the outrageous scene at Virginia City. Among the heads making the three-hour drive to weekend party and drop acid at the Red Dog were Great Society guitarist Darby Slick, Quicksilver Messenger Service lead-guitarist-to-be John Cipollina, poster superstar-to-be Rick Griffin, rock-impresario-to-be Chet Helms, and Kesey and his Pranksters. The pre-Joplin Big Brother (still largely a jam band) played a gig there. A scene started to coalesce around psychedelics, music, and a kind of costumed street theater.

On August 30, 1965, the Charlatans made their San Francisco debut at the tail end of their Virginia City summer. One member of the North Beach improvisatory and satirical theater group, the Committee, booked the Charlatans to play at the showing of a film he had made. On the drive back to Virginia City the following day, car problems forced Laughlin and Wilhelm to pull into a gas station in the small town of Rodeo, outside San Francisco. Their "freaky" behavior and dress excited the suspicions of a highway patrolman, who pulled into the gas station to take a closer look. Seeing guns on the dashboard of their car—stupidly left in plain sight—the cop searched it. Finding a marijuana baggie, he arrested the two and took them handcuffed to jail.

This bust became an all-too-familiar counterculture pattern, repeated to the point of obsessive compulsion: (1) an almost in-your-face exercise of outrageousness, "freaking freely," and cosmic revelry; (2) the neighbors (or faculty) were not amused, perceiving freaking freely to be obnoxious at best and a threat to the public weal at worst; and (3) failure to rein in the excess and exercise even the most minimal, easily accomplished, common-sense restraint, thereby provoking hostile attention, which all but guaranteed reprisal and made a bust of some kind inevitable.

At this juncture—the Red Dog scene disintegrating from an excess of its own principles, and the townspeople increasingly antagonistic and hostile—Kesey and his Pranksters showed up and wired the place for one of their electric-acid party fests. A day and night of this madness convinced the Red Dog owner that the scene had become totally out of hand, causing him to shut down for a while to let things cool off.

The Red Dog summer now over, most of the revelers—Pine Streeters at their core—returned to San Francisco. As with Kesey at Perry Lane and La Honda, however, they wanted to keep the party going. The Virginia City summer had unleashed a weird, countercultural sensibility and put it into play. A number of heads were ready for a similar scene in San Francisco—something that could occasion heretofore separate pockets of oddballs, eccentrics, and underground high-timers to find each other in volatile, creative, unpredictable conjunction—not unlike what the Pranksters had been cultivating at their acid frolics.

The Charlatans were nowhere near in the same musical league of nascent groups like Jefferson Airplane, Quicksilver Messenger Service, the Grateful Dead, Big Brother and the Holding Company, and Country Joe and the Fish. Nor were they the equal of second-line groups like H. P. Lovecraft, Savage Resurrection, or Oxford Circle. But they did play a seminal role in the evolution of the Haight-Ashbury scene and the San Francisco sound. No less a personage than Bill Graham paid tribute to the Charlatans during a 1969 interview with Ralph Gleason. When Gleason dismissed the Charlatans *as* charlatans, Graham responded that "to me, the Charlatans have always been the epitome of what San Francisco really was, the way they dressed, their whole style. I love them" (Gleason 1969, 287).

Fall of 1965: The Circus Comes to Town

It is difficult to perceive just what the fuck is happening here.

—Thomas Pynchon, *Gravity's Rainbow* (1973)

There's all kinds of weird energy out there.

—Hunter Thompson, *Fear and Loathing on the Campaign Trail* (1973)

With psychedelics suddenly available in unprecedented quantities and their use spreading in certain circles, the hip underground of San Francisco was astir in the fall of 1965. Something was afoot. By that point, a number of semi-underground scenes in a variety of communities had been evolving high weirdness for years, sprouting strange blooms at L.A.'s Venice Beach, San Francisco's North Beach and Pine Street, colleges like San Francisco State and Berkeley, Palo Alto's Perry Lane and the Chateau, and La Honda. These secret gardens had been growing independently of each other, but events started to unfold that would bring these heretofore separate scenes into the mutually provocative, cross-fertilizing contact that gave birth to and achieved full flower in the Haight-Ashbury community, and set off a chain-reaction that would rock world culture from London to Katmandu, from suburban Cleveland to Morocco—creating waves that are still coming to shore nearly a half-century later.

On July 4, 1965—five days after the Red Dog opening—Mother's opened as San Francisco's first rock nightclub. The owner was rotund Frisco DJ Tom "Big Daddy" Donahue, who also co-owned Autumn Records with DJ Bobby Mitchell. The duo had fled Philadelphia for San Francisco in 1961 in the wake of the payola scandals and had promoted a number of frenetic and wildly successful teen revues that starred the likes of the Righteous Brothers and the Beach Boys. Ever the entrepreneurs, they signed a twenty-one-year-old, multitalented phenomenon from the East Bay town of Vallejo named Sylvester "Sly" Stewart (who later changed his stage name to Sly Stone), formed Cougar Productions as a vehicle for showcasing him, and christened Sly as the producer for Autumn Records.

In hopes of drawing, and potentially signing, promising material, Donahue initiated a daytime open mic policy at Mother's, overseen by Stewart. Many bands showed up at these "cattle call" sessions—the Charlatans among them—in hopes of securing an offer to record with Autumn, despite Stewart's reputation for treating auditioners with bored contempt. The pair eventually signed some of the early (and very untalented) San Francisco bands such as the Tikis, the Mojo Men, the Knight Riders, and the Vejtables (the latter, though, would evolve into a very decent group). The label's biggest group—initially recommended to Donahue by a hooker—was a band out of San Mateo, the Beau Brummels. Their single—"Laugh Laugh"—went Top 20 in 1965.

One of the bands, which auditioned at these sessions, was the Great Society, formed by rich-kid brothers Jerry and Darby Slick in the fall of 1965 after hearing the early Jefferson Airplane perform. Their lead singer, Grace Slick, was Jerry's wife. When, in the course of audition, the band made a few "psych" moves, they were openly laughed at and put down as "dorks" by Stewart, but Donahue offered them a recording contract because he wanted to impress Grace. Their 1966 single with Northbeach Records, an offshoot of Autumn, included "Free Advice" and the first version of "Somebody to Love." The Charlatans recorded four numbers with Autumn, though none ever surfaced on record. All four were from the Red Dog repertoire: "Jack of Diamonds," "Baby Won't You Tell Me," "The Blues Ain't Nothin,' " and "Number One."

Mother's never achieved much commercial success, but it served as the site of several concerts that helped jump-start the still nascent musical scene in San Francisco, the most important of which was a month-long run, beginning August 4, 1966, of the folk-rockers the Lovin' Spoonful. They played to packed houses of eager proto-hippies, who came decked out in outrageously flamboyant Edwardian and Victorian duds—an indication that the heads were beginning to find one another by way of musical happenings and a perceptual style contoured by the acid experience.

On July 25, 1965, a psychedelicized Dylan stunned the rock world—and scandalized the folk purists—by going electric at the Newport Folk Festival. The music and lyrics of his 1965 albums—*Bringing It All Back Home* (especially "Mr. Tambourine Man" and "Subterranean Homesick Blues") and *Highway 61 Revisited* (the entire album)—testified to recent forays into LSD while he woodshedded in a little town in upstate New York called Woodstock. It was none other than Dylan, who subsequently introduced John Lennon and the Beatles to marijuana.

On August 7, Kesey and the Pranksters played host to the Hells Angels at a two-day party at La Honda. In many respects, this event—which has attained near mythological status in counterculture lore—was a mind-blowing unlikelihood. Picture this: the low rumble, then louder rumble, then even louder rumble, then out-and-out roar, and finally the ear-splitting megablast of dozens of Hells Angels Harleys cruising up the highway to backwoodsy La Honda with Allen Ginsberg—a New Yorker, an intellectual, a poet, and gay (everything the Angels most loathed)—bidding them welcome by prancing about with finger cymbals and singing/chanting "Hare Krishna." For several days, a giant, hand-painted banner with red, white, and blue lettering had been hanging at the entrance to Kesey's place proclaiming: "THE MERRY PRANKSTERS WELCOME THE HELL'S ANGELS"—a last-straw outrage serving further to alarm and antagonize the distraught neighbors.

Kesey's acid-soaked event brought together a highly unlikely triad of college-educated, Day-Glo bohemians on permanent psychedelic holiday;

intellectual-loathing, brutal, black-leathered abominations; and Beat legends Neal Cassady and Allen Ginsberg, stirring them into a Nirvana/Monty Python/ *Zap Comix* mix. Interactions of this sort, catalyzed by the acid experience and amplified by an enormous amount of backlogged, pent-up, pre-orgasmic cultural energy, would send a '60s tidal wave roaring through the *Leave It to Beaver* and *Ozzie and Harriet* America to produce Haight-Ashbury and Woodstock, on the one hand, and the horrors of Charles Manson and Altamont on the other. The Hells Angels would become La Honda frequenters and—partly in consequence of this particular weekend—sinner-saint outlaw icons of the counterculture, much to the counterculture's everlasting shame. (On tapes of the Sound City Acid Test of January 1, 1966, Kesey and Babbs discuss—sometimes in near worshipful tribute and as nuggets of exemplary wisdom—the Hells Angels/Prankster connection, replete with Angel anecdotes, sayings, and carrying-ons.)

About this time, independently of La Honda, the Hells Angels stood at their peak of near hysterical media notoriety, being hailed and damned as profane, murderous outlaws given to rape, pillage, and desecration of everything valued and aspired to by upstanding, red-blooded Americans. Much to their pride and satisfaction, they had become the superstars of scum, the subject of sensationalized spreads in national publications such as *Life*. For the Kesey crazies to *invite* them to La Honda was the last straw for the neighbors—and for the police. There already had been a drug bust, and as the Pranksters well knew, the police had them under surveillance and the neighbors had planned vigilante actions. Ginsberg, who also became a La Honda regular, penned an impromptu poem on the Kesey/Prankster scene that later appeared in *Kesey's Garage Sale* (Kesey 1973, 213).

With the San Mateo police dying for a chance to bust Kesey, the Pranksters and their compatriots brazenly and literally went out of their way to taunt them, thereby inviting a bust that became all but inevitable. Hunter Thompson, whose piece on the Hells Angels in the April 1965 issue of *The Nation* would evolve into his pre-Gonzo book, *Hell's Angels: A Strange and Terrible Saga of the Outlaw Motorcycle Gangs*, nicely captures the mood of the cops during this weekend-long Pranksters/Angels bacchanal at La Honda: "The cops stood out on the highway and looked across the Creek at the scene that must have tortured the very roots of their understanding. Here were all these people running wild, bellowing and dancing half naked to rock-n-roll sounds piped out through the trees in massive amplifiers, reeling and stumbling in a maze of psychedelic lights . . . WILD, by God, and with no law to stop them" (Thompson 1967, 294).

The cops/Kesey relationship wasn't exactly enhanced by the spectacle of a zonked, amped-out Neal Cassady shouting insults at the cops, who were stopping and searching every car that drove up. Kesey describes Cassady standing: "Naked on the private side of the creek and scream[ing] off a long, brutal diatribe against the cops only twenty yards away. He was swaying and yelling in the bright glare of a light from the porch, holding a beer bottle in one hand and shaking his fist at the objects of his scorn: 'You sneaky motherfuckers!' " (Thompson 1967, 296).

Thompson's career and renown were just then beginning to take off, and he was also working on a piece (never published) about Kesey and the Pranksters for *Playboy*. He had met Kesey through their joint appearance on a public TV program in San Francisco. In a bar afterward, Kesey had cajoled Thompson, who was researching (read: living with, partying with, hanging out with) the Angels, into introducing him to them. In the course of that afternoon, Kesey extended the invitation that resulted in this weekend-long bacchanal.

Thompson offers a peek into this scene in a letter to Murry Fisher of *Playboy* that is dated August 9, 1965—the Sunday of the Hells Angels weekend at La Honda: "Last night I was grabbed by the gendarmes at Ken Kesey's loony bin in La Honda (I introduced him to the San Francisco Angels last week and he decided to have a party for them; the locals flipped and the road in front of Kesey's house was swarming with cop cars). They stopped everybody either coming or going and went over the cars for possible violations. My tail-light lenses were cracked, so they cited me" (Thompson 1997, 536).

That August 7th to 8th party involved a cadre of the San Francisco chapter of the Angels. Before long, the Oakland chapter (and others) became regulars. According to Thompson, "La Honda quickly became a mecca for Angels from all over northern California. They would arrive unannounced, usually in groups of five to fifteen, and stay until they got bored or ran out of LSD . . . Once introduced to acid, the Angels—as with everything else they prized—went whole hog, taking mega-doses, doubling and tripling 'the recommended maximums' " (Thompson 1967 298, 301). Thompson later contended that his all-time favorite LSD experiences were those he had during parties at La Honda with the Hells Angels present. He claims that, were he given "a choice of repeating any one of the half dozen" LSD experiences he was able to recall, he would choose "one of those Hells Angels parties in La Honda, complete with all the mad lighting, cops on the road, a Ron Boise sculpture looming out of the woods, and all the big speakers vibrating with Bob Dylan's 'Mr. Tambourine Man' . . . Dropping acid with the Angels was an adventure; they were too ignorant to know what to expect, and too wild to care. They just swallowed the stuff and hung on" (Thompson 1967, 301–302).

However, in his May 2, 1965, letter to Don Cooke, Thompson described the La Honda scene as depressing, embarrassing, and somehow sad—likening it to "a kid's home circus, a Peter Pan kind of thing." A mere three months later, he'd characterized it as a King Hell bacchanal representing one of the high points of his life. This disparity is instructive. As with the fabled 1964 bus trip, the mythology remembered and delineated for public consumption doesn't always jibe with the less glorious, actual event assessments offered on the immediate observational spot.

Another instructive glimpse of this disparity can be seen in the altogether different view of Kesey and Cassady offered by writer and former wife of Neal Cassady, Carolyn Cassady, in *Off the Road: My Years with Cassady, Kerouac, and Ginsberg* (1990). In contrast to their consistent near canonization in counterculture lore, Carolyn Cassady reveals them to be sometimes pathetic, sometimes frankly reprehensible, crass jerks. Far from mean-spirited, antagonistic, or banally middle-class, she sometimes comes off as borderline masochist in her New-Agey willingness to "understand" and forgive Cassady's cruelties and betrayals and Kesey's inanities. Her account provides a much-needed balance to the quasi-deifications afforded the Beats and other '60s frontrunners. It serves as an indispensable companion and counterweight to such erstwhile counterculture gospels as *On the Road* and *The Electric Kool-Aid Acid Test*.

Another type of restlessness engulfed the Watts section of Los Angeles. Two days after the Prankster/Hells Angels bacchanal in La Honda, massive rioting, looting, and pillaging broke out in the Watts section of Los Angeles, an enclave of African Americans. From August 11 to August 16, 1965, African Americans rioted in Watts as rumors spread about police brutality aimed at African American Marquette Frye and his mother. Authorities eventually quelled the riot using 14,000 California Army National Guardsmen. When the smoke cleared, thirty-four people lay dead and more than a thousand were injured amid $40 million in property damage. In vivid contrast to the wild time at La Honda, where the participants were white and middle-class with leisure time to spare, in Watts, recalled eyewitness and jazz pianist Hampton Hawes: "Whole blocks were crackling with flames. Must have been the way Rome looked like back then, except that these citizens were all a funny color and none of them were wearing togas.

Never saw so many people on the street at one time—and this was five in the morning" (Hawes 1974, 140).

Amid the Watts riots, on August 13, Berkeley activists launched the weekly underground newspaper, the *Berkeley Barb*. It was published by the heavily bearded, genial-looking Max Scherr, former owner of a bistro called Steppenwolf that was a favored hangout of radical politicos—in fact, the HUAC protests of 1960 were planned largely in his bar. Scherr sold the bar to raise the funds to start the *Barb*. Going on fifty years old, he was an anti-war activist in the Berkeley-based Vietnam Day Committee, which began in late May 1965, as a protest against the war by students, labor unions, and pacifist groups. The first issue of the *Barb* was eight pages, had a press run of 2,000, of which 1,200 were sold, largely by Scherr himself by hawking them on the street. By 1970, it would have a peak circulation of nearly 90,000. Scherr utilized largely unpaid writers as a survival strategy and acquired a reputation for being a tyrannical manipulator. (In 1969, the *Berkeley Tribe* was started by disgruntled Scherr employees and reached a circulation of more than 50,000.) The *Barb* continued publication until 1980, though in later years it was little more than a vehicle for porno ads.

Also, on August 13, the Matrix—San Francisco's second rock night spot—opened at the foot of Fillmore Street in the Marina district. Graphic artist, folk musician, and rock-star wannabe Marty Balin wheeled, dealed, and finagled his friends into buying into the Matrix for $9,000 as a venue for showcasing his newly formed band, the Jefferson Airplane (still in its pre–Grace Slick incarnation).

Once again, Hunter Thompson afforded a peek into this pre-Haight-Ashbury scene. Thompson caught the Airplane's debut at the Matrix (as did the soon-to-be musician threesome of Jerry, Darby, and Grace Slick) and was sufficiently bowled over to telephone Ralph Gleason at 2 a.m. to demand that he check them out. Gleason—a forty-year-old liberal-leaning Columbia University alum—was the cultural critic for the *San Francisco Chronicle*. He devoted his usually brief, but widely read, column to mostly to jazz name-dropping and tidbits of gossip tipping readers off to hip events and happenings. Thompson accompanied Gleason to the Matrix to check out the Airplane, and it was in part by virtue of Thompson's goading that Gleason took interest in the countercultural scene that was just then beginning to galvanize and coalesce into something larger than the sum of its scattered parts. Gleason went on to write a now underground classic of sorts about the Jefferson Airplane—*The Jefferson Airplane and the San Francisco Sound*, which encapsulated the early days of the psychedelic dance-concert phenomenon.

In yet another chance happening so typical of the era, Gleason co-founded the magazine *Rolling Stone*, to which Thompson later would contribute.

On September 25, 1965, Thompson mentioned the Airplane in a letter to his fifteen-year-old brother, Jim: "If you're looking around for some action on the folk-rock scene, get set for a group called the Jefferson Airplane, which works out of The Matrix. They will lift the top of your head right off. A really wild sound. It won't be out for a while; they just went to L.A. to record last week, but when it comes out it's going to go like Zaannnggg!!! They make those silly goddamn Beatles sound like choirboys" (Thompson 1997, 542). Thompson significantly refers to the band as folk-rockers—the San Francisco sound was still being born.

The San Francisco/Haight-Ashbury Connection

Toto, I've a feeling we're not in Kansas anymore.

—L. Frank Baum, *The Wizard of Oz* (1939)

That is at bottom the only courage that is demanded of us: to have courage for the most strange, the most singular and the most inexplicable that we may encounter.

—Rainer Maria Rilke, *Letters to a Young Poet* (1929)

Located on a hillside high above the ocean (rarely visible due to an ever-present fog bank), San Francisco State University (SFSU) played an integral part in the evolution of Haight-Ashbury. In 1953, the college moved its campus to its present location on 19th Avenue near Lake Merced. The new campus had a dearth of housing, so students typically lived off campus in whatever accommodations they could hustle up—most typically in boarding houses and apartments. In the early '60s, SFSU students began discovering the Haight-Ashbury district. They learned that, by pooling their resources, groups of friends could live there cheaply in relative splendor.

During the 1963–1964 school year, the SFSU student body began exhibiting an increasingly hip and countercultural bent. There was a sudden and significant escalation of marijuana usage, which tripled in a very short time. By the spring registration of 1964, SFSU students passed joints up and down the registration lines. Hank Harrison, a Grateful Dead stalwart and father of Hole singer Courtney Love, reported that in the fall of 1963,

"LSD hit San Francisco like a bomb" (Harrison 1986, 89). It first took hold on the SFSU campus by way of a coterie of Jungian devotees in the psychology department. SFSU soon became known as "Acid U," and a goodly number of the figures, who would be the psychedelic frontrunners in the Haight-Ashbury scene either attended SFSU, were SFSU alums, or were taking (or had taken) a course or two there. SFSU ended up figuring more prominently than even Berkeley in the Haight-Ashbury evolution.

By 1965, the SFSU film department had become a very trippy enclave, in which heads joined with art department heavies like Alexander Epote and Seymour Locks (the later the inventor of the light show) to stage Wednesday night showings of incredibly strange and imaginative foreign films—the freakier the better. It became de rigueur for heads to "group freak" at these Wednesday night gatherings. Kesey, Babbs, and early Prankster Roy Seburn became regulars; Jerry Slick, husband of Grace and later drummer for the Great Society, was an SFSU film student at this time.

In the fall of 1965, the SFSU's Experimental College—a kind of college-within-a-college program—began. This program afforded students an opportunity to suggest courses on whatever subject they wished and, if they could get a faculty member to sponsor the course, find a teacher to teach it, and pay the teacher, they were in business. These courses received no official academic credit, but the program proved immensely popular. (Some of the classes were pretty wild. Marco Vassi, who taught at the Experimental College, wrote about some of its courses, incidents, and teachers in *The Stoned Apocalypse* [1972].) It was instrumental in bringing Buckminster Fuller, architect, futurist, and inventor of the geodesic dome, to SFSU in the spring of 1966. In true countercultural spirit, a number of SFSU students dropped out of the official university to load up on courses in the experimental, noncredit college—yet another example of how young people were increasingly viewing the counterculture as more exciting, relevant, and educational than officially sanctioned establishment culture.

All this while, increasing numbers of Acid U students discovered and moved into a twenty-five-block neighborhood known as the Haight-Ashbury district. The trolley system made the SFSU campus easily accessible, and the neighborhood was pleasantly adjacent to the Panhandle, an eight-block, mile-long, two-block-wide outcropping of Golden Gate Park. Paralleling the Panhandle three blocks to the south was Haight Street, which began at the eastern edge of Golden State Park, ran through the Fillmore district, and continued on to Market Street.

In the '20s, this neighborhood had been a fashionable, swank enclave of Victorian mansions known as Politicians Row, but by 1965, when the city built a freeway nearby, it spiraled on a downward slope to ghettodom, with at least eighteen of the thirty-odd neighborhood storefronts vacant. A highly diverse, but largely blue-collar community, it included an array of Chinese, Filipino, Japanese, Hispanic, Portuguese, and African Americans. Though fraying and decaying, the mansions retained their high-Victorian trappings and accoutrements. Students found that they could live at relatively low rent in shabby, roomy splendor. Somewhat along the lines of Perry Lane at Stanford, the neighborhood began evolving into a semi-intellectual, quasi-bohemian ghetto of choice. Acid-amped, college move-ins took delight in decorating their abodes in Victorian and art nouveau authenticity, in part accounting both for the early-on popularity in Haight-Ashbury culture of paisley and Edwardian fashions (à la George Hunter of the Charlatans), and for why so much of psychedelic art—including the Avalon and Fillmore rock posters—had such an art nouveau-ish and Aubrey Beardsleyan fin-de-siècle flair.

A number of the apartments and rooming houses in the Haight-Ashbury district were managed by older SFSU student-bohemians and folk veterans in return for free rent. 1090 Page, for example, was managed by Rod Albin, whose uncle was part owner of the building. Albin lived in the attic while taking psychology classes for three semesters at SFSU. Danny Rifkin, who with Rock Scully became co-manager of the Grateful Dead, studied German at SFSU, and managed a boarding house at 710 Ashbury that would eventually become "the Dead house," which was owned by the mother of artist Robert Crumb. For four to five years prior to his *Zap Comix* days, R. Crumb lived in the basement of 710 and rented the rest of the house to the Dead horde.

Bill Ham, a former abstract expressionist who was using these Pine Street basements to pioneer and experiment with light shows, managed both 2111 and 1836 Pine Street—rooming houses popular with musicians. 1836 Pine Street—the now-famous Dog House—would be the birthplace of the Family Dog, the group which staged the initial psychedelic dance concerts at Longshoreman's Hall.

The movement toward the Haight-Asbury district helped germinate a scene among eager students, who were predisposed to a new way of looking at reality. What emerged was a community of disgruntled middle-class, laid-back, mentally adventurous, relatively well-read, slightly older (low- to mid-twenties) bohemian-inclined student types, heads, rock musicians, artisans, and drop-out sophisticates, with a liberal sprinkling of candle-making, astrology-oriented, clueless-but-harmless airheads, who shared a cheerful, Dr. Strangean taste for the oddball, the bizarre, and the marvelous. The district started to assume an upbeat ambience of charming weirdness, open-ended possibility, and intelligent eccentricity grounded in a general appreciation of the psychedelic experience as a catalyst and common denominator. To Claude Hayward, a recent migrant to the Haight, the scene attracted "alienated suburban kids" like himself, who emphasized "creating your own reality. Live the reality you want. Make your own space. Do your own thing" (Babcock 2021, 9). In 1967, the less flattering Hunter Thompson characterized the Haight hippies as "white and voluntarily poor. Their backgrounds were largely middle class; many had gone to college" (Thompson 1967).

LSD, still legal, fostered a mindset, sensibility, and perceptual style linked to psychedelics among the Haight-Asbury residents and became the central, formative factor in the neighborhood's evolution. In the early days, especially from early 1964 to the first half of 1966 (the scene's golden era), a still largely underground, very local and circumscribed, but exceedingly hip psychedelic culture arose. The bands, artists, and merchants residing there were simply local residents and initiates sharing similarly adventurous and unsanctioned tastes, aspirations, and outlooks. The district represented a very loose, self-contained, informal conglomeration of heads, students, and like-minded aficionados of high weirdness and eccentric charm who started finding each other and gathering into tribes and/or families in a locale where rents were communally low, ideas were on the fly, and something was in the air. Hank Harrison describes the Haight-Ashbury scene of those days in *The Dead Book:*

> These were the pre-hippie summers, when hippie was a word equivalent to "groovy." One day was worth a lifetime of memories, when young and old Bohemians got together, when Alan Watts wrote about his acid trips in *The Joyous Cosmology* and Ale Ekstrom sang sea shanties with his ocarina. When the blacks from the Fillmore brought their drums to the Panhandle and blasted away all afternoon on Sundays . . . drums cutting through racial barriers, flute players, free grass. . . .
>
> In a crowd, the joint never came back to you, so you had to take a big toke and hold it and pass it on. Bigger and bigger joints were rolled, and the parties went on in the sun. . . . Kesey's bunch would show up between acid tests and look at home in the eucalyptus-studded Panhandle. (1986, 105)

This transpired within a highly volatile social, historical, and cultural context. Across the Bay at Berkeley, the massive political upheavals of the Free Speech Movement were still sending aftershocks, the civil rights movement was rocking American society as a whole, and the "war" in Vietnam was just beginning to heat up. More and more people began to see what was evolving in Haight-Ashbury as a quasi-utopian, countercultural alternative affording the possibility of living among interesting, creative heads in an experimental environment, where amazing ideas and modes of seeing were on the wing, under exploration, and being put into daily practice. This was the scene-at-large, when the fall semester of 1965 at Berkeley and San Francisco State University got underway, hard on the heels of the Red Dog summer.

7

The Flowering of the Haight

Haight-Ashbury Happens

People say that what we are all seeking is a meaning for life. I don't think that's what we are really seeking. I think that what we are seeking is an experience of being alive.

—Joseph Campbell, *The Power of Myth* (1988)

The psychedelic culture seemed to sprout a new weird bloom with every passing week during the fall of 1965. There was a burgeoning desire to play, to share and celebrate the psychedelic experience in a community of intelligent, interactive creativity and adventurous experimentation. With the exception of the Prankster circle, however, no one yet thought of themselves as part of psychedelic culture as such. Nevertheless, a variety of events, scenes, and art forms were being created to facilitate and provide opportunities for this kind of play. The heads were beginning to find each other, and they were open to suggestion. They were all dressed up and looking for somewhere to—as Dean Moriarty/Neal Cassady put it in *On the Road*—"GO."

On September 13, The Committee Theater, an improvisational comedy group started in 1963 by Alan and Jessica Myerson, had Monday evenings free and contracted for multimedia presentations of "America Needs Indians." This show simultaneously projected 600 slides and two different motion pictures on the wall, accompanied by four soundtracks, flowers, food, such Native American luminaries as Eagle Bone Whistle and Thunderstorm, and members of the Cheyenne, Chippewa, Sioux, Blackfeet, Tlingit, Makah, Pomo, and Miwuk tribes. These showings largely prompted the early popularity of Native American motifs in rock poster art and fashion (headbands, moccasins, feathers, and beads) and gave rise to the "tribes" paradigm (as in "gathering of the tribes" and the *Berkeley Tribe*). One of the producers of and the main force behind this show was Stewart Brand, a Midwesterner and graduate of a high-powered eastern prep school with a degree in biology from Stanford. During his Stanford studies, he lived with the Siletz tribe in Oregon and the Navajos in the Southwest (with whom he participated in peyote ceremonies). Brand was a proto-Prankster and would later found and publish *The Whole Earth Catalog* (1968–1971). In conversations at Brand's North Beach apartment on Vallejo Street, Brand and his friends hatched the idea for the Trips Festival, and on the roof of his apartment building Kesey got busted a second time for possession of grass.

Three weeks after "America Needs Indians" opened, on September 30, the Open Theater, which was launched by Berkeley drama department dropouts Ben and Rain Jacopetti, opened in Berkeley in an odd Victorian building—its inside walls were painted black—on College Avenue. In a series of Sunday night "spontaneous happenings," this group began experimenting with multimedia shows called "Revelations," wherein they projected film clips and light shows onto nude bodies to the sound of multiple soundtracks. Sometimes, the cast members and the audience cavorted together, sometimes both naked. These shows, it goes without saying, couldn't be performed publicly (no matter that San Francisco was in the national spotlight at the moment for its explosion of topless bars and nude beaches), so "Revelations" became quasi-underground happenings for the edification of heads and insiders. Out of largely insider, underground events of this sort presented by The Committee and the Open Theater—attended mostly by students, avant-garde artists, actor-provocateurs, counterculture politicos, prankster surrealists, and hipster intellectuals—light shows first gained popularity and began spreading.

The Open Theater became renowned for its performances of *The God Box*, a play focused on a high-frequency generator that that produced purple sparks and made fluorescent bulbs glow, when it was brought near the actors. It also became famous for: (1) the hilarious, mock/serious, dramatic readings of a nineteenth-century sermon outlining the gruesome effects of masturbation; (2) the trio, the Jazz Mice, headed by saxophonist Ian Underwood (later of the Mothers of Invention); (3) "Beatle readings"; and (4) the presentation of an amazing passage from a sermon by '20s West Coast female evangelist Aimee Semple McPherson (rumored to be a sex aficionado) that exhorted the audience to "come in numbers, come in Deuteronomy."

Open Theater booked the irreverent social comedy of the Congress of Wonders, comprised of Winslow Thrill (aka Richard Rollins) and Karl Truckload (aka Howard Kerr). The Congress became a near-fixture at the early Family Dog productions, and it was one of the featured acts at the Trips Festival. Their routine, "Pigeon Park" (Jerry Garcia and Phil Lesh meeting in a park in their near-senile, but still stoned-out dotage), has cult status among many now-grayed and/or balding heads. (Later comedy groups like Firesign Theatre were off-shoot imitators of the Congress of Wonders.)

In another two weeks, on October 15 and 16, the Vietnam Day Committee at Berkeley, started by activists Jerry Rubin and Stephen Smale, organized antiwar protests all over the US called the International Days of Protest against American Military Intervention. By July 28, the U.S. had upped its troop involvement in Vietnam from 75,000 to 125,000 and doubled the number of draftees. Escalating rapidly, the war became a very real thing in the very real lives of draft-eligible college-age males. The largest of the antiwar protests nationally coalesced around Berkeley. There was an all-day "teach-in" on campus with entertainment interspersed here and there, all in prelude to a mass march on the Oakland Army Terminal, where men and materials were carted off to Vietnam. The rally featured the first performance of "I-Feel-Like-I'm-Fixin'-to-Die-Rag" by the short-lived Instant Action Jug Band, whose two members—Barry Melton and Joe McDonald—became the core of Country Joe and the Fish. On this day, they were barely known neighborhood residents and quasi-folkies performing from the back of a pickup truck, selling EPs of their song for fifty cents (collectors now pay in excess of $300 for a mint copy). Less than 100 copies of the record had been pressed on McDonald's Rag Baby Records label by the Berkeley *Free Press*. That song became one of the anthems of the '60s and a highlight of the Woodstock festival.

Kesey and the Pranksters showed up at this rally, their psychedelic bus painted a blood red. While the other speakers delivered firebrand diatribes to raise the adrenaline levels of the audience for the march to the Oakland Army Terminal, Kesey, who was the next-to-last speaker, suggested that the anti-war firebrands seemed as fascistic as the pro-war advocates they were criticizing. Rather than exhort the crowd to march and raise hell, Kesey wheezed through a rendition of "Home on the Range" on his harmonica and urged the assembled multitude to "just fuck it."

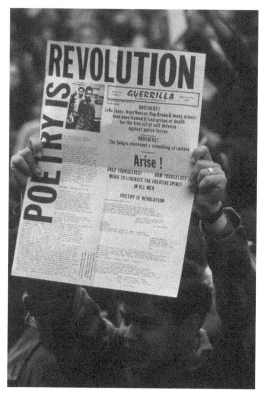

Figure 11. "Poetry Is Revolution," 1968. Photo: Bernard Gotfryd. *Source*: Library of Congress Prints and Photographs Division, public domain. https://lccn.loc. gov/2020737206

The march went as planned, some 10,000 to 15,000 marchers leaving the Berkeley campus up Telegraph Avenue toward Oakland around 8 p.m. At the Oakland city line, the procession was met by a phalanx of 400 police dressed in riot gear and armed with night sticks. To avoid a confrontational bloodbath—and counter to the sentiments of many of the marchers—leaders (Jack Weinberg at the fore) turned right and diverted the march to Civic Center Park in Oakland.

The next day, the between 2,000 and 5,000 antiwar marchers made a second attempt to reach the Oakland Army Terminal, setting out from where the previous night's march had ended at Civic Center Park. When a wall of riot-geared police again blocked their route to the Army Terminal, the marchers sat down with Allen Ginsberg singing "Hare Krishna" and playing his finger cymbals. At this point, a handful of highly hostile, hippie-hating, chest-beating Hells Angels charged the marchers, despite the Angels having been only recently psychedelicized by Kesey and the Pranksters by downing acid and partying at Kesey's. Casting themselves in the roles of America-defending patriots, the Angels physically and verbally attacked the "commie" war protesters.

The police beat back the Angels and arrested one of them, but the melee raised a bewildering question. As would become so characteristic of the era, the news media was confused: Who were the "good guys" and who were the "bad guys" here? Were the good guys these smelly, profane motorcycle outlaws "defending America" and proclaiming their patriotism while stomping the leftist students? Or were the good guys the unpatriotic, college kids denouncing the war as evil and unjust and getting beaten up by cop-hating motorcycle thugs? This question got really confusing, when

Figure 12. Anti-draft protest at IRS with peace sign on helmet, 1970. *Source*: Library of Congress Prints and Photographs Division, public domain. https://lccn. loc.gov/2015647163

the ultra-right-wing Berkeley chapter of the John Birch Society took up a collection to bail out the Hells Angel who had been jailed for attacking the students. This scenario suggests a highly ironic and complicated situation, which reveals the layers of nuances that defined the era: the Hells Angels, who viewed themselves as the ultimate social outlaws, being hailed as heroes by both the psychedelic, countercultural left and the ultra-patriotic, ideologically hyperventilating, beatnik-hating conservative right.

From Red Dog to Family Dog

The night of October 16, 1965—the same night as the second day of the anti-war rally and march in Berkeley—marked the first-ever psychedelic rock concert. No one had any way of knowing it during the event, but it would be this kind of dance concert that would largely stimulate and become the spiritual focus and driving force of the Haight-Ashbury counterculture and psychedelic scene. This communal performance, the first of these events, represented a landmark and the birth of the Family Dog from the adventurers who had been prominent in the Red Dog Saloon.

Among the key players in the Red Dog Saloon venture of that summer—which had ended only a month-and-a-half earlier—had been future poster artist Alton Kelly and Ellen Harmon, a couple cohabiting in the Dog House, a Pine Street bohemian enclave managed by Bill Ham. In 1963, when Janis Joplin hitchhiked to San Francisco from Austin with Chet Helms and got seriously strung out on speed (as did Helms), Ellen Harmon became one of Joplin's closest friends, the two spending a lot of time doing speed together.

Among their fellow Dog Housers were Jack Towle, a marijuana dealer, and Luria Castell, a former Berkeley politico, who had recently checked out the scene in Los Angeles, where the Byrds and the Lovin' Spoonful were all the rage. Castell had been one of the people who had been washed down the marble stairway of San Francisco's City Hall in 1960, when firemen turned their hoses on demonstrators protesting the HUAC hearing.

A very tough-minded, no-nonsense woman, Castell put her boyfriend and Chet Helms under a two-week house arrest, during which they managed to kick their speed habits. Shortly after kicking speed, Helms became a habitué of 1090 Page, where he started the jam sessions that led to the formation of Big Brother and the Holding Company.

These four Pine Streeters—Kelly, Harmon, Towle, and Castell—wanted to continue the sense of play, costume, and theater that they had enjoyed so much at the Red Dog that summer, and they concocted a scheme. Earlier in year, the Byrds had performed two weeks at the Peppermint Tree, a North Beach nightclub that allowed dancing, and the Lovin' Spoonful had just played a month-long August engagement at Mother's. Both engagements had been successes. In hopes of piggybacking on and building off those concerts—and of keeping the Red Dog party going—the foursome pooled their resources, named themselves the Family Dog, and rented the umbrella-shaped, echo-laden, octagonal meeting hall of the International Longshore and Warehouse Union, located in the Fisherman's Wharf neighborhood.

The four friends planned to hold a dance concert. Ideally, the event would afford an occasion for Bay Area weirdos with an appreciation for the outrageous to come into catalytic contact. With any luck, it might bring in some money, too. They booked the Charlatans (naturally), the newly formed Great Society (who had had only one gig to date), and the Marbles, an Oakland group, which embraced the British Invasion blues style. For emcee, they hired Russ "The Moose" Syracuse, a DJ with station KYA whose show, "All Night Flight," had gained popularity with the heads. Because they very much wanted to attract heads, and because light shows had been proving very popular with that crowd, the foursome hired fellow Pine Streeter Bill Ham to stage a light show at their dance concert.

The foursome dubbed their dance concert "A Tribute to Dr. Strange." Kelly fashioned an advertising handbill—the rudimentary precursor of the psychedelic poster phenomenon—and they had several hundred printed up at Joe Buchwald's Rapid Repro Shop and posted them anywhere in the Bay Area that they would likely be seen by people appreciative of weirdness and play. Sure enough, the event attracted a surprisingly large and very freaky crowd decked out in theatrically outlandish attire, ready to get weird among the fellow weird. The attendees that night included Allen Ginsberg and a highly approving Ralph Gleason. This kind of organized (sort of), planned out (sort of), publicized "happening" was unheard-of up to this time. The heads were discovering one another. A scene was coalescing and acquiring a life and momentum of its own.

In some ways, the first Family Dog production is analogous in ultimate import to the now legendary Six Gallery poetry reading of the Beats almost exactly ten years earlier on October 13, 1955, at which Ginsberg gave the first public reading of "Howl." In October of 1954, six painters wanting to try out the multimedia idea of combining art exhibits with poetry, music, and film pooled their resources and converted an old automobile repair garage on Union and Fillmore streets into the Six Gallery. The gallery became a kind of motivating force in the local art scene. At the time of Ginsberg's reading, the gallery was riding the notoriety of having recently staged Robert Duncan's controversial play *Faust Foutu* (Faust Screwed). Six Gallery was the mid-'50s precursor to mid-'60s venues like the Open Theater and The Committee Theater, combining art forms and mixing scenes to create a provocative, potentially volatile brew.

Also reading on this night were Gary Snyder, Michael McClure, Philip Whalen, and Philip Lamantia (though invited, Kerouac declined to read); Kenneth Rexroth emceed. None of that night's readers were as yet known beyond their respective inner circles. Ten years later, Ginsberg, Snyder, and McClure would become key figures in the Haight-Ashbury scene, and all three would be on stage at the January 1967 Be-In. Snyder served as the model for Japhy Ryder in Kerouac's *Dharma Bums*.

To publicize the reading, Ginsberg posted handbills in a number of North Beach bars and printed hundreds of postcards bearing the message: "Six poets at the Six Gallery. Kenneth Rexroth, M.C. Remarkable collection of angels all gathered at once in the same spot. Wine, music, dancing girls, serious poetry, free satori. Small collection for wine and postcards. Charming event." The event drew a festive, standing-room-only audience of more than a hundred eager for the happening promised by the posters. The audience passed around gallon jugs of wine at the event to increase the anticipation and excitement.

Ginsberg's reading of "Howl" created an absolute sensation. He started out calmly and quietly, but gradually began to sway to the swing and beat of his cadence, his performance escalating into a demented saxophone wail in the let-it-loose peak of primal scream therapy. Kerouac, standing to the side of the stage, began pounding the stage with a gallon wine bottle, yelling "GO!" at the end of each line, and the audience began screaming encouragement in the manner of a jazz crowd exhorting a soloist in the middle of a particularly wild improvisatory riff. By reading's end, Ginsberg was sobbing like a mad rabbi in the throes of a Rimbaud-esque mescaline binge and the wall-to-wall, standing-room-only audience was going nuts.

This happening launched what the media dubbed the San Francisco Poetry Renaissance and put North Beach and City Lights (which would publish *Howl and Other Poems*) on the national cultural map. As would happen to Haight-Ashbury in the fall of 1965 and spring of 1966, the sudden infusion of media attention altered and inflated the nascent scene. *Mademoiselle* and *Life* did photo essays about the so-called San Francisco poets, and in 1957 Grove Press founder Barney Rosset started *Evergreen Review,* which in the second issue devoted the magazine entirely to the so-called San Francisco Renaissance. In a piece called "West Coast Rhythms," Richard Eberhart enthused about this scene in a manner oddly parallel to the way Ralph Gleason would enthuse about the "A Tribute to Dr. Strange" ten years later. In his article, Eberhart described the "new, vital group consciousness now among young poets in the Bay region . . . They have exuberance and a young will to kick down the doors of older consciousness and established practice in favor of what they think is vital and new" (1956).

Significantly, Ginsberg also appeared, almost ten years to the day, at "A Tribute to Dr. Strange," which would have even more of a galvanizing effect on underground culture both locally and nationwide. This particular conjunction exemplifies the extent to which Ginsberg bridged the Beats and the '60s, and how the latter was an extension in spirit and perception of the former. Mid-'50s works like Ginsberg's "Howl," Kerouac's *On the Road,* and Burroughs's *Naked Lunch* largely set the stage and primed the pump for mid-'60s events like "A Tribute to Dr. Strange." What Ginsberg later said of the Six Gallery reading could be said every bit as validly about the "A Tribute to Dr. Strange" event a decade later: "It succeeded beyond our wildest thoughts. In fact, we weren't even thinking of success; we were just trying to invite some friends and potential friends . . . Poetry suddenly seemed useful in 1955 San Francisco. From that day to this, there has never been a week without a reading in the Bay area" (Schumacher 1992, 215).

Once the Family Dog core launched the series of happenings in the fall of 1965, there would hardly be a weekend over the next five or so years without several psychedelic dance concerts in the Bay Area. In its way, "A Tribute to Dr. Strange" succeeded beyond the wildest imaginings of Harmon, Castell, Kelly, and Towle.

In the weeks following the antiwar/Family Dog weekend, various countercultural luminaries met with a Hells Angels delegation in an attempt to dissuade them from disrupting and/or attacking subsequent antiwar events. One meeting took place in the Oakland home of Ralph "Sonny" Barger, president of the Oakland pack of Angels. Among those present were Neal Cassady, Michael McClure, Hunter Thompson, and, of course, Ginsberg, who was teaching at Berkeley that fall via a $6,000 Guggenheim Poetry Fellowship. (His classes in 123 Wheeler Hall were packed to the rafters.) During the evening, everyone talked philosophy, argued politics, smoked grass, dropped acid, chanted mantras, and listened to records by Bob Dylan and Joan Baez. In what has become a fabled moment in counterculture lore, Ginsberg reputedly confronted Barger in a manner reported by Terry the Tramp (an Angel, who would later stomp Thompson half to death): "That goddamned Ginsberg is gonna fuck us *all* up. For a guy that ain't straight at all, he's about the straightest son of a bitch I ever met. Man, you shoulda been there when he told Sonny he loved him. Sonny didn't know *what* the hell to say" (Whitmer 1987, 182). Apparently the antiwar faction prevailed that night. On November 19, the Angels called a press conference, at which Barger read a letter to President Lyndon Johnson, in which he volunteered the services of the Angels for behind-the-line "guerilla" action in Vietnam. Having demonstrated the Angel's "patriotism," Barger added that they would "absent the scene" and stop attacking the "despicable Un-American . . . mob of traitors" known as the antiwar marchers (Bay Area Television Archives website, n.d.).

The October 16 "A Tribute to Dr. Strange" lost money, but it proved such a popular success that the Family Dog foursome booked the hall for the following Sunday night, October 24, for another dance concert. Hoping to keep the ball rolling, they billed this event as "A Tribute to Sparkle Plenty," with the Charlatans and the Lovin' Spoonful as headliners. The revelers from the previous week returned in force, this time with friends in tow. Among the attendees were members of the Jefferson Airplane and the Grateful Dead, but as audience members, not performers. At this event, John Cipollina first met Gary Duncan and Greg Elmore, three future members of Quicksilver Messenger Service. The music scene and the underground psychedelic scene were uniting.

The common denominator at play at these concerts was a shared appreciation of the playful, the oddball outrageous—combined and honed, of course, by an almost jubilant let-'er-rip discovery of and experimentation with psychedelics. Persons having this sensibility, this mode of seeing, came to be dubbed hippies, a semi-putdown term initially meant to connote a minor-league, junior-grade, not-to-be-taken-seriously hipster (much the same way that beatnik was originally a putdown-diminutive of beat). The term *hippie* is attributed to *San Francisco Examiner* journalist Michael Fallon, who used it in a September 1965 article that was ostensibly about a hangout/ eatery in the Haight-Ashbury district called the Blue Unicorn on 1921 Hayes Street, just north of the Panhandle, but really focused on the strange sort of folks beginning to congregate in the Haight-Ashbury neighborhood. Owned by a Hawaii-born Naval Academy dropout named Bob Stubbs, the

Blue Unicorn was the first "hip" venue to surface in Haight-Ashbury. It afforded the denizens a place to hang out. It offered food, coffee, books, music, art, chessboards, sewing kits, a secondhand clothes box, and a big saggy sofa on which to lounge about while chatting. It was decidedly hippie in vibe and decor. The Blue Unicorn would eventually be hounded out of business by health department officials.

Hippies, unlike their beatnik antecedents[1] didn't drape themselves in and project an insular, ingrown-toenail, internal-grumbling, existential funk. Unlike beatniks, who wore black clothing and shades (even at night, in imitation of their bop heroes such as Thelonious Monk) at solitary tables in coffeehouses and darkened jazz dives, hippies reveled in color and costume during mass-participation communality. They embraced a much more upbeat, celebratory awareness and non-cynical sophistication. They also differed from their Beat precursors in that they weren't committed to writing novels and poetry. (Kesey, in fact, gave up novel writing at the top of his fame, claiming it to be an archaic and outmoded device.) They tended to be well-educated, well-versed, and well-read—they looked to Beat works like "Howl," *On the Road,* and *Naked Lunch* as their holy texts—but they were oriented less to authors than to actively participating in a playful, make-it-as-you-go sensibility and exploring new modes of consciousness, ways of seeing, and styles of being, through LSD. "LSD was new then," recalled Grace Slick of Jefferson Airplane. "It opened up our heads and gave us new insight into the fact that reality isn't just one thing" (Myers 2011).

The hippie orientation, compared to the beatnik locus, involved a more spontaneous, moment-by-moment responsiveness, which unfolded by way of yahoo exuberance radiating in the music that originated at this time in San Francisco. This sound at its peak is conspicuous in the Big Brother performance of "Combination of the Two" at Monterey or "Oh Sweet Mary" on *Cheap Thrills;* in Jefferson Airplane's performance of "The Other Side of This Life" and "The Ballad of You and Me and Pooneil" at Monterey; in the Grateful Dead's rendition of "I Know You Rider" on *Vintage Dead* and of "St. Stephen" and "Turn On Your Love Light" on *Live Dead;* in Quicksilver Messenger Service's performance of "Who Do You Love?," "Mona," and "Calvary" on *Happy Trails;* in Oxford Circle's rendition of "Baby Please Don't Go," "Mystic Eyes," and "You're a Better Man Than I" on their live performance at the Avalon. Any number of examples could be added to this list. The psychedelic dance concert at which this music was performed became a massive, mutually provocative interplay of the bands, the music, the light shows, and the Dionysian celebrants—all of it unfolding in the discovery, creation, and celebration of this particular attitude, mode of seeing, and style of being.

Back to the Haight

We live in a rainbow of chaos.

—French painter Paul Cézanne

The maturity of man means to have reacquired the seriousness that one had as a child at play.

—Friedrich Nietzsche, *Beyond Good and Evil* (1886)

On November 1, 1965, in the wake of the first two Family Dog productions, the San Francisco Mime Troupe held a fundraising event to defray legal fees incurred by Troupe founder R. G. Davis. Davis had been arrested for defying a Parks Commission edict prohibiting the staging of *Il Candelaio*, a sixteenth-century play by Giordano Bruno that had been "modernized" by future Digger Peter Berg. The Parks Commission deemed it in too poor taste to be staged in a public park.

The Mime Troupe was a street-theater venture that blended radical politics with social satire. They especially achieved notoriety for their black-face production of *A Minstrel Show, or Civil Rights in a Cracker Barrel*. The Troupe considered it its mission to stir up controversy and constantly remain at loggerheads with the authorities. Many individuals and groups key to the Haight-Ashbury scene—chief among them the Diggers—had roots in this group. Their business manager was a theater wannabe named Bill Graham, who had quit his $25,000-a-year management job with heavy-machinery producer Allis Chalmers Manufacturing Company to manage the Troupe at a subsistence salary.

Graham staged the Mime Troupe benefit without any prior experience with rock music—he literally assumed the Family Dog was a "dog act"—other than a local band, the Jefferson Airplane, which sometimes used the Mime Troupe loft as a practice venue. Graham, though, had a flair for his role as the Troupe's business manager. He reeled in the donated talents of Ginsberg, the Fugs, and the Jefferson Airplane for this "Appeal" (Graham's term for the event).

Hard on the heels of the Dr. Strange and Sparkle Plenty tributes, the scene at the fundraiser was decidedly freaky with costumes and flamboyant apparel on abundant display. Upon entering the Calliope Warehouse loft, revelers were presented Christmas-wrapped, knickknacky gifts of whistles, noisemakers, raisins, and little mirrors. Apples, oranges, grape clusters, and sticks of chewing gum hung from the rafters for participants to pluck as they wished, and anyone could dip a cup of electrified (acid-laced) Kool-Aid from aluminum foil-lined garbage cans. To Graham's astonishment, the Appeal raised an unheard amount of $4,200 (more than $38,000 today)—something which gave him pause and considerable food for thought.

That same night, the Family Dog staged its third dance concert at Longshoreman's Hall, billed this time as "A Tribute to Ming the Merciless." The featured band was the Mothers of Invention, headed by the iconoclast Frank Zappa. This third concert attracted far more high-school kids than the previous two productions, in large part because many of the heads and hippies flocked to the Mime Troupe benefit. The kids were hopped-up, antagonistic, belligerent, anti-hippie, and looking for (and getting into) fist-fights; Zappa incorporated the fights into his songs. This event, freaky, but unpleasantly so, had an edge of menace to it. Despite the troubles at this concert, Ralph Gleason began touting these dance concerts in his *Examiner* column as something altogether new and revelatory—which they were. With the possible exception of Mardi Gras, there had never been anything like these events in this country. It seemed like something out of the Beaux Art balls of Paris or the carnivals and street fairs of medieval Europe. Word was spreading. Something was afoot, and there was a demand for it.

Three weeks later, Kesey and crew decided to capitalize on the new weirdness in the air by taking their acid parties public. The Pranksters held their first public, non–La Honda "acid test" in a bookstore in Santa Cruz—admission one dollar. The first time out, the only non-Pranksters in attendance were Ginsberg (note how he *invariably* pops up at every historic moment) and a group of friends he brought from San Francisco. On December 4, Kesey and the Pranksters held their second Acid Test at a private house in San Jose; the Warlocks performed for the first time at this event. While the first acid test attracted several dozen people, this one drew 400 eager participants. The heads were finding one another, and people of a certain bent were hearing stories, checking things out, and bringing friends with them.

Less than a week later, Bill Graham produced a second Mime Troupe benefit, this time at the Fillmore, a second story ballroom at 1805 Geary

Street in a largely African-American neighborhood. The Fillmore had heretofore featured mostly African-American entertainment and essentially served as the San Francisco equivalent of Harlem's Apollo Theater. Performers at this benefit included the Jefferson Airplane, the Great Society, Mystery Trend, the jazz group the John Handy Quintet, Sam Thomas and the Gentlemen's Band, and the Grateful Dead (performing for the first time under their new name—Graham insisted that their billing include the words "formerly the Warlocks"). Admission was $1.50. A continuous block-long double line of people had already formed, when the doors opened at 9:30 p.m., and there was still a line when the doors closed at 1:00 in the morning. On this night, Graham and Helms discussed the possibility of collaborating to produce dance concerts. Interest in this scene was escalating rapidly, a fact not lost on Graham, who was preparing to leave the Mime Troupe to produce dance concerts on his own.

A week after the San Jose event, the Pranksters held their third acid test at the Big Beat in Palo Alto, featuring the Grateful Dead, Stewart Brand's multimedia Indian show, and a light show. The next week, the Pranksters held their fourth acid test at Muir Beach Lodge with music provided by the Grateful Dead, by now the acid-test house band. At this event, Owsley freaked out, scraping a chair on the floor to create a nonstop, hideous screech for two hours. While fleeing the scene, he ran his Maserati sports car into a tree and just sat in it until dawn, gunning the engine. The following week, the Kesey band moved their operations up the West Coast to Portland, Oregon, for yet another acid-drenched test.

About the same time as the acid tests and the psychedelic concerts, the Beatles released the album *Rubber Soul,* which demonstrated the evolution of the band from a bright, pop sensation to an increasingly trippy, psychologically sophisticated and exploratory group. The music and cover art of *Rubber Soul* would strongly influence psychedelic aesthetics. In late 1965, Haight residents party-hopped all night long with *Rubber Soul* being played nonstop at every party.

The Golden Year: Winter 1966

When you follow your bliss, and by bliss I mean the *deep sense of being in it,* and doing what the push is out of your own existence . . . doors will open where you would not have thought there'd be doors and where there wouldn't be a door for anybody else.

—Joseph Campbell, *The Hero's Journey* (1990)

No explanation, no mix of words or music or memories can touch
that sense of knowing that you were there and alive in that corner of
time and the world . . . We had all the momentum; we were riding
the crest of a high and beautiful wave.

—Hunter Thompson, *Fear and Loathing in Las Vegas* (1971)

Bliss it was in that dawn to be alive,
But to be young was very heaven.

—William Wordsworth, "The Prelude" (1850)

In 1966, the proto-wave of psychedelia in the Haight turned into a tsunami.
On January 3, the Psychedelic Shop opened at 1535 Haight and became
the prototypical head shop, specializing in tripping aesthetics and various
doodads and paraphernalia that heads would find interesting and useful.
Initially, books, magazines, and records were also sold. The Shop became a
major Haight-Ashbury hangout, neighborhood cog, and socializing center.

Figure 13. "Be Free" sign, 1535 Haight, Psychedelic Shop, 1967. *Source*: © The Regents
of the University of California. Courtesy Special Collections, University Library, University of California, Santa Cruz. Ruth-Marion Baruch and Pirkle Jones Photographs. Collections. https://digitalcollections.library.ucsc.edu/concern/works/vq27zn49p?locale=en

The shop included a room for people to meditate, though it was frequently used for screwing. Messages and notices about events could be left on the bulletin board. As in a Parisian bistro, the Psychedelic Shop had seats positioned near the front window for patrons to watch the street scene unfold.

The Shop was the brainchild of brothers Ron and Jay Thelin. One-time Eagle Scouts, the Thelins had most recently been owners and proprietors of a parking lot and a boat-and-umbrella rental business in Lake Tahoe. When they were initiated into LSD by Allen Cohen, one of Owsley's dealers, the Thelins had their conceptual maps redrawn. (The Thelins would later provide the financial assistance that allowed Cohen to start and publish the *San Francisco Oracle*.) The experience radically changed their lives' course. The brothers sold their Lake Tahoe store, moved to the Haight, and opened the Psychedelic Shop. They hired Allen Cohen as the store clerk.

On January 8, Kesey and his disciples staged an acid test at the Fillmore with grandiose aspirations. The most multimedia of the tests to date, it was produced by Bill Graham and attracted 2,400 people. There was so much electronic equipment—everything from closed circuit television to microphones and tape machines—that an ongoing electric hum pervaded the ballroom. The festivities included Ron Boise sculptures, live music, films, improvisatory happenings, and spontaneous theater.

At the event, it became apparent that the psychedelic culture was gathering serious momentum and just beginning to crest. Attendees sampled still legal LSD that resulted in hundreds (possibly thousands) of tripping revelers "freaking freely" in an environment created for the express purpose of enhancing, celebrating, and facilitating a mass, communal, who-knows-what'll-happen psychedelic experience. Jerry Garcia recalled this particular acid test:

> For sheer unmitigated total all-out craziness, you couldn't beat the Acid Test. Nothing has ever been like those. They were really the most fun of any of those kinds of things. I remember the one at the old Fillmore was tremendously successful.
>
> There was absolutely no paranoia—there's no law against being weird. The police were like big buffoons, some kind of dog police or something. . . . Then the cops were in the balcony. They were going around in a little official knot, sort of inspecting. All of a sudden these freaks are there with this ladder, and they're putting this ladder up to the balcony, and they're climbing it, and they're hollering, "Hug the heat! Hug the heat!" It was amazing! (Troy 1994, 78–80)

Among the many who began converging on the acid tests about this time was a Berkeley undergraduate, who would soon begin writing a column in the *Daily Cal* under the nom de plume of Mr. Jones (as per the Dylan song) about the strange goings-on in the local rock and underground scene. His real name was Jann Wenner, future cofounder and publisher of *Rolling Stone.*

In a demonstration of mind-boggling stupidity, a mere nine days after the Fillmore Trips Festival and three days after a conviction for marijuana possession, Kesey got busted for marijuana again. He was arrested with Mountain Girl (pregnant with Kesey's child; Kesey was still married and living with his wife, Fey) on the rooftop of Stewart Brand's North Beach apartment, where they had gone to smoke grass. Even more stupidly, the only reason the cops showed up was because he and Mountain Girl were tossing pebbles over the rooftop edge onto the sidewalk below, prompting someone to complain to the police. After the police pulled up in front on the street below, their police lights revolving, instead of splitting, Kesey stayed put until the police showed up on the roof. Only then, after it was too late, did he try to run for it and get rid of the grass. Perhaps, Kesey *wanted* to be taken out of "the action" by getting busted, realizing that the bus was now driving him, and things were careening beyond his control. He may have been trapped in a script that was escalating in craziness. Consciously or unconsciously, he applied the brakes before the bus went soaring over the yee-haw, eee-yikes cliff edge.

Even without Kesey, the acid-propelled wildness continued on the weekend of January 21 and 22 at the now legendary Trips Festival, a watershed moment in psychedelic culture. Held at Longshoreman's Hall, it was co-organized by Stewart Brand, visual artist/composer Ramon Sender, photographer and Open Theater cofounder Ben Jacopetti, and author/activist Jerry Mander, and co-produced by Bill Graham. They strove to concoct a mass acid test along the lines of what Kesey and the Pranksters had been doing all along, but bigger and more inclusive than ever. This event incorporated all the groups, scenes, organizations, and happenings that had been actively contributing to the head scene in recent months to put the entire mix into potentially explosive, who-knows-what contact. The weekend festivities included an acid test, the Open Theater, light shows, Brand's "America Needs Indians" extravaganza, Boise's "Electric Thunder" sculptures, and dancing to live music provided by Big Brother and the Holding Company, the Loading Zone (formerly the Marbles), and the Grateful Dead, which had essentially stopped performing outside of acid tests while they retooled their heads and their repertoire. The organizers set up tanks of nitrous oxide (laughing gas) rigged with octopus hoses and provided balloons to inhale the stuff, so enthusiasts could walk around with quacking voices. Ken Kesey appeared in a gold lamé space suit, Neal Cassady swung from the rafters. Many were tripping on LSD. Laird Grant, long-time member of the Dead circle, went around popping tabs of White Lightning in people's mouths. The two-evening event attracted 3,000 merrymakers each night and turned a then-gargantuan $6,000 profit.

Figure 14. "Can You Pass the Acid Test?": The Acid Test poster, 1965. *Source*: Wikimedia Commons, public domain. https://commons.wikimedia.org/wiki/File:-Original1965AcidTestFlyerPrint.uncolored,unmodified.jpg

Writing of it in his *Chronicle* column, Ralph Gleason panned the Friday evening festivities as "a bust, a bore, a fake, a fraud, a bum trip," but praised "the variety, imagination, degree of exoticism and just plain freaky far-outness of the thousands who thronged the Longshoreman's Hall" on Saturday night, adding that what he witnessed "defies all description" (Gleason 1966).

Many have cited the Trips Festival as the moment, when psychedelic culture moved from an underground phenomenon to the primary youth paradigm. The festival built upon the advent of weekly psychedelic dances as multimedia happenings involving music, dancing, freaky dress, light shows, Day-Glo colors, etc. The beginnings of a mass sensation, it transformed a local phenomenon created by highly intelligent, creative, and original explorers into a highly publicized scene to be plugged into, cashed in on, imitated, and appropriated by far less-octaned wannabes wanting to party, much the same way that realtors and affluents moved in and appropriated "scenes" created by long-term residents (in Greenwich Village, North Beach, Taos, etc.), driving out and displacing the natives. Ironically, the huge success of this event—the sudden fruition and public full-flowering of a new sensibility that had been coalescing and gathering momentum in recent months—ultimately led to the demise of the Haight-Ashbury scene that was just then peaking. Its glorious freewheeling spirit attracted an outpouring of media attention that prompted thronging hordes of outsiders to move into Haight-Ashbury in hopes of crashing the party. That invasion would doom the very essence the latecomers hoped to plug into and emulate.

Tom Wolfe only slightly overstated the case in *The Electric Kool-Aid Acid Test*, when he wrote that the Kesey acid tests catalyzed and directly served as a model for the Trips Festival:

> The Acid Tests were the *epoch* of the psychedelic style and practically everything that has gone into it. I don't mean merely that the Pranksters did it first, but rather, that it all came straight out of the Acid Tests in a direct line leading to the Trips Festival of January 1966. That brought the whole thing full out in the open. "Mixed media" entertainment—this came straight out of the Acid Tests' combination of light and movie projections, strobes, tapes, rock 'n' roll, black light.
>
> For the acid heads themselves, the Trips Festival was like the first national convention of an underground movement that had existed on a hush-hush, cell-by-cell basis. The heads were

amazed at how big their own ranks had become—and euphoric over the fact that they could come out in the open, high as baboons, and the sky, and the law, wouldn't fall down on them (1968, 250–251).

However, despite Wolfe's somewhat sensational account, the Haight-Ashbury era did not begin with the Trips Festival, which more likely signaled the beginning of the end for the real (as opposed to the hyped media myth) Haight-Ashbury. The scene would flourish more than ever—at least on the surface—in the coming months, but the Trips Festival gave rise to media exposure that would turn Haight-Ashbury into a ludicrous imitation of the original concept. But in January 1966 the Haight-Ashbury scene was at its peaking, cresting height with the heads riding a breaking wave like a surfboard.

In February, the psychedelic train gathered steam and moved onward. On February 4, the original Family Dog foursome produced their fifth and last concert, this time at California Hall. By now, Rock Scully, soon-to-become manager of the Grateful Dead, helped stage the event. Though this extravaganza turned a $1,500 profit unlike the previous Family Dog dances, the original Family Dog core was floundering. The Pine Streeter four—Kelly, Harmon, Towle, and Castell—were embroiled in personal antagonisms and relationship breakups, and they abandoned ship after this dance. Chet Helms, a friend of Castell, who already managed Big Brother, took over the Family Dog helm. He and buddy John Carpenter, who was manager of the Great Society and a friend of Bill Graham, arranged to rent the Fillmore with Graham on alternate weekends, an arrangement that would be short-lived.

The same day, an acid test was held in Los Angeles in a Unitarian church ministered by the hip, new-agey, and young turk Paul Sawyer, who viewed Kesey and the Pranksters as quasi-religious prophets. The church was cylindrically shaped, with a round stage in the middle of the sanctuary. The performance was in full tilt—light show, movies, blaring speakers, and so on—when Cassady made his entrance, having just completed a round-trip drive to San Francisco for a court date to stand trial for having run up twenty-seven traffic violations in a single month. (He ended up talking the judge into dropping the charges for every single ticket!) He made his entrance by noisily wheeling a dishwasher he had found somewhere to the stage in step-by-step fashion, dishes inside clattering and clanging, doing one of his patented semi-comprehensible, hilarious narrative riffs, talking into a hose and opening and closing the dishwasher front door.

At the same time, Owsley lived in L.A. in a spacious house (at 2205 Lafler Road) at the edge of the ghetto next door to an African-American nightclub and gambling den. He housed, fed, bankrolled, and equipped the Grateful Dead, and he had set up a tabbing machine in the attic of the house, cranking out a massive supply of acid tabs. For business purposes, he called his operation the Bear Research Group. He had hitchhiked to L.A. to circumvent the San Francisco police, who had already tried to bust him for amphetamine production. In the course of this several-month stay, the Dead played several sparsely attended concerts but found the L.A. scene and the kinds of music popular there much different than the sound, feel, and attitude in San Francisco.

Also on February 4, based on the immense popularity of his Mime Troupe benefits, Bill Graham—sensing some major bucks to be made—produced his first independent, non-benefit dance concert. The light show consisted of films taken of the Trips Festival projected on the Fillmore walls. A number of the dancers twirled and tripped away in the Fillmore as these films of themselves dancing and tripping away in Longshoreman's Hall played—a "mind blower" eminently appropriate for the times.

Two days later, in hopes of avoiding impending prosecution for his drug bust, Kesey faked a suicide near the California/Oregon border and then split to Puerto Vallarta in Mexico. Without him, the Merry Pranksters became befuddled and ineffective. Babbs became the de facto leader and went on a mean-spirited and nasty power trip, excommunicating even Cassady. The Prankster influence in the burgeoning San Francisco scene largely derailed at this point.

About a week later, without Kesey, the Pranksters conducted an acid test in L.A. on the fringes of Watts/Compton in a warehouse that was part of a Youth Opportunities Center, only five months after the cataclysmic Watts riots. They secretly provided Kool-Aid laced with LSD for the 200 participants, who didn't realize they were taking it, precipitating a number of "freak-outs" and the hospitalization of seven people. At the event, peace activist and hippie persona Hugh Romney (aka Wavy Gravy), one of the night's celebrants, dubbed the acid-laced Kool-Aid as "electric Kool-Aid."

On February 19, Helms produced his first Family Dog production, a dance at the Fillmore entitled "A Tribal Stomp." Exemplifying the hippie fascination with Native Americans, he "gave everyone a little leather thong with a little Indian bell and a long white turkey feather tied to it" so "everyone was a member of the tribe" (Goldberg 1989, 95). Jefferson Airplane and Big Brother were the featured bands.

Figure 15. "Krishna Consciousness Comes West": Mantra rock dance poster with Allen Ginsberg, the Grateful Dead, Big Brother, and Moby Grape, 1967. *Source*: Courtesy Harvey W. Cohen, from Wikimedia Commons, public domain. https://en.wikipedia.org/wiki/File:1967_Mantra-Rock_Dance_Avalon_poster.jpg

By now, and all of a sudden, psychedelic rock dances appeared everywhere each weekend. Even quasi-Beat poet Lew Welch got into the act, putting on a few dances at California Hall. The local music scene exploded in a way rivaled only by Liverpool several years previously. To quote eyewitness Charles Perry:

> You could see the phenomenon expand and refine itself week after week. The dance posters went through exciting artistic development. The light shows moved from brilliance to brilliance. The bands improved all the time, too, and had an even more exalted place than the poster or light-show artists.
>
> The audience made its own contribution to the event. Many individuals came in costume, painting their faces and carrying on more like a running Beaux Arts ball than a spectator show. People brought things to share, such as food or Day-Glo paints with which to decorate each other's bodies or paint designs on the floor.
>
> Not everyone involved with psychedelics went to the dances every week, but many hundreds did, and their lives revolved around them.
>
> How fast it had happened, this creation of a whole way of life centered around psychedelic dances. (Perry 1984, 55–56)

"In early '66," recalled, Spencer Dryden, a Jefferson Airplane drummer "the Haight was heaven for anybody with long hair. About 800 dyed-in-the-wool hippies and that's it. It was a family thing. No tourists. Everybody *did* live together and *did* help each other out" (Hoskyns 1997, 87). This "family thing" phenomena—this sense of being part of a tribe—made Haight-Ashbury work during the early years and was only possible when it remained at a level of 800 or so "dyed-in-the-wool hippies."

Precisely this juncture—early- to mid-1966, when it was still an organic, homegrown, relatively insider thing—the Haight-Ashbury scene was most vital and golden. For Quicksilver Messenger Service guitarist Gary Duncan, the early Haight district seemed like a wondrously idyllic scene:

> What was really going on in San Francisco in the early '60s was a whole other thing most people don't know about. The underground scene was really a lot heavier than what was publicized and what people think happened—you know, hippies playing music with flowers in their hair, all that crap.

Basically, it was an outgrowth of the Beat Generation in the North Beach section of San Francisco. If you knew the right address and knocked on the door, you could walk through that door into a whole other world.

You'd go to, say, 1090 Page Street, open up the door, and there'd be a fourteen-bedroom Victorian house with something different going on in every room; painters in one room, talking to each other, musicians in another room. It was really cool, and to all outward appearances, there was nothing happening. It was like a secret society. Things like that have to exist secretly.

There was a while when the place was just totally free. You could go anywhere, do anything you wanted, and nobody hassled you. The spotlight wasn't on everybody. As soon as the spotlight came on and there was money to be made, then it went the way of all things. (Henke 1997, 25)

As the scene grew in renown and media hype, and as outsiders, wannabes, hangers-on, and dysfunctionals saw it as a groovy amusement park and began flocking in, both the scene and the cohesive, crucial sense of community weakened and declined. By mid-year 1966, Haight-Ashbury harbored an estimated 15,000 hippies, many of them little more than transients. Once the neighborhood began attracting media coverage (the media is always on the lookout for "local color" to spice up the drab pap of its Sunday supplement, or to enliven its television eyewitness-news superficiality at 10 p.m.), it also attracted legions of runaways, teeny-boppers, and a wide array of youth, many of them teenagers, with problems ("freaks"), not to mention a variety of cultists, gurus, drug addicts, pushers, hustlers, motorcycle outlaws, and predatory opportunists who saw the hippies as easy marks. Though the new migrants to the Haight may have spelled its demise, it provided the number of residents to foster a new acid rock scene.

8

Acid Rock

The Folk Roots

Everybody must get stoned.

—Dylan, "Rainy Day Women #12 & 35"

In early 1966, the premier acid rock groups were the Grateful Dead (which, even at this late juncture, had only about fourteen songs in their repertoire, all but one of them covers of blues, soul, bluegrass, Rolling Stones, or Dylan numbers), Jefferson Airplane with folkie Signe Toly Anderson as singer, the Great Society with lead singer, Grace Slick (who would later that year jump to Jefferson Airplane), Quicksilver Messenger Service, Country Joe and the Fish, and Big Brother and the Holding Company. These bands, still mostly fledgling groups and comprised of unknowns (to the larger public), lived in the neighborhood and played at parties, benefits, pizza joints, bars, and dance concerts mostly for fun. Typically, these bands made little or no money—at least not at first. Often, they performed for free just to play. Haight-Ashbury rock groups considered their music more of a community interaction/recreation than an entrepreneurial venture.

Performances were audience-participation affairs with the dancers and light shows as much a part of the act as the bands, each celebrating and egging the other on.

"In the early days," says Big Brother guitarist Sam Andrew, "the audience and the bands were on the same plane. It's an understatement to

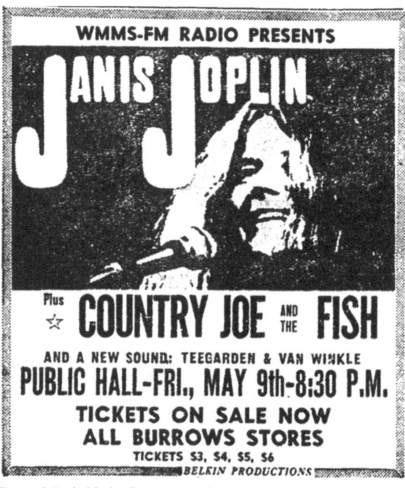

Figure 16. Psychedelic headliners: Janis Joplin and Country Joe and the Fish, 1969. *Source*: Wikimedia Commons, public Domain. https://commons.wikimedia.org/wiki/File:WMMS_Presents_Janis_Joplin_-_1969_print_ad.jpg

say that the vibe at the shows was exuberant—it was *rhapsodic*. It felt like everyone was joined by this electric current, and they were all part of it" (Hoskyns 1997, 83). It is important to keep in mind how unprecedented and unscripted this scene was: the mass, celebratory communality; the unabashed out-front strangeness; the en masse use of psychedelic drugs;

and the shared psychedelic experience. Everyone had to more or less invent their path while walking it.

This scene was so new that even a large number of the musicians, who forged acid rock, were relative newcomers to rock music. After the initial revolution of Elvis, Chuck Berry, and Little Richard, rock 'n' roll became more sanitized and tame. By the early to mid-'60s, folk music and the blues were largely considered far more hip, sophisticated, and underground than rock 'n' roll. A surprisingly large number of the San Francisco rock luminaries circa late 1965 and early 1966 had until only recently been folkies.

Many of the Bay Area rock pioneers first met by gigging on the local coffeehouse circuit. Quicksilver vocalist and bassist David Freiberg was a folk veteran, who had been in a duo called David and Michaela, and before that in a political trio called Folksingers for Peace. Jorma Kaukonen was a finger-pickin' acoustic blues semi-legend in the coffeehouse circuit in and around the Bay Area for several years prior to joining the Airplane. He performed his first-ever paid gig with a then still-unknown Janis Joplin at the Folk Theatre in San Jose. Fellow Airplane member Marty Balin had been in quasi-folk groups the Town Criers and the Gateway Singers. Joe McDonald and Barry Melton were political folksters, and Jerry Garcia played and sang in a string of bluegrass groups and jug bands. Prior to joining Big Brother, Peter Albin and his brother Rod played ukulele, fiddle, and finger-picking guitar in a bluegrass band called the Liberty Hill Aristocrats, which performed at the San Francisco Folk Festival in 1963. Big Brother lead-guitarist-to-be and Pine Streeter James Gurley had played in a progressive bluegrass band. David Freiberg, a fan of Pete Seeger and the Weavers, remembered that "we were all finger pickers. And Jerry Garcia [played] banjo. All those guys were folk singers too, the Grateful Dead" (Schwartz 2019).

In her hometown of Port Arthur, Texas, Janis Joplin became entranced by folk and blues, idolizing Bessie Smith. "Janis didn't just happen to start singing folk music and be discovered by the media," recalled a childhood friend. "She worked very hard at it." She joined the Waller Creek Boys and sang in local coffeehouses (Echols 1999, 48).

Joplin first came to Frisco in January 1963—well before anything remotely resembling the psychedelic Haight-Ashbury era had evolved—in the company of fellow-Texan Chet Helms to check out the beatnik/coffeehouse scene. On her first night in town, she sang at the Coffee and Confusion in an open mic session. In Frisco, she got so seriously strung-out on speed that she tried to commit herself to a hospital mental ward, but they refused to accept her. Out of control, her weight down to eighty-eight pounds, her mental health in genuine peril, and frightened to death, in May 1965, Joplin returned to Port Arthur to get "straight" and be a "good girl."

As she gradually regained her bearings and once again grew bored with Port Arthur, Joplin commuted to Austin to sing in the clubs, including a benefit for the ill Texas bluesman Mance Lipscomb. During this period, she was invited—and was reputedly on the verge of accepting the offer—to be lead singer for the 13th Floor Elevators. In June 1966, Helms dispatched Travis Rivers to Austin to retrieve her for a tryout with Big Brother and the Holding Company, which he was managing. Leaving the university in her last semester, the singer accepted the offer and returned to San Francisco to eventually belt out the psychedelic blues. If folk rock happened when folk met rock 'n' roll, acid rock happened, when LSD was dropped into a simmering broth of folk, blues, and rock. Listen attentively to Jefferson Airplane's first album—*Takes Off* (1966)—and you can actually hear instances of folk rock in the process of becoming psychedelic, though the crossover hasn't yet fully happened.

Many of the acid rock bands originated in the communal houses of Haight-Ashbury. Big Brother and the Holding Company evolved out of a series of open jam sessions conducted in the basement of a large house at 1090 Page Street, instigated and organized (in the loosest sense of the term) by Chet Helms, an erstwhile marijuana-legalization activist, who largely supported himself by selling underground Mexican imports and "antiques" liberated from the dumpsters of Victorian houses undergoing renovation. Helms became a 1090 habitué by virtue of a love affair with a woman, who lived there.

The house on Page Street, 1090 (as it became widely known), was built in 1898 as a fourteen-bedroom, twenty-eight-room family mansion with hardwood paneling, leather-and-paper walls, and a ballroom in the basement. During the '40s and '50s, it became a boarding house and became so dilapidated by the '60s that it was on the verge of being condemned by the city (eventually, it *was* condemned). Also by the '60s, the building had amassed an extensive underground bohemian history. For one, the Sexual Freedom League (whose motto was "love thy neighbor") had been formed there. Also, someone scrawled a phrase onto the wall of one of the 1090 bathrooms that read: "May the baby Jesus shut your mouth and open your mind," which Helms saw and later inscribed on the front of the stogie-smoking, top-hatted Indian in the poster advertising his fifth Family Dog production, the concert of April 22–23, 1966, that featured the Blues Project and the Great Society.

At the time the jam sessions at 1090 began, the place was being managed by Rod Albin, the banjo player and harpsichord virtuoso, who had figured large in the coffeehouse scene in Palo Alto. With Albin as 1090 manager, the place turned into a haven for musicians and hip SFSU students (both brothers were attending college there). One 1090 frequenter was Mike Ferguson, the pianist for the Charlatans and former owner of the head shop, the Magic Theatre for Madmen Only, which had been situated just down the street on Divisadero. Another 1090 frequenter was Sam Andrew, the son of a career military man. Andrew had lived in Okinawa, where he had his own rock band. At this juncture, he was a graduate student in English at SFSU. Walking past 1090 one day, he heard someone wailing away on a guitar and went inside to investigate.

The basement of 1090 harbored a Roaring '20s-esque gazebo bandstand with moonstone glass windows. Helms envisioned the location as a perfect venue for jam sessions by which to utilize and galvanize the abundant musical talent hanging around the place. He initiated Tuesday night jams featuring Andrew and Peter Albin, who had learned bass. These sessions proved immensely popular, attracting up to three musicians per night to play, and up to three hundred people to listen. In a preview of things to come, Helms began charging fifty cents admission.

Once the sessions had been established, Helms introduced a Pine Street acquaintance named "Weird Jim" Gurley. Gurley, to say the least, had a colorful background. Back in Detroit, his father was a stunt car driver who, as part of his "Thrill Show" act, strapped his fourteen-year-old son to the hood of a car, mounted horizontally, his head to the fore like a harpoon. With his son so mounted and strapped in, dad drove the car at high speed through burning plywood walls—which resulted in Gurley losing a couple of his front teeth.

Though like other mid-'60s guitar aspirants, who had a folk background via the North Beach coffeehouse circuit, Gurley did not want to play guitar in the style of the Beatles or the Rolling Stones. He hoped to transpose John Coltrane's saxophone improvisations onto the guitar. He would sit in the dark of his Pine Street bedroom closet for hours on end, playing with one end of a stethoscope taped to his guitar, the other end plugged in his ears. To achieve the wild, driving, and passionate Coltrane sound, he threw his Standel amplifier to the ground for screeching, Coltrane-esque feedback to end a song. Fish guitarist Barry Melton hailed Gurley as "the founder of psychedelic guitar . . . the first man in space" (Hoskyns 1997, 197). And he's absolutely right.

The contrast between Gurley and his wife, Nancy, illustrates how wonderfully odd, varied, and far-ranging the original Haight-Ashburians often were. Where Weird Jim's father was a stunt driver using his son as a strapped-to-the-hood battering-ram for his act, Nancy's father was a doctor, who had season tickets to the opera, ballet, and symphony. She earned a master's degree in English by age twenty and wore velvet gowns with lace and tiers of necklaces and bracelets—a hippie-gypsy look that Janis Joplin would emulate. Nancy and Joplin became close friends (both were Pine Streeters) in spite of the fact that Joplin early on conducted an affair with Jim and did everything in her power to entice him to leave Nancy for her. But he moved in with Joplin for only a few weeks. Weird Jim and Nancy had a baby son they named Hogo Ishi after Gurley's transcendent experience eating mushrooms with Indians in the mountains of Mexico. Translated, the name means "mushroom man."

Big Brother's original name had a bluegrass spin: Blue Yard Hill. The far more psychedelic name, Big Brother and the Holding Company, evolved out of a stoned conversation that somehow managed to intertwine the subjects of the George Orwell book *1984,* monopoly capitalism, and the connotations of the term *holding*, which carries resonances both of totalitarian corporate America and possession of marijuana.

Like many of the other acid-rock bands, Big Brother was a literate crew. Andrew graduated from San Francisco State, attended the Sorbonne for a year, and had planned to attend graduate school at UC Berkeley in linguistics. "I was coming out of a very academic, linear, abstract, scholarly, Western European tradition," he explained (Echols 1999, 123). Jim Gurley had been inspired to leave his native Detroit to hitchhike to San Francisco and become a beatnik after reading *On the Road.* The group's future drummer, David Getz, was a Fulbright Fellow—he studied in Poland—and a painting instructor for four years at the San Francisco Art Institute and also headed to San Francisco after reading *On the Road* and other Beat novels. Chet Helms, the group's organizer and future manager, attended the University of Texas in Austin, and Peter Albin was a SFSU student who had grown up in and around Palo Alto.

During the spring of 1966, Big Brother began toying with the idea of bringing in a female lead vocalist in the fashion of Jefferson Airplane and the Great Society. They auditioned Lynn Hughes, who had sung with the Charlatans (she sings on a couple of their album cuts), and Mary Ellen Simpson of the all-girl group Ace of Cups. At that point, Helms hit upon the idea of trying out his old running buddy, Janis Joplin, and dispatched

Rivers to Austin to retrieve her. She left Austin for the tryout on May 31, and on June 10 made her first public appearance with the band at the Avalon. A year later, she would drop a bombshell on the rock world with her volcanic performance at the Monterey Pop Festival.

Quicksilver Messenger Service evolved out of a friendship between David Freiberg and John Cipollina. The son of an influential and well-connected contractor and real-estate salesman in Mill Valley and godson to well-known classical pianist José Iturbi, Cipollina was one of the few acid-rock frontrunners whose background was in rock rather than folk. He had played guitar in teenage bands the Penetrators and the Deacons. He was, though, a lazy, incorrigible reprobate; in the fall of 1965, when he met guitarist Gary Duncan and drummer Greg Elmore, he lived in his eleven-year-old Plymouth car parked on Mt. Tamalpais. Older and more experienced in the ways of the world, Freiberg was the son of a magazine editor and illustrator and had played guitar and sang on the folk circuit. He had also been roommates with Paul Kantner and David Crosby in L.A. during their pre-rock folk days.

Cipollina and Freiberg met through a mutual friend—singer and harmonica player Jim Murray—at a Sausalito folk club situated in a scuttled ferryboat called the Ark. Both Cipollina and Freiberg played lead guitar—Freiberg would later switch to bass—and on October 16, the two were on the lookout for a drummer to jam with the night they ran into drummer Greg Elmore and guitarist Gary Duncan at the "A Tribute to Dr. Strange" at Longshoreman's Hall. Duncan (aka Gary Grubb), a Pawnee/Cherokee Native American, who had been raised by a Cherokee couple, and Elmore already had a minor claim to fame by having played in a band called the Brogues, which cut a garage semi-classic 45 called "I Ain't No Miracle Worker." At the time he met Cipollina, Duncan was sleeping on the floor of a North Beach pad, and he had just recently started ingesting psychedelics.

Cipollina, Duncan, and Elmore began showing up at the Tuesday night jams at 1090. Originally, they envisioned themselves more as a vehicle for their vocalist friend, lead singer Dino Valente (his real name was Chet Powers), an underground folk legend, who wrote "Get Together," a folk-circuit standard that would be covered by Jefferson Airplane, H. P. Lovecraft, and the Youngbloods. Those aspirations suddenly changed when Valente got busted for marijuana. (Freiberg spent time in the slammer for a marijuana bust, too.) While waiting for Valente to get out of jail, the rest of the would-be band lived in a dank basement in North Beach and feasted on psychedelics. Similar to Kesey in carelessness and/or stupidity, when Valente finally got out of jail, he was almost immediately busted again for the same thing, putting himself out of the musical picture for nearly two years.

Still only a would-be band at this point, the group kept casting about for and auditioning musicians who could provide some added octane and chemistry. They auditioned Skip Spence, whom guitarist Marty Balin would spot and invite, on the basis of the way he *looked,* to be the Jefferson Airplane drummer, even though (shades of Phil Lesh and the Grateful Dead) Spence had never played the drums. (After a stint playing drums with the Airplane, Spence would play guitar with Moby Grape. When his mental state deteriorated from using too much acid, he was eventually institutionalized.)

The band originally called itself Vulcan and then Cosmic Crystal Set. They hit upon the name Quicksilver Messenger Service, when they discovered that Freiberg and Cipollina had the same birthday (August 24), as did Duncan and Elmore (September 4), making all four (in astrological lingo) "quicksilver" and "messenger." Their first paying gig came about when they were commissioned by the improvisatory comedy group, The Committee, to make a tape of a rock version of "The Star-Spangled Banner" in return for an ounce of grass. (Formerly, The Committee had been using the Kate Smith rendition.) Their variant featured a cowbell and a quasi-psychedelic swirl of guitars. The Committee liked it so much that they offered the group $200 and two ounces of grass to play at their 1964 Christmas party in Muir Beach. A genuine gig under their belt, they considered themselves a band.

Quicksilver was as unfocused and undisciplined as it was hip and talented. While the Grateful Dead typically practiced four to eight hours every day (Garcia got up at 6 a.m. every day to practice on his own and would pour obsessively over guitar exercise books), the Quicksilver bunch were less interested in practicing than in taking lots and lots of drugs, screwing as many women as possible (even though most of members were married, with kids), and projecting themselves as outlaw heroes, making their loathing of the straight world a kind of lifestyle theatric that they used to justify their ongoing debauchery as defiant heroism.

Ambrose Hollingsworth, proprietor of a school of psychic magic (he did astrological readings and his wife did Tarot readings), served as their first manager. Hollingsworth moved the band out of their rural Larkspur shack into a place in downtown Mill Valley that became famous as a haven for runaway, would-be hippie girls. During this period, Elmore was so traumatized by a horrific acid experience that he stopped talking, other than giving one-word answers and using short as possible phrases. When Hollingsworth was crippled in a car accident, Ron Polte—a friend of Hollingsworth's from

Chicago, where they had both been petty gangsters became manager. Polte had fled Chicago for San Francisco after accidentally shooting (and killing) his best friend and had become an acid convert.

Polte moved the band to a deserted dairy farm near Olema, at which point Cipollina acquired his famous pet timber wolf. They lived near the Grateful Dead, which were ensconced in Rancho Olompali, a temporarily vacant home for mentally challenged children. Like many other San Francisco sound leaders, the Quicksilver bunch frequented Olompali and participated in the legendary six-week, acid-drenched debauch that took place there in 1966 with the Dead and many other revelers. Quicksilver would eventually be run off their Olema headquarters by armed vigilantes, angry that Cipollina's wolf and Valente's great dane teamed up to chase horses, kill sheep, and strew garbage everywhere.

Quicksilver lost their highly unique dual guitar brilliance that gave them such a sensationally intricate psychedelic sound when Duncan left the band the day following their New Year's Eve gig at Winterland in 1968. Badly strung out on speed, the guitar wizard Duncan became tired of the band's lack of ambition and decided to take off with Valente to ride motorcycles, womanize, and start their own band, even though Quicksilver had just recorded *Happy Trails,* one of the all-time great psychedelic albums.

Prior to forming Country Joe and the Fish, Barry Melton and Country Joe McDonald joined a group called the Instant Action Jug Band. Melton and McDonald were both products of families that espoused radical left-wing politics. McDonald was a third-generation radical. When he was twelve years old, his father lost his phone company job of eighteen years, when FBI informants tipped off his employer that he was a card-carrying communist. McDonald enlisted in the navy at seventeen. When he got out, he went the typical veteran route, attending Los Angeles State College and getting married. Restless, McDonald quit college, left his wife, and moved to Berkeley, when the Free Speech Movement started. At Berkeley, he took up with a circle of protest singers and began a magazine devoted to folk music called *Rag Baby.* Melton also came from Los Angeles, and his father, a union organizer, was a radical. Melton had a folk background via the L.A. coffeehouse circuit and came to the Bay Area to attend San Francisco State University. School fell by the wayside, when he decided he wanted to be a musician.

Melton and McDonald crossed paths at the Berkeley Folk Festival. Both of them folk politicos, both in a kind of betwixt-and-between limbo, they struck up a jamming friendship and collaborated on an EP recorded in the

Berkeley living room of Chris Strachwitz, founder of the folk/blues record label, Arhoolie Records. This four-song EP, titled *Songs of Opposition,* included the initial versions of "Superbird," a parody of President Lyndon Johnson, and "I-Feel-Like-I'm-Fixin'-to-Die Rag," probably the first anti-Vietnam war anthem. Melton, McDonald, and several other musicians, who rounded out the Instant Action Jug Band, performed the latter song on a flatbed truck during the legendary Vietnam Day march of October 16.

Bruce Barthol, one of Melton's friends from high school in Van Nuys, joined with McDonald and Melton. Barthol had a left-wing background, his father being a psychology professor with radical sympathies. Like McDonald and Melton, he had dropped out of school—in his case, Berkeley. The three started rooming together in an apartment behind a folk club near the Berkeley campus called Jabberwock. McDonald and Melton began doing psychedelics, prompting them to shift (à la Dylan) from folk to rock. They formed Country Joe and the Fish, the "Fish" portion of the name chosen in allusion to Chairman Mao's dictum, "A revolutionary should move among the people like a fish in water." Ed Denson, McDonald's compatriot in publishing *Rag Baby,* became the group's manager, and the band began packing them in at Jabberwock and the Cabale in Berkeley. McDonald's songs became increasingly acid-amped, as in "Bass Strings" and "Section 43"—arguably the most psychedelic music done in 1966. (I consider *Electric Music for Mind and Body,* with its blend of hip wit, leftist politics, and acid-inspired psychedelic sensibility, one of the foremost—and most underrated—albums of the era.) McDonald and Janis Joplin struck up an affair for a season, but it was doomed because McDonald was an acid devotee with leftist sympathies whereas Joplin was apolitical and only took psychedelics two or three times, her drugs of choice being alcohol, speed, and heroin.

In mid-'60s San Francisco, everyone had the freedom to invent him or herself anew—to create a persona and become it. (Witness the Prankster monikers and Bill Graham, whose original name was Wulf Wolodia Grajonca.) The Jefferson Airplane provided a case in point. The group was largely an invention of Marty Balin (whose birth name was Martyn Jerel Buchwald), a heretofore folkie, dancer (he danced in *West Side Story*), sculptor, painter, and graphic artist, who, like so many of the early frontline musicians, had just discovered LSD and recently separated from his wife and child. Balin created the Jefferson Airplane in both a literal and figurative sense. Not only did he pick the band members, he helped build the stage for the group and do the interior decoration (some of it using his own art pieces) at the venue that he operated, where the band made its debut: the Matrix, formerly a Fillmore Street pizza parlor. Balin both designed and printed the first non-Charlatans rock poster of the Haight-Ashbury era for an appearance of the Airplane at Longshoreman's Hall on October 16, 1965. Only three copies of that silk-screened poster were made.

As with so many of the Haight-Ashbury legends-to-be, Jefferson Airplane began as a quasi-folk endeavor modeled on the folk rock of the Byrds. Balin had most recently been with the Town Criers, a folk-lounge trio sporting matching suits and ties. Several years earlier, he had heard Dylan sing at Gerde's Folk City in Greenwich Village, and since then he had dropped acid and—inspired by the Beatles' appearance on the *Ed Sullivan Show*, and having seen *A Hard Day's Night* "about nine times or something. I about died when I saw it" (Gleason 1969, 87)—Balin had aspirations to sing as a rocker. He began forming an acoustic group to back *him*. In Balin's own words: "I was going to get a band to back me. So I got involved with music. We started out acoustically, all these different musicians. The musicians couldn't play well enough and I kept dropping guys and getting guys, and dropping guys" (Gleason 1969, 91).

While trying to assemble a band the summer of 1965, Balin talked a friend into investing $1,300 to become part owner of the newly formed Matrix club, where Balin's band would play a set number of times (an agreement the band never fulfilled) with the management getting a percentage. On August 13, 1965, the band made its public debut at the Matrix. Balin, meanwhile, went about literally *inventing* a band (as compared to putting one together). According to Marty: "I went around telling everybody in town, everybody. I said, 'I've got the best group in town.' But nobody heard it and not even me because I had nobody in the group! But I figured if I told everybody I had the best group, the best musicians would come and try to get into it. Which they did!" (Gleason 1969, 99–100).

Considering what the band would eventually become, Balin's criteria for selecting personnel was astonishingly haphazard. Recalling how George Hunter assembled the Charlatans, Balin's approach to inventing the Jefferson Airplane was as much visual—based on a hip look—as musical. Take, for example, his discovery of the group's first drummer, Skip Spence. As Balin recounted it:

> Skip had never played drums in his life. But I saw him sitting in a club one day and I was looking for a drummer and I saw Skip Spence. I'm very struck by images of people. And I saw him and I said, "That's my drummer." And I went up to him

and I said, "What are you doing?" He was auditioning for The Quicksilver at the time. And he said, "I play the guitar and I sing." I said, "Do you play drums?" And he said, "No." I said, "Why don't you get some sticks and work with them, you know? You'd be a great drummer, I can tell." He said, "I don't play drums." And I said, "Play for a week and see what happens. If you can play in a week, you can play in our group." So I called him a week later, and I said, "Do you think you could do it?" And he said, "I'll try it." (Gleason 1969, 91)

He based his finding of guitarist Paul Kantner on an equally ludicrous looks criteria. Balin claimed that one day he spotted this guy "walking into a folk club [the Drinking Gourd], I just saw him, and I said, 'That's the guy!' I just knew it. He had a twelve-string and a banjo and he had his hair down to here and an old cap and I just went right up to him and I said, 'What are you doing?' He said, 'Nothing.' I said, 'Let's go to dinner.' I had never heard of him, but I *knew* he was good" (Gleason 1969, 87).

Kantner had moved to San Francisco from San Jose only the day before with his girlfriend, Ginger Jackson, and one of his buddies, David Freiberg. The trio moved into a Fillmore commune. Back in San Jose, Kantner had been performing in a folk venue called the Off Stage, and working a day job in a cannery with the aid of amphetamines. He had also been attending the festivities at La Honda.

Kantner's coming aboard, Balin noted, catalyzed the band's transition from folk to rock:

And then I found Paul and we jelled. And it was just beautiful. We had the same level of communication like what we wanted to do musically. So we started working out, and we were still acoustic. Then Paul said, "I'm going to have to get an amplifier on my guitar to compete with the drums," and then we got this pickup and an amp. We always considered ourselves folk people. Then Paul and I said, "No, this is rock." And that's where it's at. So we started playing with it. (Gleason 1969, 91)

Jorma (originally Jerry) Kaukonen came to the Bay Area in 1962 to attend Santa Clara, a private Jesuit college. Earlier, he had attended Antioch College in Ohio and had been playing guitar since 1956. In his teenage days in the Washington, D.C., area, Kaukonen performed in a band called the Triumphs.

By 1962, Kaukonen had developed a reputation in the Bay Area coffeehouse circuit as a finger-picking acoustic blues guitar virtuoso. He remembered:

> There was a place called the Folk Theatre that was the precursor to The Offstage,[1] which was on First Street in San Jose, and the first weekend that I was in California there was a hootenanny. Many of the people who became "somebody" later on were at this particular hootenanny, and that was my welcoming, my first weekend in the Bay area. As I recall, Jerry [Garcia] was there and a bunch of Palo Alto people. After we met, Jerry and I would occasionally play together because I knew a lot of old-timey songs and I liked to play rhythm guitar behind people like Jerry who were playing that stuff. (Troy 1994, 38)

As Kaukonen recalled about the early days of the Airplane—an observation applicable to all the groups connected with the San Francisco sound—"none of us had any idea that we would be at least partial creators of a psychedelic sound. Heck, I barely knew what psychedelics were. In the beginning," he said, "I wanted us to sound like a blues band: Jack Casady was the only member [of the band] who had played in a rock band . . . I had a Rickenbacker twelve string that Paul made me get, and I was using a lot of folk-blues techniques. Later on, beginning with *Surrealistic Pillow* and moving into *After Bathing at Baxter's* [both released in 1967], I began to learn about the electric guitar" (Henke 1997, 57).

Casady came to the band by way of Kaukonen, who had met him in Washington, D.C., as a member of the Triumphs. Since then, Casady had been playing guitar in blues bands and strip joints in the D.C. area. He agreed to join the Jefferson Airplane only after the band offered him a $50-a-week salary and a plane ticket to San Francisco. Casady took acid for the first time the night of the second Family Dog Production, "Tribute to Ming the Merciless," and Melissa Cargill became his girlfriend after Owsley got busted. Spencer Dryden, the son of an assistant film director in Hollywood, joined the band after the increasingly erratic and undependable Skip Spence got the boot just prior to the recording of *Surrealistic Pillow*. Before joining the Airplane, Dryden had primarily been a jazz drummer, playing in Sunset Strip strip joints in L.A. He became interested in rock through the Byrds and the Lovin' Spoonful. Early on with the Airplane, Dryden had a wife and child in L.A., a girlfriend in San Francisco, and an open affair with Grace Slick, who was still married to Jerry Slick.

Signe Toly, recommended by Kantner after he saw her sing at the Drinking Gourd in the early fall of 1965, became the original female vocalist for Jefferson Airplane. That fall, she married Jerry Anderson, a one-time proto-Prankster, who worked the lights at the Matrix. Eventually, the band began having second thoughts about her place in the group. She got pregnant and had a baby that demanded her attention, and her outspoken and alcoholic husband, who felt the Airplane was doing his wife wrong, proved difficult. Other band members began thinking about replacing her, and Kantner and Casady lobbied for Grace Slick, the more sexually charged, large-voiced lead singer for the Great Society.

Grace Slick (aka Grace Wing) was a rich kid. Her father worked at Weedon and Company, an investment banking firm. Her mother had once been a Hollywood understudy to Marion Davies, the '20s actress, who had been bankrolled by William Randolph Hearst, and had done some nightclub singing. Both parents graduated from the University of Washington, and Grace grew up in affluence, most recently in Palo Alto. She had a number of high-powered friends as a young girl and excelled as a cheerleader in high school. Grace attended Finch College, which she described as a swank all-female "finishing school for girls from wealthy or prominent families who went there (if they didn't have the grades to get into Vassar) to learn the basics of how to get and keep a Yale or Harvard man." She studied at Finch for two years, with a year at the University of Miami in between, where she "cut [her] hair short, bleached it blonde, got a Coppertone tan, wore white shorts and tennis shoes" (Slick 1998, 53–54, 65).

Her parents, the Wings, were close friends with their neighbors, the Slicks. In the fall of 1958, when she moved back to San Francisco, Grace married the boy next door, Jerry Slick. For a semester, he attended San Diego State, but then switched to San Francisco State University to study film, where he won first prize in an Ann Arbor film festival.

In the fall of 1965, the Great Society formed when Grace (who at the time was modeling clothes at I. Magnin), her husband, Jerry, and his brother, Darby, went to the Matrix to hear the newly formed Jefferson Airplane. Assessing the San Francisco scene, they saw a dearth of talent—the Matrix and Mother's were the sole rock venues at that time, and most of the future Haight-Ashbury frontrunners had yet to be heard—so they decided to start a band with Grace as lead singer, Jerry on drums, and Darby on lead guitar. The band gave their second-ever performance at the "A Tribute to Dr. Strange" event at Longshoreman's Hall on October 16, 1965.

The Great Society quickly started to implode. Neither Jerry nor Grace was particularly monogamous, and both began having affairs. Darby was using heroin, and he and bassist Peter Vandergelder increasingly drifted toward Indian music (they took lessons from master tabla player Ali Akbar Khan) and started thinking about going to India to study the sitar. When Grace got the invitation to join the Airplane in September of 1966, the band and the Grace/Jerry marriage already had started to dissolve. Her husband, Jerry, advised her to accept the offer, and the Great Society never performed again. Two of Jefferson Airplane's top hits—"Somebody to Love," written by Darby Slick, and "White Rabbit," written by Grace—were originally Great Society songs.

After Slick joined the Airplane, Casady and Kaukonen got heavily into speed, idolized the blues-based power trio Cream, and became increasingly hostile toward Balin for what they believed to be his "wimpy" compositions and vocals. The band factionalized: Kaukonen and Casady in one corner openly critical of Balin; Dryden and Slick in another conducting their affair, and Balin semi-ostracized from both camps. Kantner basically got along with everyone (he would father a child with Slick) and was the driving force behind one of their best album: *After Bathing at Baxter's*. Through it all, the band evolved musically into what many psychedelic aficionados consider the premier Haight-Ashbury band.

The Grateful Dead, one of the Airplane's major competitors, evolved largely out of the Bay Area coffeehouses and folk scene. In his pre-Dead incarnation, Jerry Garcia was a bluegrass banjo and guitar-picking phenomenon in a number of groups, including the Sleepy Hollow Hog Stompers, the Hart Valley Drifters, the Thunder Mountain Tub Thumpers, the Black Mountain Boys, and the Wildwood Boys—the latter group actually winning the amateur bluegrass competition at the Monterey Folk Festival in 1963. (Janis Joplin also performed at this festival that year during her first San Francisco sojourn.)

Garcia's girlfriend, Sarah, was a musician and film student at Stanford, who was friends with, and had been a classmate of, Joan Baez at Palo Alto High. She and Garcia almost reluctantly married when she got pregnant. On December 8, 1963, the Garcias had a daughter, Heather. As a new father, to help make ends meet, Garcia began giving guitar lessons at Dana Morgan's Music shop in Palo Alto. Giving drum lessons there at the same time was Bill Kreutzmann, who had grown up in Palo Alto (his choreographer mother taught dance at Stanford). That New Year's Eve, sixteen-year-old Bobby Weir was wandering the streets, looking for something New Year's Eve-ish to do. Then he heard someone wailing away on the guitar in the back of Dana Morgan's Music. It was Garcia, who had forgotten what day it was and was passing the time playing while waiting for a student to show up for his weekly lesson. Weir talked Garcia into letting him in, and they took some guitars down from the wall displays and played for a few hours. On the basis of the fun they had together, they decided to form a jug band, Mother McCree's Uptown Jug Champions, with keyboard player and vocalist Pigpen (Ron McKernan, whom Garcia had met at parties at the Chateau) and Bill Kreutzmann. Weir, still too inept at guitar, played washtub bass.

Being the hootenanny era, Mother McCree's gigged on the peninsula folk circuit. They went electric, when Dana Morgan Jr. became their bass player and put electric instruments at their disposal. They soon evolved into a blues/rock group (the direction blues aficionado Pigpen wanted to go), changed their name to the Warlocks, and combined up-tempo bluegrass with gin-joint blues numbers in imitation of the Rolling Stones, which offered a white British version of African-American Chicago blues. When Dana exited the group (Garcia needed to tell him what notes to play), Garcia invited his buddy Phil Lesh to become the bass player, despite the fact he had never played bass and didn't particularly care for rock. Lesh, a college student who played trumpet and studied and composed avant-garde electronic music, accepted the invitation to play bass for the Warlocks largely due to his friendship with Garcia during their Chateau days.

In May 1965, the group first performed as the Warlocks at Magoo's Pizza Parlor in Menlo Park, after which they began gigging in the bars of Redwood City, the East Bay, and in North Beach strip joints. Garcia's bluegrass compatriots couldn't believe he had gone electric.

The same year, the group began experimenting with LSD. They did a group "drop" (except Pigpen, who eschewed acid entirely) on the day of the second Family Dog production at Longshoreman's Hall. Stoned on acid among hundreds of other tripping fellow heads, the Warlocks decided they wanted to refashion themselves from a bar band to a counterculture, acid-amped group. They cut a demo under the name Emergency Crew for Scorpio Records on November 3, 1965, but it wasn't released until June of 1966. The 45 consisted of "Stealin'" and "Don't Ease Me In," reworked bluegrass standards they had performed as Mother McCree's. Their early repertoire also featured ten- to fifteen-minute covers of Motown numbers like "Dancing in the Streets" and Bob Dylan songs such as "It's All Over Now, Baby Blue."

The band's comanagers, Rock Scully and Danny Rifkin, were Haight-Ashbury originals and students at San Francisco State University. The son of a college professor, Scully grew up in highly affluent Carmel-by-the-Sea and attended boarding school and college in Switzerland. He came to San Francisco to attend graduate school at SFSU, during which time he lived in Haight-Ashbury, managing the fifteen-room pad at 710 Ashbury that would become the "Dead House." Scully met Rifkin, also an SFSU student, when they took the same trolley to school. When he became the Dead's co-manager—appointed to that position by Owsley, who was the band's patron at the time—Scully was maneuvering to become manager of the Charlatans and partnered with erstwhile Family Dog cofounder Luria Castell to stage dances at California Hall.

The transition of the largely folk-based bands to leaders of a San Francisco psychedelic sound occurred for several reasons. To be heard in the clubs, they abandoned their acoustic guitars for electric ones and cranked up their amplifiers to assault their audiences with ear-numbing volume. "The only way you were going to impress anybody is to have a stack of amplifiers and then you could make the place rock," explained Barry Melton of Country Joe and the Fish. "The only way that you could propel music to a really big crowd, in the '60s, was with amplified music" (Unterberger 2003, 35).

The San Francisco groups, having expanded consciousnesses from psychedelics, also dished up an experimental, improvisational sound. "LSD, it made me want to hear longer sounds and be freer musically," noted Garcia (Szatmary 2019, 137); "We'd do songs and they'd suddenly be 10 or 15 minutes long" (Watrous 1989, 42). Such an improvisational sound perfectly suited dancers at the ballrooms, who did not want the music to be interrupted. "The dancers didn't want the songs to end," stressed Rock Scully. "Dancing was a real important part of it and the band wasn't always the focus of attention" (Troy 1992, 115).

Open to a range of possibilities, the psychedelic sound also incorporated many different elements including bluegrass, blues, rock 'n' roll, jazz, and country. Chris Darrow of the group Kaleidoscope recounted that "what we did is we took the elements of different musical styles and genres that we liked, and tried to incorporate them into our particular viewpoint of the world" (Unterberger 1999, 8). Likewise, the Dead concocted a sound that integrated and assimilated everything from bluegrass, blues, Indian ragas, and Coltrane-esque free jazz.

Acid Rock's Heyday

I was permitted to hear an incredible music. . . . I heard the gestation of the new world . . . the sound of stars grinding and chafing, of fountains clotted with blazing gems. . . . Music is planetary fire, an irreducible which is all sufficient; it is the slate-writing of the gods.

—Henry Miller, *Tropic of Cancer* (1934)

We need magic, and bliss, and power, myth, and celebration and religion in our lives, and music is a good way to encapsulate a lot of it.

—Jerry Garcia

Suddenly I realize
That if I stepped out of my body I would break
Into blossom.

—James Wright, "A Blessing,"
The Branch Will Not Break (1963)

Musically, the early days of Haight-Ashbury featured a very noncommercial, alternative scene with play—and the psychedelic experience in particular—as the primary motive and generative impetus. That sense of artistic, musical, intellectual, and psychological mutuality, interweaving and overlapping, made the community vital.

Examples of this small-scene interaction and interrelationship surfaced everywhere. Poster artists Mouse and Kelly let Big Brother and the Holding Company use their Henry Street studio as a rehearsal room. Early on, Jefferson Airplane used the Mime Troupe headquarters for a rehearsal loft. The Grateful Dead allowed their 710 Ashbury abode to be used as headquarters for HALO (Haight-Ashbury Legal Organization). Psychedelic artist/missionary Michael Bowen's apartment studio at the corner of Haight and Masonic served as an early office for the underground newspaper the *Oracle* and a community gathering place for writers, artists, and photographers. (Bowen was one of those busted when G. Gordon Liddy raided Millbrook.) The Diggers provided free food and clothing to anyone wanting it. "It was all real high in those days," reminisced Garcia, "because at the time the Haight-Ashbury was a community . . . it was just a very small neighborhood affair when we were all working for each other's benefit" (Troy 1994, 107).

Precisely that sensibility—a close-knit community of intelligent and intensely creative heads "working for each other's benefit"—differentiated the early golden period of the Haight-Ashbury community from what it evolved into by the late '60s. Those giving Haight-Ashbury its initial impetus were vibrantly intelligent, creative, interesting, and productive individuals. They were mostly in their mid-twenties (or older), many of them longtime veterans of the various local bohemian and avant-garde scenes. Initially, few of them—Kesey and Cassady being obvious exceptions—were known outside the immediate circle or community. They were a high-octane bunch, eager to create. "The joint was jumping," as poster artist Victor Moscoso observed of those early, pre-onslaught days, when Haight-Ashbury was still an in-the-making phenomenon: "The surf was up. The air was electric with things happening. You could actually walk into a room and say, 'Hey, let's start a rock & roll band,' and seriously launch yourself into rock & roll. That's what these guys did. They were garage bands. And what happened was they became famous garage bands, because they were at the right place at the right time. So was I, and so were a whole bunch of other people" (Henke 1997, 99).

Moscoso's observation was right on target. The Grateful Dead was originally a local bar band with big aspirations; Jefferson Airplane was an invention of Marty Balin; the Charlatans were essentially George Hunter's art project; and Big Brother and the Holding Company was a Tuesday night jam band. Even many of the to-be-premier bands began in so amateur and loosely organized a fashion that they relied on borrowed or rented instruments and equipment. In June 1965, the Charlatans had a single speaker and a ten-watt amp between them at their first gig on opening night at the Red Dog. At Big Brother's first gig, all the guitarists plugged into the same amp and shared a single speaker. The Warlocks initially depended on instruments, amplifiers, and speakers on loan from the music store owned by the bass player's father.

The bands quickly became an essential facet of the Haight-Ashbury community. While psychedelics served as the community catalyst, the bands provided the community cement. As Haight-Ashbury denizen, Digger, Mime Troupe artist, and school teacher David Simpson put it:

It is very important to know how closely the alternative community of San Francisco identified with the music of specific musicians—the Grateful Dead, the Jefferson Airplane, the Messenger Service, and Big Brother and the Holding Company. They were our bands, they were our musicians. Neither they nor we felt the distinction between the artists and the people, and it gave the music great strength. By 1968 nobody danced at rock concerts any more, but in 1966 and 1967 nobody sat down. It was quite impossible. The concerts were a melee of bodies. It was a wonderfully inspired sense of oneness. (Hoskyns 1997, 111)

In contrast to the community-based Haight-Ashbury musicians at this point, the touring national acts (i.e., money-making) in mainstream rock were pop groups such as the Monkees, Fabian, Bobby Darin, Bobby Vee, Gary Lewis and the Playboys, Sonny and Cher, and the like. The Rolling Stones and the Beatles (and maybe the Animals, perhaps the Kinks and the Who) proved exceptions, and they were British. Motown promoted more of a pop-soul sound, and Dylan had just begun to gain popularity but mostly as a hip, underground insider in New York. (When he played in the Folklore Center in Denver in the summer of 1964, only four people attended—I, alas, was not one of them.)

The Grateful Dead, Jefferson Airplane, Quicksilver Messenger Service, Big Brother and the Holding Company, and Country Joe and the Fish were all working bands well before the Fillmore and the Avalon Ballroom came into existence. In early February 1966, Bill Graham still managed the Mime Troupe, yet to produce his first rock concert (and totally unversed in the music). The emerging psychedelic music scene did not extend much beyond the nexus of Haight-Ashbury, San Francisco State University, the Art Institute, and—to a lesser extent—Palo Alto and the Kesey crowd.

The Fillmore and the Avalon

The four-day "Batman Dance" put on by Bill Graham at the Fillmore (from March 18 to March 22, 1966) represented a historic event for Haight-Ashbury because it marked the final Helms/Graham collaboration. Graham and Helms had been sharing the venue on alternate weekends, but Graham exercised some muscle and hustle to secure the Fillmore for his sole use.

The Helms/Graham story is integral to the Haight-Ashbury legend. Helms and Graham had a deal, in which Helms and his friend, John Carpenter, booked and managed shows every weekend at the Fillmore—their own shows one weekend, Graham's shows the next—and Graham, in return, bankrolled the entire operation by paying the Fillmore rent, fronting the money for bookings, and sharing the profits. The Fillmore was located at 1806 Geary, in a predominately African-American neighborhood two miles from Haight-Ashbury. (This venue is a different building than Fillmore West, which would open in 1968 in the former Carousel Ballroom at the corner of Van Ness and Market.)

Eventually—inevitably—friction developed. When the Butterfield Blues Band played to wildly enthusiastic crowds that packed the Fillmore to the rafters, it became clear that competition would likely develop between Helms and Graham for booking Butterfield on future weekends. Graham, far more streetwise, corporate-oriented, ambitiously driven, and ruthless than the more laid-back, hippie-oriented Helms, roused himself from bed in the early hours after the performance to call Albert Grossman, Butterfield's manager, in New York to reserve the group for productions he would stage himself.

Helms, feeling angry and betrayed, broke with Graham—which was fine with Graham. Having learned the production ropes, Graham knew by now that he could pack the Fillmore every weekend through his own efforts and pocket the entire profit for himself. Helms seemed entirely expendable, and Helms would have to fend for himself. Helms moved his Family Dog operations eight blocks east to the old Puckett Academy of Dance built in 1911 on the corner of Sutter and Van Ness. He renamed it the Avalon Ballroom and opened on April 22 with a dance/concert featuring the Blues Project and the Great Society with "lights and stuff by Tony Martin." With Helms at the Avalon and Graham at the Fillmore, a rivalry ensued between the two, and the dances they staged became the driving force and central cog of Haight-Ashbury culture and social life.

Helms and Graham had a kind of yin-yang difference of personality and vision, and the ambience of their respective venues reflected their divergent views. In Graham's own words, "The very first show we did, a statement was made right then and there as to the way they [Helms and company] do their business and the way we [Graham and company] do our business and that was the beginning of a feud that lasted quite some time" (Gleason 1969, 289). Hard-nosed and perfectly willing to play hardball, Graham eventually required bands playing the Fillmore to sign an agreement not to play at the Avalon—or anywhere else in San Francisco—for a year following their performance at his venue.

The backgrounds of Helms and Graham explain their different approaches to music in the Haight. Helms's father, who worked in a Texas sugar mill, died when Chet was twelve, after which he was raised in Fort Worth by his mother and grandfather, a fundamentalist Baptist evangelist.

His uncles were printers, who specialized in biblical tracts and advertising handbills. Helms, harboring visions of becoming a missionary, worked in his uncles' print shop and eventually used his knowledge when, as head of the Family Dog, he consorted with rock poster artists. Helms fell into ungodly ways (what his grandfather and uncles called backsliding) when he went away to the University of Texas to study engineering. In 1961, he got caught up in the civil rights movement and dropped out of school.

Forsaking his fundamentalist background, he gravitated toward the bohemian life, wandering without direction between Austin, Mexico, and the Beat haven of San Francisco. In the course of hanging out in the bars and coffeehouses of Austin, he became friends with Janis Joplin, who had left her evangelist-laden upbringing in Port Arthur to sing and pursue a beatnik lifestyle in the far more worldly city of Austin. In January 1963, the two became friends (but never lovers) and hitchhiked to San Francisco together to do on a hipper scale in North Beach essentially what they had been doing in Austin. When Joplin temporarily returned to Texas, Helms remained in San Francisco to experience and participate firsthand in the transition from the North Beach beatnik era to the Haight-Ashbury hippie scene. After becoming manager of Big Brother and producing rock concerts, in late May 1966 Helms recruited Joplin as singer for Big Brother. His increasing involvement with Family Dog productions eventually required him to give up managing Big Brother.

Favoring shoulder-length hair, a beard, and sandals, Helms *was* a hippie, and he cultivated a hippie vibe and ambience at the Avalon, donning duds every bit as outlandish as his customers, walking about amid the general melee, relishing the hippie theater (for instance, the puppeteer named Demetrious who hung life-sized puppets from the balcony and manipulated them to dance with girls). Helms staged his productions as quasi-theatrical events, titling them "Tribal Stomp," "Euphoria," "Laughing Cure," "Earthquake," and the like. He became "very interested in the scene's potential for revolution. For turning things upside down, for changing values" (Perry 1976, 83).

Graham was born in Berlin, Germany, in 1931. His father died suddenly two days after his son's birth, and his mother perished in the Auschwitz concentration camp. He and his sister Tolla spent a good portion of their early years living in a Berlin orphanage, placed there by their mother in hopes that it would keep them out of the Nazi's clutches. At age ten, Graham and his sister were among sixty-three Jewish children, who fled through France on foot, only eleven of whom survived (his sister not among them). From France, he moved to New York City to live with a foster family in the Bronx. He put himself through City College by working as a cab driver and as a waiter in the Catskills, and served in the Korean War, earning the prestigious Bronze Star and Purple Heart for being wounded in action. After playing a few roles in theater groups in and around Long Island, Graham harbored serious enough acting aspirations to move to Los Angeles, where he worked as a waiter and took acting lessons. He came close to a breakthrough when he was a finalist for the role of James Whitmore's sidekick in the TV series *The Law and Mr. Jones* (1960–1962), but he lost the part because his face seemed too heavily "Jewish" to the director.

Fed up, Graham abandoned acting for the corporate world. He took a well-paying regional office management position with a heavy-machinery company. The allure of the floodlights still beckoned enough for Graham to give up his $21,000 salary ($194,250 in today's money) to manage the Mime Troupe at a subsistence level. Unlike his fellow Troupers, Graham wasn't primarily motivated by politics. His interest in the Troupe was entirely theatrical, and he promoted the group's business and financial interests. Gradually, the Troupe's dearth of business success began to wear thin for Graham, despite his love of the theater world, and he began thinking with increasing seriousness about leaving the Troupe for something else—what, he didn't know.

Just at this time, Mime Troupe founder R. G. Davis was busted for defying the Parks Department ban of a racy sixteenth-century commedia dell'arte production, prompting Graham to head up a series of fundraising benefits to help Davis with his legal expenses. These benefits were quickly followed by Graham's productions of the Fillmore Acid Test and the Trips Festival. These events brought in far more money than Graham dreamed possible, opening his eyes to an entrepreneurial future. Since he had wanted to leave the Mime Troupe anyway, Graham decided to freelance and try his hand at producing rock concerts patterned on the acid test and Trips Festival model—even though he was almost totally unfamiliar with rock music.

Applying the knowledge and skills he had acquired during his stint in the corporate sector, Graham ran the Fillmore in a hard-nosed, all-business, make-the-trains-run-on-time, I'm-here-to-make-money spirit. He hired security guards to enforce order, dressing them in green and yellow uniforms, and he forbade the Hells Angels from wearing their colors inside. He prohibited the use of drugs at the Fillmore (so no one did them in his presence—they waited until he was out of sight). Unlike Helms, Graham despised hippies. More than once, he and Kesey had to be pulled apart to prevent fisticuffs. In the initial encounter between Graham and Kesey at the Trips Festival, when Kesey, having just been busted, attended (against the judge's express orders) incognito, Graham saw Kesey in a silver spacesuit with a space helmet, holding open the exit doors to let people into the hall. Just ushering people into this circus that I'd been trying to organize for the past four days. So I rushed through the hall to the exits yelling, "What the fuck is going on? What the hell are you doing?"

Then at the peak of my madness, when I'm ready to boil over, ready to burst, screaming, "So do you know what I mean? Do you damned well know what I'm saying?" Space Captain flipped the lid of his space helmet shut and walked away.

At first I was stunned. I couldn't believe it. People don't do that. Then I began to laugh. My temper was broken. That was the first time we met. (Anthony 1980, 82–83)

Graham also exploded into other screaming fights at this same production with Luria Castell and an acid-zonked Sam Andrew—both for letting people in for free (in Castell's case, it was the Charlatans).

On another occasion, Janis Joplin did an interview with a local counterculture publication stating that she preferred the "vibes" of the Avalon to the Fillmore, saying Fillmore audiences had too many army guys wanting to get laid by "hippie chicks." Graham saw the interview, and the next time he noticed Joplin in the Fillmore, he had her bodily thrown out of the building. At the time, a thoroughly blitzed and stunned Joplin could not believe she was being given the bum's rush. In another incident, she and Graham ended up in a shouting match. While Helms relished the hippie theater of his productions and sometimes gave free passes to entire communes, Graham carried around a clipboard and made damn sure nobody snuck in free. His motto: "I get up early."

Dance concerts turned up at other venues around town, but they were no match for the Fillmore or the Avalon in terms of vibes, aesthetics, and acoustics. Longshoreman's Hall was a concrete bunker used as a union hall. A popular venue for conventions, it had abysmal acoustics—music reverberated in layers of echoes, making it difficult to hear. California Hall, a large brick building two blocks from the Civic Center and owned by the German-American Association, had a dismal, grim, and gloomy ambience. Winterland wouldn't come into use for a year or so more, and the Straight Theater wouldn't come into being until May, when three partners leased the old and badly dilapidated Haight Theatre, which had at one time been a neighborhood cinema, then a homosexual movie house, and then an Assembly of God church. They renamed the venue the Straight Theater, possibly in wry allusion to its gay-movie house days of yore. The Straight Theater was beset by so much strategic red tape and obviously orchestrated resistance from the various city bureaucracies that it never really got off the ground.

During the beginnings of psychedelic rock, the Fillmore and the Avalon became the major venues for dance concerts, each in competition, each holding dance concerts every weekend, each hosting incredible groups, and each producing now-legendary posters to promote their productions. Both places had a legal capacity of just less than 1,000. A typical concert drew 500 to 1,500 customers, but neither Helms nor Graham hesitated to pack in 2,000 to 3,000 patrons if a large audience came to the door.

Situated like the Fillmore, on the second story of a building, the Avalon dance floor was built on springs that made the floor bounce when the audience rocked out. The stage was close to the ground and situated in a corner. A balcony partially surrounded the dance floor, bordello-style red-flocked wallpaper covered the rooms, and lots of mirrors, gilded booths, and columns graced the Avalon like a Victorian mansion.

The Fillmore's location in a largely African-American neighborhood resulted in trouble from time to time, especially after African Americans became increasingly hostile to the hippie hordes inundating Haight-Ashbury. Patrons entered the Fillmore from Geary, whereupon they walked up stairs to the ticket hut on the second floor landing, and then up more stairs to the second-floor ballroom. On either side of the dance-floor entryway, they could sample penny candies or apples, provided free by Graham. A balcony ran along the rear wall, as well as along one of the side walls, of the dance floor.

The Avalon came to be regarded as the more low-key, less strictly regimented, more drug-tolerant, and generally more hippie venue. Paul Kantner of the Jefferson Airplane believed that Helms was "more in tune with what San Francisco was at that time—sybaritic, hedonistic, party-loving people. Chet didn't get up as early in the morning as Bill prided himself on doing, but the Family Dog in its own way was a better operation for the scene, and much more embracing" (Hoskyns 1997, 81).

In the view of fellow Airplane member Jorma Kaukonen: "Both promoters put on a good show, but their styles were different. Chet was a hippie who was part of the Haight-Ashbury scene, and he knew the musicians. Though Chet wanted to make a profit, the Avalon was more psychedelic and a hippie scene. Bill was a money-sucking capitalistic pig who had real security, and you could get your ass kicked there" (Hoskyns 1997, 82). According to Quicksilver bassist David Freiberg: "The Fillmore was fine. Winterland was nice, too. It was all good, but the Avalon really had a good vibe. It was like playing in your living room there" (Henke

1997, 94). Boz Scaggs (originally a member of the Steve Miller Blues Band, which played at the venues) said much the same thing. "The Avalon," he recalled, "was the really special place. It just had the right vibe. It was real comfortable and relaxed. Something about the room—it was the right size and the right vibe" (Henke 1997, 83).

To Quicksilver guitarist Gary Duncan:

> As far as the musical scene, the Avalon Ballroom was the place to be. It was a lot cooler place than the Fillmore.
>
> Chet Helms was more instrumental in the beginning for creating the atmosphere. Bill Graham didn't come till a while after that. I'd have to say honestly that the real scene was at the Avalon . . .
>
> Graham was a businessman. He put San Francisco on the map, he brought a lot of big talent to San Francisco. If you look at it from that respect, he had a lot to do with making rock & roll concerts a common thing [but] the Avalon was just a lot looser. We'd play the Avalon at least twice a month, sometimes more. (Henke 1997, 91)

Graham would go on to produce concerts for six years—long after the Avalon folded and the Haight-Ashbury scene was over. He held auditions at the Fillmore on Tuesday nights, charging a buck to anyone wanting to listen. He remains a complicated figure in Haight-Ashbury history. Graham initiated dance/concert weekends around which the Haight-Ashbury culture thrived, and he brought in some top-line, eclectic talent, but his business practices could be very non-Haight-Ashburian: cutthroat and hostile to competition. In a seeming contradiction, Graham served as a great promoter of the music, but never relished it. He booked Cream, for example, because he had heard so much *about* them—at the time of booking them, he had never so much as listened to one of their records and didn't even know what the band sounded like.

The Evolution of the Light Show

Let the seer bring down his broad eye to the most stale and trivial fact, and he will make you believe it a new planet in the sky.

—Henry David Thoreau, *Journals*, November 5, 1839

The light show, an essential element of the dance concerts, was produced by projecting light through glass slides, petri dishes, or watch covers enveloped with liquid pigment. The colored liquid was stirred, swirled, and otherwise manipulated in ways that cast radiant bursts of colored light onto the wall in ever-shifting shapes and patterns. Done with skill, the effect could be spectacular. Strobe lights, film clips, and black lights were gradually added into the mix. The most skilled practitioners became very sophisticated in these techniques, elevating the practice into an art form. Eventually, the frontline light-show artists became almost as well-known with coteries of fans and followers as the rock groups. They even got billings on posters.

Ozoned celebrants loved the psychedelic quality of these swirling, spinning, blobbing, oozing, overlapping, melding, zoom-in/zoom-out patterns as they melted on the walls to the soaring, surging, rocking, and rolling feedback explorations of the Jefferson Airplane, the Grateful Dead, Kaleidoscope (which also used belly dancers in their shows), Quicksilver, Big Brother, Country Joe and the Fish, and H. P. Lovecraft—everyone all the while outlandishly decked out, freaking freely and dancing in an en masse, communal good time. The light-show phenomenon had been evolving as an underground art form in its own right for years prior to the advent of psychedelic dance concerts—long before the fall of 1965, long before La Honda, the acid tests, "America Needs Indians," and the Open Theater. It proved immensely congenial to the psychedelic experience, however, and it ended up both catalyzing and synching perfectly with developments in the psychedelic music scene. The convergence of the music and the light shows reflected yet another intermingling of disparate scenes occasioned by psychedelic dance concerts. The experience spawned an interdisciplinary connection between the film avant-garde with the poets, the coffeehouse folkies, the heads, the street-theater politicos, the painters, the bohemians, and the students.

The psychedelic light show originated with a San Francisco State University professor named Seymour Locks. In 1952, Locks attempted to revive experiments in "projected scenery" that composer Igor Stravinsky had introduced in his ballet *The Rite of Spring* during the '20s for a presentation at an upcoming conference of art educators. One of the facets of projected scenery involved projection of colored-light designs on dancers running in and out of view. In the course of preparing his show, Locks discovered that he could project interesting patterns of color onto a wall by using an overhead projector to shine light through colored liquids while he stirred and swirled them in a transparent dish. Locks's students, including Elias Romero, picked up on the technique and ran with it, putting on a few performances of their own. In 1955, Romero journeyed to San Francisco specifically to learn more about the technique, after which he became a kind of Johnny Appleseed of the light show, performing them to the improvised music of jazz combos.

In 1958, Romero staged a light show to music for the Los Angeles Beat crowd with Christopher Tree, an old college classmate, on drums. By 1962, Tree and Romero lived on Pine Street, performing light shows at parties and coffeehouses, and Tree and Romero began collaborating on regular Sunday night light shows in an old church in the Mission district for R. G. Davis when he formed the Mime Troupe—heralding the interconnections between street theater, art, politics, music, film, and light shows.

Bill Ham, a devotee of "action painting," managed Romero's Pine Street apartment building. Romero passed his light-show skills on to Ham, who began experimenting and putting on shows for festively stoned Pine Streeters. Encapsulating the sensibility of the Haight, Ham considered his work instant, spontaneous, transitory, shared art that captured moments in time. In January 1966, the *San Francisco Chronicle* characterized Ham's light show as "action painting that ceases with the action." The same month, the *San Francisco Examiner* raved about Ham's "instant art. This is a remarkable happening; a brilliant and beautiful collection of instants" (billhamlights. com/history/). Ham eventually did the light shows for the original Family Dog productions.

Other light-show luminaries were Ben Van Meter—a SFSU graduate and would-be musician (he auditioned unsuccessfully for the Charlatans) who was into filmmaking (his films included the notorious "Poon-Tang Trilogy")—Tony Martin, who did many of Graham's original dances; and Roger Hilyard, who did the light shows for the Trips Festival. Yet another Pine Streeter, Travis Rivers, imported light-show techniques to Texas, where he did light shows for 13th Floor Elevators concerts. Some of the leading light-show groups were Holy See, which specialized in mandala imagery, Head Lights (snatches of their work can be seen in the film *Monterey Pop*), the Brotherhood of Light, Optic Illusion, Dr. Zarov, Crimson Madness, Little Princess 109, Dry Paint, and Sunburst.

The Psychedelic Poster

Chet Helms provided the initial impetus for development of the rock-poster art scene, when he upgraded the posters commissioned for his dances from black-and-white to color. "I wanted to create an advertising vehicle that would have a life beyond the actual event," he reasoned (Drucker 1997, n.p.).

For his posters, Helms originally chose Wes Wilson, an ex-philosophy major at San Francisco State University, who had almost no art training but, as owner of an ancient 17-by-22-inch hand press, had done some printing for the Mime Troupe. Wilson had also previously created several handbills for Helms, as well as the handbill and the program for the Trips Festival while he was working at Contact Printing, a small press. In some ways, he seemed ideally suited for Helms's needs. Wilson exemplifies the nature of the Haight-Ashbury community: Wilson became Helms's poster artist less because of his artistic credentials than because they knew each other. In doing eleven of the first twelve Family Dog posters, Wilson all but invented the psychedelic rock-poster genre as he went along. For his part, Helms supplied the themes—such as "Sin Dance," "Euphoria," "Tribal Stomp"—and found the photo of the Indian that was used as the Family Dog logo; he spotted it in *The American Heritage Book of Indians*. He also discovered Avalon's motto ("May the baby Jesus shut your mouth and open your mind"), which he saw on the walls of 1090 Page Street. Wilson also produced many of the early Fillmore posters for Graham until May 1967.

Before Wilson, very few templates existed for acid-rock posters. The placards in the Haight ostensibly informed the public about a rock concert, but in the true spirit and style of psychedelic aesthetics, Wilson heaped flair upon function and turned the rock poster into a sophisticated, highly creative genre in its own right. He conceived of the psychedelic rock poster in the same sense that the bands invented the music they were playing in front of light shows each night. Wilson began experimenting with distorted, flowing, vibrant lettering in the style of Art Nouveau artists such as Alphonse Mucha and Viennese Secessionist artist Alfred Roller by squeezing the lines together to make the letters bulge—a difficult-to-read look that became integral to psychedelic poster art. His technique resulted in posters that could be easily read only by the hip-insider members of the Haight community. Wilson also used vibrant, pulsating colors to replace the initial black-and-white posters to make the posters even more difficult to decipher. Paul Kantner of the Jefferson Airplane called the posters a "secret code." They "were the flags of the incipient republic" (Drucker 1997, n.p.).

Like many other elements within the Haight, poster artists developed the psychedelic postings based upon their experience with acid. "When I started doing posters, especially the posters in color," Wes Wilson conceded, "I think I selected my colors from my visual experiences with LSD." Bob

Fried, who started his posters in 1967 in the Haight, owed the same debt to psychedelics. "I wanted my posters to convey feelings of dimensional space, like what you feel when you trip on acid. Passing from one reality to another," he explained. "I wanted to express a kind of space network, rushing, floating, going through time. I wanted people to feel in my posters the sense of discovery I myself was experiencing" (Grushkin 1987, 72, 83).

The acid-inspired rock posters became works of art in their own right, almost for their own sake. The lettering was sometimes psychedelicized and ultra-aestheticized to the point, where the posters were nearly unreadable but artistically stunning, a development that drove practical-minded Bill Graham up the wall. When collectors began scooping these posters up—the competition for obtaining them became cutthroat, collectors gathering

Figure 17. Joe Gomez drawing a poster for the Avalon Ballroom concert with Big Brother and Mount Rushmore, November 25–27, 1967. *Source*: © The Regents of the University of California. Courtesy Special Collections, University Library, University of California, Santa Cruz. Ruth-Marion Baruch and Pirkle Jones Photographs. https://digitalcollections.library.ucsc.edu/concern/works/qb98mf45k

like vultures to liberate them the second they were tacked up—Helms and Graham began making them available for purchase at their venues. Poster sales became one of the primary sources of income for the Avalon, the revenue generated by their sale sometimes keeping the Family Dog solvent. At one point, Graham threw in a free poster of the night's event with each ticket purchase.

Some of these posters now sell for thousands of dollars, with prices literally escalating by the week. The artists who created them, however, were scandalously underpaid—typically getting between $25 and $100 per job. A poster artist couldn't make even a minimal living through their art. Until the height of his Haight-Ashbury superstardom, Rick Griffin and his wife lived in a van. Graham and Helms, meanwhile, not only reaped advertising dividends from the posters, but made money selling them. The problem faced by the artists was that if they weren't willing to work for $25–$100 a pop, a long line of other artists were eager to do so.

Wilson and Graham parted ways, when Wilson eventually gave Graham an either/or ultimatum to pay him better for his work. As would be his wont over and over—and as he would do several years later, when the light-show artists issued a similar ultimatum—Graham chose Wilson's "or." Wilson largely pioneered the psychedelic-rock poster scene, but with an increasing number of talented and creative poster artists in the wings and unable to support himself without Graham's commissions, Wilson moved to the Missouri Ozarks and passed away in 2000 at the age of eighty-two.[2]

After sending Wilson on his way, Graham replaced him as regular poster artist with his own wife, Bonnie MacLean. He had hired MacLean as his secretary when he worked for Allis-Chalmers, and she had moved with him to his new career producing rock concerts. Trained at the Pratt Institute in New York City, she had been doing the chalkboard posters in the Fillmore lobby all along, so Graham put her to work doing the art posters as well. Her style looked similar but more polished compared to Wilson's approach.

Wilson's successor as featured poster artist at the Family Dog was Pine Streeter Stanley Miller (aka Stanley Mouse, later just Mouse, named after his quiet demeanor). The son of a Walt Disney artist, he had migrated to Berkeley from Detroit in 1964 at the age of twenty-five after attending art school for eight years and having made a name for himself doing hot-rod posters and tee-shirts at drag races and indoor hot-rod shows in a style derivative of Ed "Big Daddy" Roth. Miller moved to San Francisco after making the acquaintance of some Pine Streeters, one of whom was Alton Kelly (an original Family Dog artist; Mouse would eventually team with

Kelly to create some of the most legendary psychedelic rock posters). In 1965, Miller got drafted into the army but managed to get out by early 1966, returning to San Francisco in a rented hearse the same night as the Trips Festival. He created his first rock poster for the Captain Beefheart/Oxford Circle show with a head of a steer (June 17–18, 1966) and subsequently would produce twenty-six of the next thirty-six Family Dog posters, a number of them in collaboration with Kelly.[3]

The work being done by Mouse and Kelly reputedly made Rick Griffin take an interest in rock posters, prompting him to move from L.A. to San Francisco in 1966. Griffin grew up in the surf culture of Southern California. He developed a surfer cartoon character named Murphy or "Murf the Surf" that became widely known in surfer circles, and he joined the staff of *Surfer Magazine* upon graduating from high school. Griffin joined a musical hipster family called the Jook Savages and attended the Watts Acid Test. After ingesting acid, he and the Savages moved north to San Francisco. Griffin launched his poster career, when he drew the poster for an art exhibition put on by the Savages at the Psychedelic Shop. In another example of the early Haight-Ashbury community, Griffin's second-ever assignment came when he delivered his Jook Savages poster to the printer. In the printer shop at the same time, the organizers of the upcoming Human Be-In saw the Jook Savages poster, liked it, and on the spot commissioned Griffin to produce the Be-In poster, which resulted in a now-legendary poster of an Indian saint with a third eye in his forehead. Helms, so taken by both these black-and-white posters, asked Griffin to create Family Dog posters.[4]

Victor Moscoso, who attended Cooper Union Art School in New York City for three years and then studied for another two years with Josef Albers at Yale, had far more training than most of the psychedelic poster greats. After reading Kerouac's *On the Road* in 1959, he journeyed to San Francisco to attend the Art Institute and stayed there to teach. One of his trademarks was making his posters extremely difficult to decipher. Reversing the rules that he learned from his mentor Albers, he combined two colors from opposite ends of the color scale with equal intensity to achieve "vibrating colors," so "your eye will not be able to tell which one is in front of the other." At the same time, he lettered words in the negative space to make them "as difficult to read as possible." With these two techniques, he hoped to "hang the viewer up for as long as you can! A week! A month! A year, if you can! An hour will do." "What happens," he explained, "is the poster becomes a thing of entertainment unto itself! You don't even have to go to the concert" (Groth 2011).

Like so many other Haight-Ashbury insiders, Moscoso reveled in the neighborhood vibe of the early scene and the intelligent, creative productivity driving it. What made it an exciting place, he recalled, was the widely shared aspiration to create amazing new ideas, sounds, sights, and events without worrying about money. Though crashing in your van or playing for free in the park, the artist lived in a state of intensely creative vitality in a way valued and appreciated by your equally creative, intelligent, and contributing peers. Artists delighted in a vitalizing sense of competition, less in the sense of defeating the opposition than in rising to new heights. They created posters to energize the community to make it an even more amazing and fun place to live. "It was all happening at the neighborhood level, where you knew the musicians and the people in the audience," related Moscoso about how the scene developed among the poster artists. "Within seven days of having done a piece, I'd get feedback about a poster from people who were at the dance and from the musicians. I could immediately put the feedback into the next poster," he reminisced. "All the artists were doing this. We're watching each other's work. We're competing with each other. Wes Wilson would do a poster for Bill Graham. I might do a poster for Family Dog. Somebody would do a poster for California Hall. Somebody else would do one for Straight Theater. So there were four, six, eight posters coming out each weekend." "You could take whatever you wanted from anybody," Moscoso gushed, but "you had to add your own twist; otherwise, it was just taking. And we weren't into taking; we were into creating" (Henke 1997, 99).

Within several months, Fillmore, Avalon, black-light, and many other posters with swirling designs and exploding colors graced the bedrooms of most Haight residents to aid them on their consciousness-raising journeys. In December 1966, the Print Mint opened a second store on Haight Street, trying to quench the thirst of heads for posters, which added to the psychedelic ambience of the district. In addition to reprints of Family Dog posters and other images, the store became a gathering place and source of information for hippies.

The posters also beckoned nascent hippies along the West Coast. Mickey Hart, soon to be a percussionist for the Grateful Dead, owned a music store in San Carlos, about forty-five minutes from the Haight, and posted psychedelic posters in his storefront window. "The psychedelic posters became the totem," he remembered, "that was the call, you know, the call of the weird. They were just as much art as they were a clarion call . . . The word was going up the peninsula" (Silos, 2003, 169–170).

Soon psychedelicized happenings appeared in other cities along the coast. By 1967, hippies in Portland, Oregon, had staged two of their own trips festivals. The psychedelic energy was mounting.

9

The Trip Intensifies

The flowers appear on the earth; the time of the singing of birds is come, and the voice of the turtle is heard in our land.

—The Song of Solomon 2:12

It's revolutionary growing your own food instead of supporting the profit system. . . . It's revolutionary to learn how to fix stuff, rather than junk it or take it in to be replaced.

—Stephen Gaskin, cofounder of the Farm in 1971, *This Season's People* (1976)

The Diggers

As the spring turned into summer, the activity in the Haight intensified. In July, a group emerged out of the Mime Troupe calling itself "Diggers" after the seventeenth-century English utopian reformers, led by Gerrard Winstanley and William Everard, who wanted to abolish money and ownership of private property to "restore Creation to its former condition" (Burton Wolfe 1968, 63). The Haight-Ashbury Diggers were a highly political bunch—but psychedelic/anarchist, non-ideological politicos—who saw themselves as gadflies promoting the "ideology of failure," by which they meant a total renunciation of "winning" as a life goal. "When Love does its thing," as a Digger broadside put it, "it does it for itself, not for profit." "Freedom," they said, "means free" (in the double sense of "liberated" and "not for money"). The Diggers promoted true anarchy, unpredictability, and self-determination, preaching that all institutions—from the family to the church, from rock venues to motorcycle gangs—were "horizontal and vertical pyramid hierarchies boxed and frozen for coordinating programmed corpses" ("A Digger Manifesto" 1967).

The Diggers loved to create spontaneous, unscripted, see-what-happens, invent-it-as-you-go street theater, usually grounded in some kind of challenge to authority, sacrosanct ideal, or cherished self-image. The idea of Digger theater—somewhat akin to the Kesey-circle prank—lassoed passersby into the in-the-making play in hopes of evolving some kind of outrageous, Dadaistic situation that made a sociopolitical point and prompted the participants to reexamine their day-to-day roles, values, and assumptions. Nor was their prankish theater directed solely at the "straight." As often as not, it was directed at the sacrosanct roles, values, assumptions, and pieties governing the Haight-Ashbury.

The Diggers organized and staged free concerts in the parks and provided free food in the Panhandle at 4 p.m. daily. The women made large pots of soup and baked bread in an old bakery with the operative slogan: "It's free—because it's yours!" Whenever anyone—including the police—demanded to know who was in charge, the answer was "You are—it's yours!" They also opened a free store called the Free Frame of Reference (later called the Trip Without a Ticket), at which they dispensed food and household items (some donated, some stolen, some retrieved from dumpsters) at no charge. To get into the Digger store, one needed to pass through a nine-by-nine-foot yellow square made of bolted-together two-by-four boards to both symbolically and literally enter and pass through the Digger frame of reference to get in line for free food. The Yippies, organized in 1968, modeled themselves after the Diggers, but the Yippies were much more blatantly political, New York cynical, and seekers-out of media hype and individual renown. The most prominent Diggers were Peter "The Hun" Berg, Peter Cohan (the present-day actor, who now goes by the name Peter Coyote), Billy Morrott, and Emmett Grogan (the latter two originally from Brooklyn). Grogan wrote the autobiographical *Ringolevio: A Life Played for Keeps,* much of which describes his Digger experiences. He was found dead of a heroin overdose in a New York subway on April 1, 1978.

By July 1966, a tidal wave of newcomers flattened the Haight, a victim of its own success. What six months ago had been a local neighborhood scene was turning into a countercultural refugee camp and circus with increased crime and disease. What had been a close-knit community was becoming a parody of itself—a place to "be a hippie." The heart of the scene started to fracture. With the Haight so saturated with and overrun by newcomer wannabes that new arrivals could no longer be easily assimilated, the Diggers responded to the "emergency" by dispensing free food, trying to locate adequate housing, offering twenty-four-hour counseling services, and operating a runaway location site. "The Diggers are practicing the Cardinal Virtues, because that's the right thing to do," stated the Diggers (Perry 1976, 150).

On October 31, the Diggers held a Full Moon Public Celebration. It began at 5:30 p.m. at Haight and Masonic, the busiest intersection in the Haight, with "the intersection game." At the Digger's behest, a crowd of approximately 600 hippies (many of them costumed for Halloween) began milling around at random in the middle of the intersection, doing silly walks amid nine-foot puppets, and the Diggers chanting, "the streets are public; the streets are free." Traffic tied up, cops arrived, and a number of arrests were made amid the improvised Digger street theater. At one point, the cops actually engaged in an argument—to the wild delight of the Diggers—with one of the cryptically wisecracking, Zen storytelling puppets, as though it were a person.

On December 16, the Diggers conducted the Death of Money and Rebirth of the Haight Parade. Festivities began at 5 p.m. with the Mime Troupe passing out pennywhistles, automobile rearview mirrors, flowers, lollipops, incense, candles, and bags of lawn clippings (grass, get it?). Six pallbearers wearing Egyptian-esque animal masks carried a black-draped coffin. Approximately 1,000 people joined in, led by a phalanx of Hells Angels. Less than two weeks later, the Diggers hosted a feast that served more than 500 people.

In early 1967, the Diggers continued their community-focused creativity. On February 17, they offered a crafts class at the being-remodeled Straight Theater, wherein a Mime Troupe actress taught a still relatively unknown technique known as tie-dying. Soon after classes commenced, neighborhood boutiques began accepting tie-dyed wares on consignment. One could, in effect, wear a light show. Within months, tie-dye became a countercultural fashion fad and spread like wildfire throughout the country. Prior to the Digger-sponsored community class, it had been mostly an insider, local skill/craft.

Other groups catered to the growing horde of heads in the Haight. On November 22, a merchants association calling itself the Haight Independent Proprietors (H.I.P) was formed by the craftspeople in the Haight, who had been excluded from the more traditional Haight Merchants Association. H.I.P would figure significantly in neighborhood events over the coming year and defended the hippies against the police. "The Haight-Ashbury represents a cultural renaissance and creative surge that is changing the bruted face of America," they contended, and the Haight residents should not be harassed by the authorities (Daloz 2017).

A few weeks later, the Drogstore Cafe moved to Haight and Masonic, the Haight's busiest intersection, and became a major hippie hangout. It was originally called the Drugstore, but the police wouldn't stand for use of the word *drug*, so the name was changed to accommodate the authorities.

Like the Haight in general, the Diggers found their spontaneous creativity through acid. "I don't think the psychedelic rebellion would have happened without LSD," contended Digger Peter Berg, an impetus behind the Free Store. "LSD was so undeniably a consciousness-changing agent, and to go on that consciousness change, to undergo it, and to come out on the other side, and not be ravingly insane, meant that you could turn reality upside down" (Babcock 2020, 80).

The Hippie Press

A series of publications about the counterculture in the Haight arose to cater to the swarm of incoming hippies and to spread the psychedelic word to other parts of the country. During the fall semester of 1966 at Berkeley, a student named Jann Wenner began writing a weekly column in the *Daily Cal* called "Seamy Signs of Rock and Roll." He took the angle of covering, and alerting readers to, the most bizarre happenings and strangest music around. A year later, on November 9, 1967, Wenner borrowed $7,500 from his family and teamed with journalist Ralph Gleason to launch a newsprint magazine called *Rolling Stone*. In the inaugural issue, he wrote that "we have begun a new publication reflecting what we see are the changes in rock and roll and the changes related to rock and roll" (Wenner 1967, 2).

September 20, 1966, marked the inaugural issue of the *San Francisco Oracle*, a pivotal underground newspaper that reflected the Haight ethos. There had been several earlier—and abysmal—issues of this magazine/newspaper under various titles, including *P.O. Frisco* and the *Haight-Ashbury Ash*. The *Oracle* came into being, when a marijuana dealer with literary/journalistic aspirations named Allen Cohen met brothers Ron and Jay Thelin. The Thelins urged Cohen to pursue his magazine dreams and partly bankrolled him, along with contributions from Bill Graham, Peter Tork (of Monkees

Figure 18. A man named "Jesus" selling the *San Francisco Oracle*, 1967. *Source*: © The Regents of the University of California. Courtesy Special Collections, University Library, University of California, Santa Cruz. Ruth-Marion Baruch and Pirkle Jones Photographs. https://digitalcollections.library.ucsc.edu/concern/works/jm214p16v?locale=en

fame), the Grateful Dead, and various marijuana dealers. "We were going to fill our newspaper with art, philosophy, poetry and attend to this change of consciousness that was happening in the Haight-Ashbury and, we hoped, the world," related Cohen (Perry 1976, 44).

The *Oracle* became progressively wilder and wonderfully weirder as it went along. Printed on February 14, 1967, *Oracle* No. 6 used a technique that caused the ink on each page to blend into a variety of colors, so that every single paper was slightly different from all the others. It focused on coverage of psychedelic festivals and included an astrological debate over when the Age of Aquarius would begin. *Oracle* No. 7 (March 1967) featured a panel discussion in which Allen Ginsberg, Gary Snyder, Timothy Leary, and Alan

Watts argued, contemplated, and proposed some unbelievably airhead ideas: Gary Snyder predicting, for example, that New York City would be covered over by grass within forty years. The debaters gave serious flight time to some amazing, far-out musings, which now seem so ludicrous as to be entertaining in a smack-the-forehead, hoot-out-loud fashion—à la *Reefer Madness*.

The eighth issue (June 1967) had a cover showing a mountain with "San Francisco" written on the snowy peak, over which three flying saucers hovered. In the background, an op-art pattern of purple rays shaded into violet, in which was placed the face of Chief Joseph of the Nez Perce. The inside pages were swirls of colored patterns with most of the text columns arranged into shapes rather than in conventional straight columns. Each copy had a unique color scheme, and the entire press run of 100,000 copies was scented with Jasmine Mist perfume. Most of the stories in this issue dealt with Native-American topics: Indian psychedelics, rights, and lifestyles.

The *Oracle* operated on such a tight budget that it took several press runs to publish each issue. Typically, a batch of copies would be printed for sale on the street, and the proceeds would be used to pay the bills so that another, larger run could be printed—that process sometimes repeated several times per issue. Of the total twelve issues, the largest run of the *Oracle* was 117,000 papers. As with many Haight-Ashbury endeavors, the *Oracle* was largely a labor of love, something done for the fun and "the trip." The staff largely went unpaid.

In another venture, on January 10, 1967, New York Beat poet and science-fiction novelist Chester Anderson and Digger Claude Hayward scraped together $300 and started the Communication Company, envisioned as a kind of instantaneous newspaper (printed on mimeograph machines) to dispense the Haight news via broadsides, bulletins, announcements, notice of events, commentary, occasional poetry, often sarcastic and mocking interpretations of recent events (sometimes only minutes after the actual event), commentary on local stores and personalities, exhortations, and Digger pronouncements. Communication Company bulletins became fixtures in the daily life of the Haight scene and complemented the sporadically published *Oracle*. The more than 600 items printed by the company "was the blog of Haight Street," contended Hayward. "It had that immediacy, that nowness" (Babcock 2021, 14).

The Communication Company charged very little for their services. According to Anderson, "Our policy, stated most simply, was this: we'd print anything for anyone for whatever they were willing to pay, including no pay at all, and everything for the Diggers [was] free."

To support themselves, the five-member staff relied on the Haight residents. "The community supported us after an odd fashion," mentioned Anderson, "bringing in groceries and stolen paper, paying our rent and some of our bills, keeping us extravagantly high, and letting us in on everything that happened."

Like most of the psychedelicized Haight, the Communication Company espoused fun and spontaneity. Anderson contended that it "remained untainted by any leanings toward linear organization." "We came as near to anarchy" as possible, except for the staff living together. Rather than hardcore and direct political action, he focused on loose-knit "revolutionary gangs," and at one point "playfully" corrupted the mayor's son to produce "more and lasting change" rather than a political assassination of the mayor. Anderson felt that "revolutionary Joy, it's not only fun, it's religion" (Babcock 2020).

Beginning in late 1968, the Print Mint became a haven and distributor for a new type of publication called the underground comix. Initially, the shop published the weekly tabloid *Yellow Dog*, edited by poet and Print Mint owner Don Schenker. Soon, it branched out to carry the classic *Zap* comix, a creation of Robert Crumb, which Crumb's then-wife Dana Morgan sold on the streets of the Haight for thirty-five cents from a baby stroller. The inaugural issue of a thousand copies sold out to Haight residents. By the second issue of *Zap*, Crumb had enlisted the help of poster artists Victor Moscoso and Rick Griffin as illustrators. Using an enlightened business model, Print Mint owner Schenker paid for the printing but shared the profits equally with the artists.

Surreal, sometimes astonishingly vulgar, often hilariously funny, *Zap* and subsequent underground comix became a source of numerous catch phrases, images, and posters that had wide currency in the late '60s and early '70s. The genre yielded cult classics among the college crowd with such famous characters as the holy man, Mr. Natural and his neurotic sidekick Flakey Foont, Angelfood McSpade, the sewer snoids, and the Furry Freak Brothers: Freewheelin' Frank, Fat Freddy, and Phineas (and their cat).

Acid-Rock Festivals and Free Concerts

THE BE-IN

As the Haight scene became increasingly visible, psychedelic concerts continued and peaked by 1967. During the first weekend of October 1966, the Awareness Festival at San Francisco State University was produced by Stewart Brand, who had coproduced the Trips Festival in January. The comedy duo of the Congress of Wonders performed, the Grateful Dead played, and Bill Ham presented a light show in the women's gym. Conga players drummed for fifteen hours nonstop in a flea market outside. The event revolved around an acid test in which it was rumored that Kesey—at the time a fugitive from justice—would make a disguised appearance. He did, but via a broadcast from a secret location on campus, and even then not until 2 a.m. on the last day, when only a handful of the hardcore (and very acid-zonked) inner circle remained. By then, even the FBI had gone home.

Less than a week later, LSD became officially illegal. As a reaction to the new law, hippies staged a Love Pageant Rally in the Panhandle as a we're-still-here, nose-thumbing of the authorities and as a dress rehearsal for an upcoming Be-In.

On New Year's 1966/1967, the Hells Angels and the Diggers cosponsored and financed the New Year's Wail outdoor party in the Panhandle. The Angels took the lead at the event in tribute to the Diggers, which had raised bail money for two Angels, Hairy Henry and George "Chocolate George" Hendricks at the Death of Money Parade a month earlier. They dispensed free beer on an unseasonably sunny day to two thousand participants who danced to the music of Big Brother and the Grateful Dead. So impressed by the collaboration of the Angels and Diggers at the event, Chester Anderson decided to start the Communication Company. The *San Francisco Chronicle* captured the irony of the gathering when reporter David Swanston observed "a hippie with shoulder-length hair and two civil rights buttons pinned to his jacket chatted with an Angel with shoulder-length hair and a small Confederate flag on his sleeveless coat" (Swanston 1967, 1).

Two weeks later, on January 14, 1967, Pow-Wow: A Gathering of the Tribes for a Human Be-In was held at the Polo Field in Golden Gate Park from 1 to 5 p.m. The idea for the happening was hatched by Beat artist Michael Bowen and psychedelic holy man/guru John Starr Cooke, who sometimes was called Charlie Brown. Cooke, reputed to be the source of the idea to exorcise and levitate the Pentagon, was well known around the streets of Haight-Ashbury. He likely first turned on Jerry Rubin by providing him first marijuana and then a 100-microgram dose of Owsley's White Lightning. The experience transformed Rubin from a man-the-barricades ideologue/activist to a leader of the Youth International Party (YIP), which, starting in December 1967, practiced a psychedelicized, anarchist, Prankster-Digger-style street theater with followers called Yippies.

Somewhat akin to Owsley, Cooke had a pretty lofty pedigree. His brother-in-law was a prominent California Democrat named Roger Kent. Kent's brother, Sherman, served as the righthand man for Secretary of State John Foster Dulles during the height of the Cold War, as well as head of the CIA's National Board of Estimates, which calculated the size and scope of Soviet military power. An avid student of the occult, in 1950 Cooke became a devotee and close confidant of L. Ron Hubbard and rose up the worldwide Scientology ranks before he started to question Hubbard. In 1962, the ever-adventurous Cooke took LSD and continued to ingest it daily for two years. When he heard about Timothy Leary, he eagerly contacted the LSD missionary, who considered him "interesting."

Cooke moved to Cuernavaca, Mexico, where he directed a group of acid missionaries named the Psychedelic Rangers. This group envisioned themselves as cosmic warriors in an all-out good guy (acid users) versus bad guy (everyone else) battle for the future of the cosmos. He sent his Rangers to do battle in various psychedelic hot spots throughout the U.S., Canada, and Europe. One of his Rangers and a confidant of Cooke was Beat artist Michael Bowen, who eventually became a frontline figure in Haight-Ashbury. Bowen lived in the same building as the *Oracle* office on the corner of Haight and Masonic, began to work for the newspaper, and even landed one of Cooke's articles in issue number 9, titled "One—that Great Architect of the Universe—designed a single Design." On October 6, 1966, the day, when LSD was declared illegal, Cooke, still living in Mexico, called Bowen in the Haight and raved to him about the Love Pageant Rally. After some discussion, Cooke suggested the notion of a Pow-Wow: A Gathering of the Tribes for a Human Be-In and eventually supported it by a group meditation of his followers in Mexico.

Many considered the Be-In to be the crowning moment of the Haight-Ashbury scene, after which the neighborhood and everything it embraced and fostered went quickly and steeply downhill. Nearly every eyewitness praised the people, performers, and atmosphere (vibes) in glowing, almost worshipful terms. Speakers and luminaries included Allen Ginsberg (was there ever an important countercultural event where he wasn't present?), poet Gary Snyder, Timothy Leary, who exhorted the crowd to "turn on, tune in, drop out," Leary side-kick Richard Alpert, and poets Lenore Kandel and Lawrence Ferlinghetti. Politicos Jack Weinberg of the Free Speech protests and Jerry Rubin also appeared. Owsley appeared with seventy-five turkeys and sandwich bread, which he sprinkled with White Lightning LSD for the 20,000 revelers. Among the bands were the Grateful Dead, Quicksilver

Messenger Service, and the Jefferson Airplane. At the conclusion of the event, Gary Snyder blew a conch shell and Allen Ginsberg led a chant of "Om Shri Maitreya" to the Coming Buddha of Love and then called for "some kitchen yoga," urging participants to stay behind to help clean up and then walk en masse down to the Bay's edge to watch the sunset. The national media attended the event in force. *Time*, *Look*, and *Life* magazines sent reporters to cover the gathering, who fabricated a slanted view for the public at large. Such attention eventually enticed thousands of runaway, desperate, confused young teens to descend upon the Haight and pervert it.

The organizers of the event hoped that it would finally unite the hippies and the political activists. In the January 1967 issue of the *San Francisco Oracle*, editor Allen Cohen predicted "a union of love and activism previously separated by categorical dogma and label mongering will finally occur ecstatically when Berkeley political activists and hip community of San Francisco's spiritual generation and contingents from the emerging revolutionary generation all over California meet." In the same publication, Leland Meyerzove offered a poem, "A Psalm upon the Gathering of All Tribes": "They shall come in ones, in two, in multitudes, and the tribes shall become one and be no more" (*Oracle*, January 1967, vol. 1, no. 5, cover and page 2). For a brief moment on an unseasonably warm day in January, the organizers seemed to achieve their vision.

On February 24, 1967, the Invisible Circus took place, the brain child of the Diggers, the Artist Liberation Front, and a hip pastor, Cecil Williams of the Glide Memorial Church, where it was held in fifty-two rooms of the five-story church. They pegged it as a "72-hour environmental community" and presented it partly as a reaction to the Be-In, which they felt focused too much on the psychedelic elite of Leary. Big Brother started the festivities with a rendition of "Amazing Grace." The Diggers provided food, Mouse painted t-shirts, Pigpen played the organ, automobiles staged slow-mo collisions in the parking lot (a planned performance/event), and Lenore Kandel read the soles of people's feet. In the basement, the Communication Company feverishly published minute-by-minute news flashes. The 5,000 attendees, who had been asked to bring drums, flutes, and bells, heard lectures about the evils of pornography and, at the same time, nude revelers passed out candles to the congregation. After thirty-six hours of partying, Pastor Williams decided to prematurely end the happening. The Glide Foundation concluded that "there were problems galore but many good things happened" ("The Invisible Circus," 1967).

In June 1967, acid rock came into full and vivid flower. On the weekend of June 10–11, the Fantasy Fair and Magic Mountain Music

Festival metamorphosed in the amphitheater on Mount Tamalpais in a bid to recreate the Be-In vibe. Organizers from radio station KFRC hoped to raise funds for Hunters Point Childcare Center in San Francisco. More than forty thousand people, traveling up the mountain on school buses called the Trans-Love Bus Lines or on the back of a Hells Angel's motorcycle, paid the two-dollar admission fee and packed into the area for an event that became the prototype for rock festivals. They walked around the fair grounds and, much like a Renaissance faire, went to art booths, watched jugglers and acrobats, and listened to poetry readings. "It wasn't a bunch of people sitting in stadium chairs," enthused festival coproducer Tom Rounds, "we got everybody really involved in the trippiness of the whole thing" (Newman, 2014).

Figure 19. Portland Trips Festival poster: The San Francisco consciousness spreads up the West Coast. *Source*: Author's collection.

The participants danced to such groups as the Jefferson Airplane, the Charlatans, the Doors, Country Joe and the Fish, and the Mojo Men, most of whom performed for free. "The concept of doing free shows for people really made a lot of sense to a lot of San Francisco bands like the Dead, us and Big Brother. We were all spiritually on the same plane," recalled Jorma Kaukonen of the Airplane. "There was never any thought of making money off of it. It's just what we did" (Newman 2014).

As with other festivals in and near San Francisco at the time, most of the bands and the crowd did LSD. "Before you go onstage, there's Owsley, the Purple Pope, and he asks you, 'Do you want the sacrament?'" recalled singer/songwriter P. F. Sloan, who performed at Fantasy Fair. "So you stick out your tongue and BOOM! And he says, 'Give it about seven minutes.' He was the loving chemist." "I do remember the entire audience turning into this undulating love jello," he added (Newman 2014).

Amped on acid and having the Haight sense of community, both the bands and audience intermingled with one another. After a set, band members walked among the crowd and enjoyed the next act. "We weren't just performers," explained Jorma Kaukonen, "we were part of the audience." "It was a real communion," agreed singer/songwriter Penny Nichols, who opened shows for Janis Joplin in the Haight. "It was the essence of the experience of being in San Francisco at the time" (Newman 2014).

THE MONTEREY INTERNATIONAL POP FESTIVAL

From Friday, June 16, to Sunday, June 18, the Monterey International Pop Festival, a watershed moment in counterculture history, launched psychedelic rock as a major force in the mass music market. An estimated 50,000 to 90,000 people showed up at a venue that could seat 7,500.

The event had been carefully planned by producer/label owner Lou Adler, Beatles publicist Derek Taylor, promoter Alan Pariser, and John Phillips of the folk-rock group the Mamas and the Papas, who expressly wrote a theme song for the festival, "San Francisco (Be Sure to Wear Flowers in Your Hair)," which provided a hit for singer Scott McKenzie on Adler's Ode Records. They established headquarters in the Renaissance Club in L.A. and lured such music luminaries as Smokey Robinson and Berry Gordy, head of Motown, to serve on a board of directors. Adler concocted a motto for the festival, "Music, Love and Flowers," and the festival organizers negotiated a deal with documentary filmmaker D. A. Pennebaker, who had scored with the Dylan documentary *Don't Look Back* (filmed in 1965). Though the festival producers staged an eclectic set of musicians on the advice of Beatle Paul McCartney, they hoped to package the new "San Francisco sound and sell it, Los-Angeles style, to the world," complained Sam Andrew of Big Brother (Szatmary 2019, 145).

Despite the corporate genesis of the Monterey festival, the Haight-Ashbury sensibility prevailed at the event. The Diggers passed out free soup and provided some accommodations to concert-goers; the Hells Angels gave rides to the stage to several of the musicians; and the Dead arranged free camping at Monterey Peninsula College for participants. The ever-present Owsley distributed free samples of his newest batch—Monterey Purple—to one and all backstage. Chet Helms observed: "We were totally out of our minds on acid and it was wonderful . . . The last night of Monterey Pop

Figure 20. Jefferson Airplane poster, 1968. *Source*: Wikimedia Commons, public domain. https://commons.wikimedia.org/wiki/File:WMMS_Presents_Jefferson_Airplane_-_1968_print_ad.jpg

everyone took a lot of Owsley acid. There were big gallon jars of Monterey Pop Festival Purple going around, and you could dip your hand in take a fistful out and stick them in your pocket, and it was being passed out to the crowd and being taken by everyone" (Troy 1994, 111).

All the bands at Monterey strove mightily to outdo one another, some resorting to new heights of sensationalism. Pete Townshend of The Who smashed his guitar. Not to be outdone, Jimi Hendrix "sacrificed" his guitar by dosing it with lighter fluid and setting it on fire and made mock love to the amplifiers. The Grateful Dead jammed and improvised. Janis Joplin skyrocketed to fame simply by virtue of her gritty, full-of-pain vocal performances, and Ravi Shankar, the only paid performer, displayed his virtuosity the entire Sunday afternoon. By and large, the San Francisco groups stole the show, radically changing the direction of rock worldwide. In addition to the Dead and Big Brother which played on the final day, on Saturday the Jefferson Airplane, Quicksilver Messenger Service, and Moby Grape enraptured the audience and cemented the psychedelic sound as the new style. Generally evoked by the media as the public start of the psychedelic era, Monterey—not Woodstock—represented the last great hurrah of the psychedelic counterculture in its truest and finest incarnation. The hippie counterculture subsequent to Monterey—including Woodstock—was an exercise in irony, a mere extension and imitation of a Haight-Ashbury that by then was in decline.

Acid Rock Goes Mainstream

Just as its huge success ensured the ultimate failure of Haight-Ashbury, the triumph of the San Francisco sound at Monterey significantly changed the Haight-Ashbury music scene—and, hence, the culture—permanently for the worse. Where, prior to Monterey, the Haight-Ashbury groups tended to be consciously noncommercial, grassroots, participatory extensions of the community, after Monterey many of the musicians adopted superstar affectations as they were courted, wined, dined, and lavished in visions of fame and fortune by agents and big-label record executives brandishing at least somewhat lucrative contracts. An element of greed entered the scene that corrupted (or at least changed) the innocence that before had given it such charm, grace, and radiance. Even before the final Sunday performance of Monterey was over, music entrepreneur Albert Grossman dangled superstar images before Janis Joplin and pressured her to dump Big Brother—which she would do within the year—and sign with him, to her sad and ultimate detriment. With the possible exception of the heavy, fuzzed-out blues of Blue Cheer (and, in my personal opinion, the Savage Resurrection), no frontline, groundbreaking groups of acid-rock emerged from the Haight-Ashbury scene following Monterey.

Monterey changed everything money-wise, too. In the fall of 1967, before Grossman became manager of Big Brother with a 25 percent commission on all earnings, the band grossed $25,000 total with each band member getting $125 a week. They agreed to take on Grossman as manager because he promised them at least $75,000 ($644,000 in present-day dollars) for the coming year. Compare this to the scene a year previous, when Cipollina lived in his car, Joplin sung for free beer, Jack Casady agreed to join the Airplane when they assured him he would earn $50 a week, and Quicksilver did a gig for $200 and two ounces of grass. As late as 1964, Robert Hunter and Jerry Garcia lived in their cars and ate meals of canned pineapple.

Figure 21. Janis Joplin belting out the psychedelic blues, Seattle, July 5, 1970. *Source*: Author's collection.

Two days after the Monterey International Pop Festival, on June 20, a solstice celebration in Golden Gate Park officially launched the Summer of Love. The Diggers barbecued a lamb and fired hamburgers in shovels over coals—all for free ("Because it's yours!"). There were archers, magicians, jugglers, and hundreds of street musicians. The bands included the Grateful Dead, Big Brother, Quicksilver, and a liturgical orchestra replete with conch shells, Chinese oboes, and six-foot-long trumpets. What a day! Spending all day in the park eating hamburgers and listening to the Dead, Big Brother, and Quicksilver. Then, that evening heading for the Fillmore, which featured Jimi Hendrix and the Airplane—the entire day's entertainment costing only $3.50. Those *were* the days, my friend.

After Monterey, record companies inked deals with many of the psychedelic bands, which soon released albums. Following a mediocre-selling, more folk-oriented debut in 1966, the Jefferson Airplane rode on the Monterey wave with the now-classic *Surrealistic Pillow* that reached number three on the chart and included the hits "Somebody to Love" and the drug-inspired "White Rabbit." Other psychedelic rockers followed suit. In early 1967,

Figure 22. Jefferson Airplane, psychedelic rock stars, circa 1970. *Source*: Wikimedia Commons, public domain. https://commons.wikimedia.org/wiki/File:Jefferson_Airplane_circa_1970.JPG

the Grateful Dead dropped their self-named inaugural record, which on the strength of Monterey reached number 73. In May, Country Joe and the Fish delivered *Electric Music for the Mind and Body* with a free release party at the Fillmore, where the band passed out five kilos worth of joints. The album eventually reached number 39.

Mainstream records rushed out the first LP of Big Brother and the Holding Company featuring Janis Joplin immediately after Monterey, which hit number 60; the next year, the band cut *Cheap Thrills*, complete with Robert Crumb artwork on the cover that snagged the number 1 spot on the pop chart. Moby Grape, the critically touted San Francisco outfit, signed a contract with Columbia Records and in early June released a self-named debut, which scaled the chart to number 26 after their appearance at Monterey. The album cover shockingly (for the time) featured one of the band members, drummer/singer Don Stevenson, giving the finger to record buyers. In a fanfare of media hype, Columbia Records released ten of the thirteen songs on the album as five singles and rented the Avalon for a press party. Two days later, three of the band members were arrested for contributing to the delinquency of a minor after getting caught with three naked seventeen-year-old girls in a parked car alongside a fire trail in the hills above Sausalito.

Quicksilver Messenger Service became the last major psychedelic band to issue a record. In May 1968, they produced a self-named, silver-foil-covered album that hit number 63. The next year, they released their crowning achievement, *Happy Trails*, which fans took to a number 27 chart position.

With acid rock records pouring in, a new type of underground radio station promoted the psychedelic trend. During the '40s, the Federal Communications Commission encouraged AM stations to create FM counterparts. In 1964, when the FCC banned new AM licenses and mandated that FM stations needed to include original programming on half of its broadcasts, new types of music started to appear on FM radio.

In San Francisco, on February 11, 1967, twenty-six-year-old Larry Miller began DJing the first FM rock show on KMPX. He was given the midnight to six a.m. slot, Monday through Saturday, and was paid $45 a week. What's more, he had to sell his own ads to finance his time slot. His show revolutionized FM radio by featuring underground, psychedelic, non–Top 40, longer-than-three-minute songs.

On the evening of April 7, 1967—on a recommendation from Ralph Gleason—Tom "Big Daddy" Donahue, one-time owner of Autumn Records and Mother's psychedelic club, assumed responsibility for programming at

KMPX and aired his first show. He felt that "there will be a change [of Top-40 radio] somewhere along the line. Some radio station owner will have the courage to come up with a new kind of radio" (Krieger 1979, 33). Donahue started to play the music of psychedelic San Francisco and asked his listeners to send him beads, bells, feathers, and posters to decorate the station offices. Almost immediately, he received the requested items, including marijuana, and residents of the Haight began to lounge around the station. Within a week, he secured his initial advertising account and in a few more weeks he hired two female radio engineers to help him. By early August after the acid-rock explosion at Monterey, Donahue switched to an all-rock format, and KMPX broadcast the sound of psychedelia to the thousands of heads in the area. As early as April 26, an enraptured listener confided that "the Ecstatic Experience flashing through my ears has led me to flamboyant changes in apparel and make-up, so that now I arrive at work in outfits normally reserved for weekend day-tripping" (Krieger 1979, 41).

KMPX continued its march to success with the addition of a unique breed of ad salesman. In May 1967, Donahue tapped Milan Melvin, a dope dealer in the Haight, who begged the radio station manager for a job. Believing that Melvin could sell ads on KMPX because he sold marijuana, he sent him to head shops, hippie clothing stores, and other Haight-Ashbury boutiques. Melvin made his rounds with a stovepipe hat over his shoulder-length hair, a purple cape, an earring in one ear, and sporting beads. Giving cut-rate deals to snag first-time customers, he slowly convinced shop owners, such as the clothing store Mnasidika, to advertise on KMPX.

Wildly successful, Melvin hired two other like-minded, consciousness-raised friends to help. He recruited twenty-seven-year-old Jack Towle, who had helped found Family Dog by taking out a loan for a batch of marijuana and selling it for a profit. Melvin also sprung Chandler Laughlin from jail in Contra Costa County, where he was serving time on marijuana charges. He had worked with Laughlin on a scheme to buy Native American pottery, resell it, and then buy Native silver-crafted jewelry. Laughlin had been a bartender at the Red Dog Saloon and had been responsible for hiring the Charlatans at the saloon as the house band. Together, the three hip salesmen cornered the Haight market and contacted some of the largest ad agencies in San Francisco for business. By the end of the year, KMPX had become an important fixture in the city and would jump-start the growth of FM underground radio stations throughout the country. Indeed, the trip in the Haight had intensified.

10

The Decline of the Psychedelic Consciousness

Style is important. Many people scream the truth but without style it is helpless.

—Charles Bukowski, "Trouble with a Battery" (1968)

The Psychedelic Bus Breaks Down

Amid the flowering of hippiedom lurked the sinister seeds of its own demise. Ken Kesey, one of the pioneers in the acid revolution, who had defied authorities to promulgate the virtues of LSD, butted up against establishment reality. In late October 1966 FBI agents nabbed Kesey following a high-speed car chase on the Bayshore Freeway south of San Francisco less than thirty minutes after brazenly appearing on a taped TV show in which he jeered J. Edgar Hoover. A few days later, on Halloween night, out on bail, Kesey held an acid graduation at the Calliope Company warehouse in the Market Street skid-row area (272 Sixth Street, just south of the *San Francisco Chronicle* building). This decaying, largely derelict facility housed the offices and rehearsal space of the Mime Troup. Originally, it had been a horse-and-buggy stable, later a hotel, a pie factory, and then a flophouse. It had once been the training camp for boxing great Jack Dempsey in preparation for one of his title fights.

Kesey organized the acid graduation to demonstrate that he had forsaken acid. "Taking acid is not the thing that's happening anymore," Kesey declared (Perry 1984, 100). "LSD has reached the stature where Babbitt begins to take it. It used to be Hell's Angels and Bohemians, but now the son of the hardware store owner in Des Moines is taking it," he complained (Ortega, 1966, np).

Neal Cassady started the ceremony by constructing an altar with miscellaneous junk from the neighborhood lit by a spotlight. Kesey followed by telling the attendees, a smattering of Merry Pranksters, Hell's Angels, and devotees, about his experience in Mexico, where he raised his consciousness without the crutch of LSD. Cassady then passed out diplomas to Pranksters who had graduated from acid.

The Haight-Ashbury community had very mixed feelings about this "graduation." Many viewed it as either a self-serving stunt (and/or prank) or an act of betrayal on Kesey's part to placate the authorities in hopes of securing a lighter prison sentence: similar, say, to Nixon attorney Charles Colson discovering Jesus in prison after Watergate. There may be some basis for this accusation. Kesey at the time had been charged with three felonies:

Figure 23. Ken Kesey, 1967. Photo: Robert James Campbell. *Source*: Special Collections & University Archives, University of Oregon Libraries. https://oregondigital. org/catalog/oregondigital:df73g992f

the original San Mateo County bust for marijuana possession, the arrest for possession in San Francisco just prior to the Trips Festival, and a federal charge of flight to avoid prosecution. In big trouble and facing a likelihood of doing major time, Kesey later described this graduation event—and his precarious circumstances—in very telling fashion:

> I came back from Mexico in 1966, and the FBI caught me. All of the San Francisco revolutionaries were waiting to see what I would do. My metaphor is this: There were guys on either side of me, each with a gun at my head. There was someone in front of me with a microphone wanting me to say something so that he would be able to record the sound of the shots. Anybody who has been through that situation knows you have to cooperate to survive. But still, through this, you are sending a message to the people, saying, "If you are paying attention, you know I have to do this." (Whitmer 1987, 206)

On November 30, Kesey went on trial in San Francisco for his rooftop bust for possession of marijuana. The trial ended in a hung jury, 8 to 4 against Kesey. The state opted to retry. In April 1967, Kesey's retrial ended in another hung jury, this time 11 to1 against Kesey. In lieu of trying him a third time, the state let Kesey plead "nolo contendere" on the lesser charge of "knowingly being in a place where marijuana is present"—which let him escape with ninety days in jail.

A month later, Kesey lost his appeal of the original San Mateo County conviction for marijuana possession (the La Honda bust). Possibly in return for his role in the acid test "graduation," he got off with six months on a county work farm, a $1,500 fine, and three years of probation: a piddling penalty by any measure. Kesey was allowed to serve both sentences concurrently. He spent his work-farm time in the prison tailor shop and was released five months into his sentence. Another Haight LSD missionary fared much worse. On September 16, 1967, Timothy Leary was fined $30,000 and sentenced to thirty years in prison for getting caught with three ounces of grass while crossing the border from Mexico into the U.S., a massive sentence for a relatively minor violation involving a non-narcotic drug. The court system blatantly sent a message to the counterculture, by making an example of Leary.

In early January 1967, when the archetypical conservative Ronald Reagan assumed the governorship of California, the crackdown on the hippies and left-wing students began in earnest. On August 20, 1967, the San Francisco City Council outlawed rock music in the Panhandle. On the first day of October, police raided the Dead house at 710 Ashbury. Pigpen and Bob Weir, the two members of the band least into drugs (Pig Pen forswearing them completely), were arrested; none of the other band members were home at the time.

The Haight Mushrooms and Implodes

By late 1967, the Haight-Ashbury was an altogether different community than it had been in late 1965 and early-to-middle 1966 when, in the estimation of Jefferson Airplane drummer Spencer Dryden, Haight-Ashbury originally harbored maybe 800 "dyed-in-the-wool hippies and that's it." By the summer of 1967—the so-called Summer of Love—at least 75,000 would-be-hippies inundated Haight-Ashbury. The community deteriorated into a carnival freak show—all circus, no bread—in celebration, imitation, and perversion of itself. "There was an explosion," remarked Jay Thelin of the Psychedelic Shop, which set aside part of its store for a calm center for confused newcomers. "People came in from all over and our little information shop became sort of a clubhouse for dropouts" (Burton Wolfe 1968, 45).

Charles Perry conducted a sociological study in 1967–1968 called the Haight-Ashbury Research Project, which provided interesting insight into the neighborhood's rise and fall. He found that the flood of newcomers fell into three primary categories. The smallest group—about 15 percent—consisted of a psychotic fringe and religious obsessives, who were incapable of contributing creatively or positively to the community, many unable even to carry on an ordinary secular conversation. They tended to come from cold, authoritarian families, and a large number of them ended up addicted to heroin and/or speed, many remaining in the Haight after it degenerated into a dangerous ghetto in 1968 and beyond.

About 40 percent were idealists, who were attracted by the Haight mystique and saw the community as a city-on-the-hill model for a new age. They came from supportive families, and most of these kids never completely severed contact with their parents. Upon leaving the Haight, they tended to either return to college, enroll in college, or move to career-type employment.

The remaining 45 percent of the migrants hoped for the media-created exaggeration of a no-hassle, dropout lifestyle involving a minimum of work and a maximum of sex, rock shows, and being stoned. They tended to come from families that demanded achievement but discouraged independence. In this group, the use of psychedelics deteriorated into a mode of recreation providing escape from the drag of nuts-and-bolts workaday existence—a problem Aldous Huxley addressed in his 1954 treatise, *The Doors of Perception*.

Poster artist Victor Moscoso complained about the sudden transformation of the Haight-Ashbury community with the rapid population increase. "If you have a neighborhood, like Haight-Ashbury," he explained, "you can have flowers out on your lawn or your window box; you could know everybody in the neighborhood and have a kind of familial community feeling. If you've got a thousand people walking up and down the Haight-Ashbury neighborhood, you have a neighborhood. If you have a million people walking up and down the Haight-Ashbury, you have anarchy. It became a zoo," he sighed (Groth 2011).

Moscoso's sentiments encapsulated the contradictory forces that figured both in the rise and demise of the Haight-Ashbury counterculture. One of the most charming, liberating, and upbeat proclivities of the early Haight-Ashbury was its "be here now" mindset, its foregrounding of the still-in-the-making "now," and in-the-moment "being" among a relatively tight-knit group of comrades. The collective, expanded consciousness of a circle of friends dissipated and became a caricature as a tidal wave of after-the-fact, appropriately costumed, poseurs, flower children, and airhead wannabes naively dismissed everyday concerns as the uptight hang ups of the straight, game-playing world. But as presciently noted by Huxley ten years earlier, even in Haight-Ashbury you woke up to "utilitarian considerations" of paying the rent, obtaining food, and keeping the electricity on and the plumbing functional. One still needed to reconcile the "timeless bliss of seeing as one ought to see" with "the temporal duties of doing what one ought to do" (Huxley, 1954, 26).

The creators of contemporary documentaries and studies, who became interested in the scene (or were assigned to write about it), witnessed it during its decline, though at the height of public attention. Examples of this press mania included the Harry Reasoner documentary, *The Hippie Temptation* (1967) (a howler on the level of *Reefer Madness*), Joan Didion's essay "Slouching toward Bethlehem" (1968), the Nicholas von Hoffman study, *We Are the People Our Parents Warned Us Against* (1968), and the Lewis Yablonsky study, *The Hippie Trip* (1968). None of these treatments focused on the people who created the scene that evolved into Haight-Ashbury. These pieces largely featured, interviewed, and analyzed mind-blown teeny-boppers, and the scenes they inhabit are indeed pathetic and depressing. Documentaries like Reasoner's and "studies" of the Didion/von Hoffman sort featured figures who were ideal for middle-class loathing, tongue-clucking, and journalistic "color." They purported to explore and reveal the "real" Haight-Ashbury, but just reassured the middle class of its superiority and rightness. Nonetheless, they accurately registered what happened to the Haight-Ashbury scene and the counterculture at large when individual creativity, intelligence, and meaningful contribution gave way to a plug-in mindset of nonstop partying and dropping out as an excuse for unmitigated self-indulgence and excess.

By late 1967, the Haight-Ashbury neighborhood had become so overrun that it was difficult even to walk down the sidewalk on Haight. Traffic stood at such a standstill or crawl that it took an hour to drive the six blocks of Haight from Masonic to Stanyan (the main patch of the street was only fifteen blocks long). Several sight-seeing buses were now giving tours for tourists from Wichita, Des Moines, Cleveland, Baltimore, Miami, and so on to see "real" hippies. Even these crassly commercial ventures such as Gray Line's Hippie Hop canceled the service within two months due to the congestion. The vast majority of residents by now had lived there four months or less; most of the original inhabitants had begun to flee. The scene had long since stopped evolving, mired in stasis and completely devoid of the springtime vitality of even six months previous.

By the summer of 1967, an estimated half of the people on the street in Haight-Ashbury were speed freaks—shooting methedrine, going three-to-four-day stretches without sleep, toward the end of which they would "space," that is, lapse into unconsciousness even while being physically awake, subject to hallucinations tending toward the paranoid and violent. "Spacing" often caused erratic, unpredictable, dangerous behavior that broke out into violence at the slightest—many times entirely imagined—provocation. Heroin became increasingly common with an estimated one out of five Haight-Ashbury denizens now either using heroin regularly or having tried it as an antidote to depression after long-term speed use. Despite the Summer of Love press hyperbole, Haight-Ashbury street life became progressively dangerous. More Haight residents than not packed guns or knives. Even the Diggers issued a broadside that read: "An Armed Man Is a Free Man."

The number of flipped-out druggies showing up at the San Francisco General Hospital jumped from 150 in February 1967 to 750 in July. Many of these people—almost all of them newcomers from the recent mass influx—used drugs for entertainment, taking *anything* they could get to keep high all the time just to be high. Rape and robbery became commonplace on the street. Various longtime LSD dealers such as William "Superspade" Thomas turned up dead as outside heavies—including Mafia stooges—moved in to co-opt the immensely lucrative drug trade. The neighborhood was being appropriated by dysfunctional, Manson-type creeps and violent thugs, who increasingly were being celebrated and canonized as outlaw saints. (The *Freewheelin Frank* (1967) biography by Frank Reynolds, secretary of the Hells Angels, and coauthored by beat playwright Michael McClure, serves as a perfect example.)

As thousands of drugged-out, desperate teens streamed into the Haight, on June 7, 1967, Dr. David E. Smith started the Haight-Ashbury Free Clinic at the intersection of Haight and Clayton Streets, which would serve as a model for all subsequent free medical clinics. The first free nonsectarian medical clinic in the United States, on the first day of operation it served more than 250 patients, most of them young, drug-addled hippies. The next day, another 350 youths came to the clinic to see Smith, who felt that "health care is a right, not a privilege." "They're confused, searching young people whose immaturity has led them into the drug world," explained clinic manager Bob Conrich about their clientele (Pearlman 2017). Staffed with volunteer doctors, nurses, and students from the University of California, San Francisco, professionals such as pharmacist Darryl Inaba established a drug treatment program in a walk-in closet "painted up in all colors, with black-light posters, pillows on the floor and lava lamps" (Bai 2017). Smith noted, "I haven't seen a kid in the clinic who hasn't used drugs, and most are using them right now. Marijuana, methedrine, DMT, LSD and, now the new one, STP. We want to tackle the drug problem here now," he proclaimed. The clinic, open twenty-four hours a day, received funding from concerts held at the Fillmore and $25,000 from organizers of the Monterey International Pop Festival.

The Diggers, scrounging for food and warm beds for the Haight onslaught, quickly recognized the danger to the Haight. "The youth of America are on their way to the Haight-Ashbury, between 50,000 and 200,000 will cross our community and enter our lives," read one Digger handbill. "The Diggers need food to feed people. The Diggers need clothes to give people. When 200,000 folks from places like Lima and Ohio and Cleveland and Lompoc and Visalia and Amsterdam and London and Moscow and Lodz suddenly descend, as they will, on the Haight-Ashbury," the handbill concluded, "the scene will be burnt down" (Daloz 2017). In early April 1967, the Diggers and others banded together in the Council for the Summer of Love to anticipate the throngs of migrants

To punctuate the worsening condition in the Haight, in October 1967, the ever-creative, playful Diggers staged a "Death of Hippie" funeral

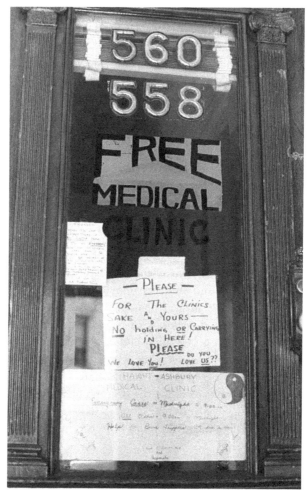

Figure 24. Free Medical Clinic in the Haight, 1967. *Source*: © The Regents of the University of California. Courtesy Special Collections, University Library, University of California, Santa Cruz. Ruth-Marion Baruch and Pirkle Jones Photographs. https://digitalcollections.library.ucsc.edu/concern/works/xd07gs73d?locale=en

procession at sunrise down Haight Street. About eighty hippies walked alongside a cardboard coffin containing a hippie effigy with one Digger carrying a sign that read "Hippie, Son of Media." They hoped to discourage the further influx of wannabes and to somehow resurrect the old scene that had gone sour. "We wanted to signal this was the end of it," asserted

Figure 25. Death of Hippie procession, Haight, 1967. *Source*: © The Regents of the University of California. Courtesy Special Collections, University Library, University of California, Santa Cruz. Ruth-Marion Baruch and Pirkle Jones photographs. https://digitalcollections.library.ucsc.edu/concern/works/mw22v5449

one Digger. "Stay where you are and bring the revolution to where you live and don't come here, because it's over and done with" (Daloz 2017). Their action was too late, though, and utterly futile. The Haight-Ashbury had become a shoddy imitation of itself.

The Exodus

Confronted by a lack of housing, sanitation, and basic services, many hippies started to return slowly to their homes across the country. By the end of 1967, with the Summer of Love over, the short-term hippies exited Haight-Ashbury en masse back to wherever they came. The streets had the seedy, deserted, exhausted air of a beach town the week after the Fourth of July. Those staying behind tended to be heavily into speed and heroin. There was a palpable sense of brooding and imminent menace. Haight-Ashbury became a heroin-infested slum, where you could literally get knifed at high noon for a bag of groceries. It was a seriously dangerous place to be after dark. For example, "Blind Jerry" Sealund ran a health food store on Page Street until 1969, when he closed it after being robbed twelve times in eleven months.

Given the dark, brooding atmosphere, many of the original Haight merchants closed shop. On October 6, 1967, the Psychedelic Shop ceased operations. The Thelin brothers left a sign in the window that read: "Nebraska needs you more than the Haight." In 1968, another mainstay merchant abandoned the Haight when she closed Mnasidika (1510 Haight), a clothing boutique owned and run by one-time Delta Airlines stewardess and sexual switch-hitter Peggy Caserta, remembered most for her affairs with Haight-Ashbury luminaries. Caserta authored the irreproachably trashy memoir *Going Down with Janis,* which begins with the immortal line: "I was stark naked, stoned out of my mind on heroin and the girl lying between my legs giving me head was Janis Joplin." Mnasidika for a while gave members of the Grateful Dead fancy threads to wear on loan, which Caserta would then sell at a premium price by advertising that the duds had been worn by members of the Dead.

About the same time, health authorities boarded up the Blue Unicorn, one of the first "hip" spots to come to Haight-Ashbury, where you could find coffee, food, books, music, art, chessboards, sewing kits, and a big saggy sofa (but no jukebox). Owner Bob Stubbs eventually moved to Hawaii to start an import business and to farm. By 1969, the Haight had thirty-six vacant storefronts, and the remaining eighteen had protective metal grates over the windows.

Other Haight linchpins rode into the sunset. In March 1968, the *Oracle* issued its final issue (number 12). The cover depicted a corpse-like boy lying atop Mount Tamalpais. Also in March, the entire staff of KMPX walked off the job to protest new management restrictions about which records could be played. Most of the strikers began work two months later for a new station, KSAN. Notably, on February 3, 1968, Neal Cassady was found dead on railroad tracks outside San Miguel de Allende, Mexico. He died from ingesting a lethal combination of alcohol and barbiturates four days short of his forty-fourth birthday.

The main acid rock venues shuttered their doors. In September 1968, the Board of Permit Appeals closed the Avalon due to complaints from the neighbors about noise. The Family Dog relocated to Denver, where they opened a branch at a locale a mere three to four blocks from my high school! Chet Helms claimed he chose Denver because it was "one of the most sophisticated towns we visited." (Tim Scully, recall, operated an acid lab in Denver for a while.) Like a nerdy goddamn fool, I never set foot in it. As the child of militantly evangelic born-again parents, at the time I didn't even like the Beatles: I hadn't so much as even listened to *Magical Mystery Tour* or *Sgt. Pepper's*! In consequence, I missed out on opportunities to hear live performances by Hendrix, the Doors, Canned Heat, the Other Half, and many others.

The Straight Theater met the same fate as the Avalon in the Haight. On September 11, 1968, Satanist film maker Kenneth Anger rented the Straight Theater to stage an "Invocation of My Demon Brother," a birthday celebration of English Satanist Aleister Crowley. Anger showed parts of an in-progress work, *Lucifer Rising,* starring Digger Bobby Beausoleil (then known as "Bummer Bob") in weight-lifter poses. In one of the less endearing connections of the era, Beausoleil would go on to become one of the primary cogs in the Manson Family. Manson lived in Haight-Ashbury for a while, on the roof of the Straight Theater, where he recruited hippie chicks for his "family," including Sandy Good, one of the original Deadheads, a regular at the acid tests and participant in the Trips Festival. A few months after Anger's event, the Straight Theater closed down.

In early 1968, a cooperative of San Francisco rock bands pooled their resources to stage shows at the Carousel Ballroom. In a truly cooperative spirit of the times, the Grateful Dead, the Jefferson Airplane, Big Brother, and Quicksilver showcased acid rock bands to compete with the Fillmore. As a sign of the times, the venture folded in less than six months, and the entrepreneurial Bill Graham snapped up the site for his Fillmore West. The final event on May 1, 1967, at the Carousel, a Free City "convention" billed as an "anarchist event," starkly exemplified what the Haight-Ashbury scene had degenerated into by then: utterly juvenile, loathsome, and airhead behavior was passed off as far-out revelry, hip "unrestraint," and hilarious and overtly carnal carryings-on.

The Fillmore survived the hippie implosion but only because Graham practiced hard-nosed, no-nonsense business tactics. When 500 or so workers in the various light shows went on strike for higher wages, Graham simply discontinued light shows, which became a thing of the past, the bottom line displacing idealism, invention, and creativity.

Hippie Hill, a gently-sloping meadow about 1,000 feet in length, just off Kezar Drive in Golden Gate Park, bordered on either side by eucalyptus and oak trees, started to receive unwanted attention from the police. It had become a favored gathering spot for hippies to (as Whitman put it) loaf and invite their souls. Though within sight from the top of a police station, the police at first stayed away, allowing those gathered to smoke grass without hounding them.

Near Hippie Hill, many listened to Ashley Brilliant, an ex-college professor (a Ph.D. in history from Berkeley) with a beard and frowzy head of hair, who became a prototypical hippie, famous for communicating with a bullhorn and for writing poem-epigrams he called "Pot Shots"—later syndicated worldwide with cartoon illustrations. He stood on a wire milk-bottle box with a shopping cart bearing an amplifier and loudspeaker, selling his songbook and a record of himself performing. He was notorious for his corny jokes: question—"What happened to the hippie who crossed IBM with LSD?" answer—"He went on a business trip." He was also known for his vapid songs sung to the Lone Ranger theme: "It's a nark, it's a nark, it's a nasty nark/ if you've got any pot, better keep it dark / to and fro let him go up the wrong tree bark/ it's a nark, it's a nark, it's a nasty nark." And probably known most of all for his silly epigrams: "Congratulate me, I don't love you anymore"; "A man could grow old waiting for his life to end"; "Why don't you take this life home for a few days and see how you like it?"; "How can I possibly respect anyone who respects me?" By 1968, Ashley Brilliant and his fellow hippies in and near the park drew constant police attention.

Even the hippies, who fled from Haight to more bucolic surroundings, faced difficulties. In 1962, Lou Gottlieb—a former member of the commercial folk groups the Gateway Singers and the Limeliters with a doctorate in musicology—purchased Morningstar Ranch as a real estate investment. Morningstar was located on thirty-one acres atop a hill situated seventy miles north of San Francisco in the Russian River country of Sonoma County near the town of Sebastopol. After attending the Trips Festival as a reporter for the *San Francisco Chronicle*, Gottlieb became psychedelicized and envisioned the ranch as an "alternate society for those who can't make it in the straight society and don't want to. It's a community being rather than doing" (Gustatis 1969, 137–138). It opened its gates for free access and became loosely associated with the Diggers, who started a large vegetable garden on it to grow produce for their Free Store. As happened over and over in the era, the scene at Morningstar—early on something truly special—was ruined by a story about the commune that appeared in the July 7, 1967, issue of *Time* magazine, causing it to be overrun by teenage dropouts who wanted to get high and avoid work. Similar to Haight-Ashbury, Morningstar became a hepatitis-ridden, garbage-strewn stink hole with an undercurrent of very real danger. Preschool kids ran around unsupervised, filth-caked, crying, and unfed while mom disappeared in the woods for a few days of tripping and sex. Little kids were given marijuana and acid. Like the Haight, Morningstar turned into a drug-ridden, depraved scene—violence, muggings, beatings, rape, and stealing were commonplace—especially after a group of violent African Americans from the Fillmore district of Frisco moved in and essentially took over with Gottlieb declining, on "philosophical" grounds, to intervene. On July 4, 1968, the Health Department, headed by the ironically named Ellis D. Sox, ordered Gottlieb to cease operation of Morningstar Ranch as an organized camp. Morningstar's fate followed a similar trajectory to Haight-Ashbury's: an initially idyllic scene was taken over, co-opted, and squeezed out by bikers, dealers, derelicts, creeps, and thugs.

Many of the original, creative Haight residents moved to the country. Upon leaving the Haight, they migrated to communes or quasi-communes in the countryside, but near enough to urban centers to allow the residents to pursue lives of marginal employment organized around crafts, families, and friends. This group continued the hippie lifestyle and maintained that frame of reference even after the Haight collapsed. "The Haight Street is no longer fun," groused Tsvi Strauch, the owner of In Gear, an original hippie shop in the Haight. "Many of us are getting away from it because of all the plastic hippies and tourists that are fouling up the whole scene . . . I think more and more the real hippie scene will move into the country, where communes will be formed" (Burton Wolfe 1968, 191).

Migrants included many of the heyday Haight luminaries, many of whom settled in areas to the north such as Marin, Sonoma, Mendocino, and Humboldt counties. Artist Ramon Sender, health-food store owner "Blind Jerry" Sealund, light-show master Ben Van Meter, Open Theater co-founders Ben and Rain Jacopetti, Peter Krug, the owner of the Haight store Wild Colors, and Communication Company founder Chester Anderson permanently settled within several miles of each other in the vicinity of Sonoma County's Russian River, living there for years in a quiet, deliberately low-key, bohemian camaraderie. Digger Peter Coyote went to Olema to ranch on a commune, and Trips Festival originator Stewart Brand bolted to the country. A number of Pranksters followed Wavy Gravy to a mountaintop outside L.A. called the Hog Farm. Still bitter over how media hype destroyed the Haight, they aggressively, deliberately—even rudely—discouraged newcomers and thwarted any sort of publicity.

More than eighty Diggers moved north en mass. They settled on the Black Bear Ranch in Siskiyou County in an old ghost town, which had been a gold-mining haven during the 1860s. Earning profits from a major LSD deal and several highly visible donors, they paid $22,500 for the ranch and vowed to provide "free land for free people." The group abolished private property and kept contact with the Hells Angels and the Black Panthers. To sustain themselves, the Diggers fought forest fires in the area, raised their own food, and planted trees for the government. In several years, the Haight-Ashbury became a fond but fading memory after their new beginning.

Even the Grateful Dead moved from their 710 Ashbury location to Camp Lagunitas in Marin County. "Haight-Ashbury was getting too crowded and the Gray Line tour buses were going past our house as part of their tour," complained Rock Scully (Troy 1991, 120). Peter Coyote did not consider the mass movement from the Haight a failure. "I don't think it ended," he reasoned. "I think it was just part of like an ongoing quest" (Graham 1992, 197).

11

The Psychedelic Legacy

The goal towards which the pleasure-principle impels us—of becoming happy—is not attainable; yet we may not—nay, cannot—give up the effort to come nearer to realization of it by some means or other.

—Sigmund Freud, *Civilization and Its Discontents* (1930)

In life all finding is not the thing we sought, but something else.

—Ralph Waldo Emerson, *Journal* (April 1863)

The answer is never the answer. What's really interesting is the mystery. If you seek the mystery instead of the answer, you'll always be seeking. I've never seen anybody really find the answer—they think they have, so they stop thinking. But the job is to seek mystery, evoke mystery, plant a garden in which strange plants grow and mysteries bloom. The need for mystery is greater than the need for an answer.

—Ken Kesey, "The Art of Fiction," interview by
Robert Faggen, *Paris Review*, Spring 1994

We shall not cease from exploration
And the end of all our exploring
Will be to arrive where we started
And know the place for the first time.

—T. S. Eliot, "Little Gidding" (1942)

I keep secret in myself an Egypt that does not exist.
Is that good or bad? I don't know.

—Rumi, thirteenth-century Persian poet,
"An Egypt That Does Not Exist"

All that was most vital and extraordinary about what transpired in Haight-Ashbury began stirring in 1964, coalesced and gained sudden momentum during the fall of 1965, and flashed like a mirror catching the sun throughout 1966, with a final feedback soar at the January 1967 Human Be-In. During this mere year-and-a-half stretch, Haight-Ashbury and environs was possibly the most interesting place on the planet for anyone pursuing a certain kind of unconventional intelligence and finely honed sense of play, a genuine desire to delve and explore, and a willingness to create a new world in which to live more fully. What happened there in that year and a half left a permanent stamp on the twentieth century that remains readily apparent.

One way or another, Haight-Ashbury and all its ramifications intimately affected anyone coming of age in the '60s and those born after the fact—even the present-day conservatives most loudly loathing everything it represents. The Haight-Ashbury mindset, approach to life, and mode of being spilled over and surfaced in not only every city and region of the U.S., but throughout Europe and Third World locales like Morocco, Tangiers, Nepal, and India.

Every time you see a tie-dye t-shirt, a Mouse/Kelly rock poster, or hear Janis Joplin singing "Ball and Chain," you bear witness to a legacy from that specific neighborhood nearly sixty years ago. Today, the shadow of the Haight appears with Silicon Valley computer whizzes, who "micro-dose" on LSD to enhance their creativity and to break on through to the other side. Echoes from the Haight emerge when doctors use psychedelics to treat victims with posttraumatic stress syndrome to free them from their fears and horrors. The focus on organic farming, health food, recycling systems, and a green future date to hippies such as Steward Brand, who foresaw the climate change crisis of today. Current jam bands such as Widespread Panic and Leftover Salmon pay tribute to the Grateful Dead for their approach to music and life.

In a heady time during a tumultuous decade, youth stretched, challenged, shattered, and discarded fundamental social paradigms and value assumptions. In 1970, the United States seemed to be a profoundly different place than it was in 1960. It would have been impossible to foresee

Haight-Ashbury in 1959. Love it or hate it, the events catalyzed by that neighborhood between1965 and 1967 make it a defining metaphor for the '60s. Those who long for the sensibility that characterized the pre-'60s Eisenhower America evoke Haight-Ashbury and the counterculture it helped create with loathing caricature. Those who prefer post-'60s America evoke Haight-Ashbury as a kind of arcadia and recall it with affection and nostalgia. No other decade stirs such passionate debate and difference of interpretation.

To have come of age in that decade and to have been caught up in the day-to-day events of its unfolding put one's understanding of the world to a constant and daily challenge. The times were, indeed, a-changin'. Radically new standards of awareness evolved, all former givens questioned and certainties suddenly examined. Was there ever a more interesting and stimulating time to be a college student? Some of us who lived through that era recall those days in the manner of Wordsworth in "The Prelude," when he reminisced about his flaming youth, when the French Revolution turned the old order, and all its underlying assumptions, inside out:

> Bliss was it in that dawn to
> be alive, But to be young
> was very Heaven!

What is one recollecting in looking back on such a "dawn?" What is being referred to by evoking it? Everyone from the diehard Deadhead with a graying ponytail to the chest-out, buttocks-clenched, hippie-loathing, born-again railing against the One World conspiracy gives a different answer to that question. My answer—and I suspect that many share it—is that the thoughts of anyone evoking the '60s are trained less on specific events or personages than on a prevailing "attitude towards the Cosmos" as poet T. E. Hulme put it. The generative impetus of this attitude produced a counterculture that emphasized play—while engaged in moment-to-moment creation of a still-in-the-making new world. This sense of play underlies Shakespeare's "The play's the thing," or Louis Armstrong's "You have to love to play," with Haight-Ashbury circa 1965–1967 being the foremost manifestation of that perception. The counterculture trappings—the Avalon, the Fillmore, long hair, and events like the Tribute to Dr. Strange, the Trips Festival, the acid tests, the Human Be-In, and Monterey Pop—reflect and manifest this sensibility, which created and gave *rise to* the events in this book.

William James's essay, "On a Certain Blindness in Human Beings" (in James 1913), wonderfully articulates my sense of "those days"—what it was like to be alive in "that dawn," the feelings aroused in us by it—and why it still matters to me sixty years later. When traveling through the mountains of North Carolina, James passed muddy clearing after muddy clearing denuded of trees. To his eye, the log cabins, corn rows, and rail fences presented a dreary, depressing spectacle of destitution, havoc, and "unmitigated squalor": a "hideous . . . sort of ulcer, without a single element of artificial grace to make up for the loss of nature's beauty."

After speaking with his driver, James realized that he "had been losing the whole inward significance of the situation." As an outsider looking in, the scene harbored an entirely different significance for him than it did for the people living in it. Where he saw ugliness, the residents saw the embodiment of heroism, future promise, and "personal victory": "The chips, the girdled trees, and the vile split rails spoke of honest sweat, persistent toil and final reward. The cabin was a warrant of safety for self and wife and babes. In short, the clearing, which to me was a mere ugly picture on the retina, was to them a symbol redolent with moral memories and sang a very paean of duty, struggle, and success" (James 1913, 631).

To further illustrate *what* one sees as a function of *how* one looks, James cites a letter in which Walt Whitman relates the enormous pleasure he takes from riding a stage down a three-mile length of 23rd Street in Manhattan on a "bright and cool" October afternoon:

> You see everything as you pass, a sort of living, endless panorama of shops and splendid buildings, and great windows; on the broad sidewalks crowds of women richly dressed continually passing, altogether different, superior in style and looks from any to be seen anywhere else—in fact, a perfect stream of people—men too dressed in high style, and plenty of foreigners—and then in the streets the thick crowd of carriages, stages, carts, hotel and private coaches, and in fact all sorts of vehicles and many first class teams, mile after mile. (James 1913, 639–640)

James uses Whitman's letter as a way to demonstrate the variability of perception. "Truly a futile way of passing the time, some of you may say, and not altogether credible to a grown-up man. And yet, from the deepest point of view, who knows the more of truth and who knows the less,—Whitman on his omnibus-top, full of the inner joy with which the spectacle inspires him, or you, full of the disdain which the futility of his occupation excites?" (640)

This relativity poses a question central to Haight-Ashbury, the '60s, and how to live our lives. If the product of one perceptual style apprehending a scene is "inner joy," and the product of another looking at the exact same scene is "disdain," which perceptual mode constitutes "the deepest point of view" and encompasses "more of the truth?" How a person answers that question will determine his or her attitude toward the '60s counterculture. To quote William Blake: "The eye altering alters all."

In "The Lantern Bearers," Robert Louis Stevenson captures the same variability of seeing:

> Toward the end of September, when school time was drawing near, and the nights were already black, we would begin to sally from our respective villas, each equipped with a tin bull's-eye lantern. . . . We wore them buckled to the waist upon a cricket belt, and over them, such was the rigor of the game, a buttoned top-coat. They smelled noisomely of blistered tin. They never burned aright, though they would always burn our fingers. Their use was naught, the pleasure of them merely fanciful, and yet a boy with a bull's-eye under his top-coat asked for nothing more . . .
>
> The essence of this bliss was to walk by yourself in the black of the night, the slide shut, the top-coat buttoned, not a ray escaping, whether to conduct your footsteps, or to make your glory public,—a mere pillar of darkness in the dark; and all the while, deep down in the privacy of your fool heart, to know you had a bull's-eye at your belt, and exult and sing over the knowledge. (James 1913, 632–633)

The implied question crucial to and underlying anyone's conception of the '60s remains: Which perceptual style, which mode of seeing, produces the deepest point of view? Which perceiver knows more? Which perceptual style brings one closer to the truth: the yea-saying view of the boys filled with inner joy provoked by ill-smelling lanterns, or the dismissive view of the jaded grown-up man disdaining the squalor and silliness? For some of us sixty years later, the '60s at their peak best remains a "secret" that we continue to carry beneath our topcoats as "our particular brand of luminary." Stevenson, James, and Whitman contend that "to miss the joy is to miss the all." To the lantern bearer, "the joy" is, in the end, "the all." But those who disdain "the secret of the lanterns" see the entire counterculture as a spectacle of unmitigated squalor, silliness, and ineffectual loafing.

This dichotomy does not answer the question of how best to live one's life. Aldous Huxley observed in *The Doors of Perception* that no matter how privy we are to "the secret of the lanterns"—"the glory and wonder of pure existence," "the manifest glory of things"—and no matter how much we see as "one ought to see," we have to live in "the world of . . . utilitarian considerations" and wrestle with "the dirty Devices of the world." "The outer world," as Huxley noted, "is what we wake up to every morning of our lives," and in which "we must try to make our living." To keep things from falling apart à la Kesey at La Honda, Leary at Millbrook, or the counterculture at Haight-Ashbury, it is essential to "reconcile [the] timeless bliss of seeing as one ought to see with the temporal duties of doing what one ought to do." To blow off the "outer world," to avoid "work and monotony," to take acid fourteen days in a row ensures a miserable life (Huxley, 1954, 26).

To address life in a manner "credible to a grown-up man" (or woman), one must learn *response-ability:* in the manner, say, of jazz saxophonist Charlie Parker launching into an improvisatory flight at high midnight in Minton's Playhouse in Harlem, but exquisitely aware of, responsible to, and in imaginative response to the contributions of the other musicians, the tempo, the key, the way "things are headed." Response-ability entails a generative, meaning-making interplay between the yahoo, sky's-the-limit vision of youth and the what-you-get imperatives of adult life.

No matter what triumphs and failures, joys and heartbreaks, solidarities and breakups, and acts of courage and failures of nerve that life has delivered and sometimes inflicted on us during the past sixty years, some of us still secretly harbor the glimmer of a bull's-eye lantern beneath our topcoats. The lantern, however, shines in two directions at once. On the one hand, it affords a secret, warming, redemptive nostalgia for that brief flash in the mirror, when everything opened up, anything seemed possible, and we viewed the world, as Huxley put it, like Adam on the morning of creation. On the other hand, it produces a haunting sense of having lost what might have been.

Poster artist Victor Moscoso remarked about this conflicting interplay between that heady, brief, improbable flash in the sun, when new worlds were being made, with that sense of impermanence:

There was a period of time in 1965 and 1966 when I thought the millennium had come. A benevolent virus had descended and happened to hit San Francisco and was spreading out. Pretty soon everybody was going to live by the golden rule and treat everybody the way they wanted to be treated. And the lion shall lay down with the lamb, etc. I really thought the millennium had come, and for about six months in San Francisco, it had. (Henke 1997, 127)

Some of us lucky enough to have experienced the heady exuberance Moscoso described—whether in Haight-Ashbury or Cleveland, Boulder or Kansas City, Madison or Miami, or . . . wherever—look back on the '60s in our advancing age (in the manner, perhaps, of Hofmann in the wake of his accidental dosing) and wonder "What happened?" "What *was* that?" A psychotic episode? A transformative epiphany? A mass delusion? A breakthrough to "the other side?" A manifestation of everything gone wrong with our culture? A new city on the hill? Was that "millennium" merely another failed myth, the same fate as *all* myths?—the Holy Grail? The Second Coming? Was Haight-Ashbury in particular and the counterculture in general merely another passing fad like raccoon coats, hula hoops, Pez dispensers, or nose rings? Did Haight-Ashbury have any significance beyond its particular time and place?·

Though the promise of the millennium of raised consciousness never materialized, most paradigm shifts constantly evolve and take shape over time. Christianity, Marxism, Hinduism, Buddhism, and Freudianism continue to flourish and mutate into new and exciting forms. The ethos of the Haight-Ashbury—the notion of a sea of possibilities and alternative ways to approach and understand the world—shape, animate, and drive our lives, choices, perspectives, and consciousness and make us most vitally alive and creatively interesting. The ongoing way of thinking started in the Haight, though not overtly transparent to everyone in day-to-day transactions, allows us to experience the joy of life.

What *did* happen—what constituted the '60s and/or Haight-Ashbury—was less a set of events or factual incidents than a sensibility, a way of seeing, and a mode of consciousness that allowed us to see beyond the workaday world to perceive a "climate of possibilities" as Chet Helms recollected (Troy 1991, 104). This awareness made us alive to "the mysteries" and gave us access—like Whitman atop his omnibus and Stevenson's pals harboring bull's-eye lanterns—to the bliss. Those of us who opted to pass through the "doors of perception" to glimpse, in Huxley's words "what Adam had seen on the morning of his creation—the miracle, moment by moment, of naked existence" were forever changed. Some of us continue to nurture a way of seeing and knowing unavailable to those, who tenaciously and stridently cling only to factual reality. That unique perspective more than a half-century later still produces a secret delight, pleasure, and joy.

Appendix

As the twentieth century gave way to the twenty-first, many of the figures who played significant roles in the Haight-Ashbury story are dead: Ginsberg, Joplin, Burroughs, Grogan, Boise, Leary, Cassady, Garcia, Pigpen, Cipollina, Helms, and Graham. Those still living have drifted into senior citizendom—hip or otherwise.

This list of brief biographies aids readers by keeping track of the many people, organizations, and sites mentioned throughout the text. Not a comprehensive list of every person or place mentioned, it serves as a guide for those who appear throughout the story.

Key Players

Albin, Peter (b. 1944) and Rod (1940–1984). The brothers founded the Boar's Head, a folk coffeehouse, in 1961. Peter later became the bass player for Big Brother and the Holding Company; Rod managed 1090 Page Street which housed many arty SFSU students.

Alpert, Richard (1931–2019). Assistant professor of sociology at Harvard, where he met Timothy Leary and became his partner in drug experimentation. Later a well-known lifestyle guru who went by the name Ram Dass.

Balin, Marty (1942–2018). Vocalist and founder of Jefferson Airplane and manager of the Matrix club.

Barron, Frank (1922–2002). Psychologist and graduate-school classmate of Timothy Leary, who introduced Leary to the use of hallucinogenic mushrooms. He pioneered the psychology of creativity and the study of human personality.

Brand, Stewart (b. 1938). Proto-Prankster, major player in the Trips Festival, producer of the show "America Needs Indians," and later the publisher of the *Whole Earth Catalog*.

Brierly, Justin (1905–1985). Teacher at Denver's East High School, who mentored future Beat icon Neal Cassady and friend of the Beats Hal Chase.

Cassady, Neal (1926–1968). Legendary Beat character, who served as the model for Dean Moriarty in Jack Kerouac's *On the Road* and Cody Pomeray in other Kerouac novels. He drove the bus for Ken Kesey's Merry Pranksters and participated in many of Kesey's acid tests. He died alone along railroad tracks in Mexico.

Chase, Hal (1923–2006). Mentored by Justin Brierly, Chase attended Columbia, where he met future Beat Allen Ginsberg and shared an apartment with Jack Kerouac.

Cooke, John Starr (Charlie Brown; 1920–1976). Co-originator of the 1967 Human Be-In/Gathering of the Tribes with Michael Bowen. He had previously lived in Mexico, where he led the Psychedelic Rangers.

Donahue, Tom "Big Daddy" (1928–1975). Radio DJ and owner of Mother's, the first rock club in San Francisco. He co-owned Autumn Records, which recorded the Charlatans among other local bands. In 1967, he became the program director for KMPX.

Duncan, Gary (1946–2019). Guitarist for Quicksilver Messenger Service. After Quicksilver dissolved in 1975, he worked as a longshoreman.

Garcia, Jerry (1942–1995). Originally a bluegrass banjo player, Garcia was the founder and guiding force behind the Grateful Dead. The band participated in many of Kesey's acid tests and lived together in a house at 710 Ashbury Street (the Dead House) in the Haight during the '60s.

Ginsberg, Allen (1926–1997). Noted American Beat poet who was an inspiration to and a participant in many key events on the Haight-Ashbury scene.

Gleason, Ralph (1917–1975) Writer and journalist, who during the '60s chronicled the San Francisco music scene. Cofounded *Rolling Stone.*

Graham, Bill (1939–1991). Concert promoter and manager of the Fillmore as well as coproducer of many seminal events during the Haight-Ashbury heyday, including benefits for the Mime Troupe. Very interested in acting and theater, he considered his early Fillmore concerts as living theater.

Ham, Bill (b. 1932). Visual artist who was one of the pioneer experimenters and producers of light shows. In 1959, he moved to San Francisco and, five years later, installed the first psychedelic light show at the Red Dog Saloon. He staged light shows for many concerts at the Avalon and Fillmore ballrooms and, in January 1968, opened the Light Sound Dimension Theater (LSD). In 1970, he left for Europe and, three years later, returned to San Francisco, where he still works.

Helms, Chet (1942–2005). Helms brought Janis Joplin to San Francisco and eventually introduced her to the musicians who became Big Brother and the Holding Company. He competed with Bill Graham as a producer of concerts at the Avalon Ballroom.

Hitchcock, Peggy (1901–1998), Tommy (1910–?), and Billy (1910–1989). Heirs to both the Mellon and the Hitchcock fortunes. The family owned a sixty-four-room mansion in Dutchess County, New York, in the town of Millbrook, that became a center for LSD experimentation under Timothy Leary.

Hofmann, Dr. Albert (1906–2008). Swiss chemist who first synthesized LSD at Sandoz Pharmaceuticals.

Hubbard, Captain Al (1901–1982). Early LSD advocate who introduced Aldous Huxley to the drug, among many others. He had deep ties within the government and industry that enabled him to become a strong advocate for the drug.

Hunter, George (b. 1942). The main impetus behind the formation of the Charlatans and early psychedelic graphic designer.

Huxley, Aldous (1894–1962). British author who was among the first to write about his experiences using LSD in the groundbreaking work, *The Doors of Perception* (1954).

Kesey, Ken (1935–2001). American novelist best-known for *One Flew over the Cuckoo's Nest* and *Sometimes a Great Notion*, and leader of the Merry Pranksters and numerous acid tests.

Just before he began serving his six-month jail sentence, Ken Kesey moved the bus, his wife, and the kids to his old stomping grounds of Springfield, Oregon. After doing his time, Kesey and family lived in a shed on his brother's farm, remaining there doing dairy farming until his death in 2001, with Mountain Girl and Babbs living close by. The Kesey family still runs Key-Z Productions out of Eugene, Oregon, selling Prankster-related videos, books, posters, music, paraphernalia, doodads, and memorabilia. The bus rusted and rotted on farm property but has recently been refurbished.

In August of 1982, while still a graduate student and teaching assistant at Rutgers, working on a dissertation about Kerouac, I attended a week-long Kerouac conference in Boulder, Colorado, that commemorated the twenty-fifth anniversary of the publication of *On the Road*. The conference was co-hosted by Naropa University in Boulder and the University of Colorado (my undergraduate alma mater). Walking through Boulder to the campus one afternoon to attend a session, I was just about to step onto the street to cross an intersection, when this dilapidated, top-down convertible pulled up to the stop sign in front of me. There, three or four feet away, was none other than a forty-seven-year-old Ken Kesey sitting in the passenger seat, his thirty-something female companion at the wheel. Both wore sunglasses with white frames and red valentine-shaped lenses, both—as evidenced by their luxuriously sprawled posture, arms-draped-across-seat and head-held-slightly-back—envisioned themselves as culture stars as they tooled through Boulder in their check-us-out movie-of-the-moment. They gave a little "ta-ta, tennis-anyone" wave as they lurched off (not waiting for me to cross) in a rattle-trap cloud of dust.

Laughlin, Chandler (1937–2012). Bartender at and cofounder of the Red Dog Saloon who hired the Charlatans as its house band.

Leary, Timothy (1920–1996). Leading proselytizer for LSD who taught psychology at Harvard and then became a major figure in the promotion of mind-altering drugs.

Throughout the '80s and '90s, he tirelessly tried to evoke the old showbiz magic, this time by way of a New Age combination of cybernetics and outer space snake oil. He joined up for a while with G. Gordon Liddy in the early '80s—the same ultra-ambitious Dutchess County district attorney who led the Millbrook raid and bust of Leary and was later a Nixon administration foot soldier and Watergate operative—to do a college tour, in which the two debated the '60s. I attended one of those "debates" in the New York University student union in Greenwich Village and have to say it was showbiz schlock at its most flagrantly opportunist, nausea-inducing, you're-beautiful-baby, have-your-people-get-in-touch-with-my-people, let's-do-lunch worst.

Both men were pathetic—Liddy in a boorish, sneering, loud-mouthed, histrionically jackbooted heil-Hitler manner, Leary in a Beverly Hills-ish, mush-minded, eighteen-hole-tanned, beautiful-people, rock-star-wannabe style. Liddy described—with unabashed macho pride and in sneering contempt of the easily baited, liberal college kids in attendance—an occasion when, to test his will and inner fortitude, he captured, killed, cooked, and ate a rat. Both Leary and Liddy performed their roles in a pathetically transparent, rile-the-crowd, boost-the-ratings, con-man fashion. Their act was obviously well-rehearsed, scripted, collaborative, and oft-performed.

No breakthroughs in consciousness occurred that night. I came prepared for a memorable evening—if nothing else, an experience with which to regale my graduate-school buddies over beers. But the occasion did little more than reaffirm and validate the showbiz-hype, rock-star, groupie/guru, Beverly Hills-esque impression of Leary I had acquired from reading his books. To fully appreciate Leary—and there *are* things to appreciate—it's necessary to turn one's bullshit censors and wretch reflex to low and practice Samuel Johnson's "willing suspension of disbelief." Leary died of prostate cancer in 1996.

Melvin, Milan (1942–2001). Dope dealer turned ad salesman for alternative radio station KMPX.

Miller, Stanley (Stanley Mouse; b. 1940). Psychedelic graphic designer who partnered with Alton Kelly in the creation of many classic rock posters.

Osmond, Humphrey (1917–2004). Psychiatrist and early researcher on mescaline and other psychedelics who introduced Aldous Huxley to the drug.

Savio, Mario (1942–1996). Leader of the Free Speech Movement at Berkeley.

Stanley, Augustus Owsley III (1935–2011). Acid guru and major manufacturer and distributor of LSD for the Haight community.

Thelin, Ron (1939–1996) and Jay. Brothers who co-owned the Psychedelic Shop and helped fund the *Oracle* magazine. Jay eventually started a company that sold wood-burning heaters.

Thompson, Hunter (1937–2005). "Gonzo" journalist and participant in Ken Kesey's acid tests.

Wasson, Gordon (1898–1986) and Valentina (1901–1958). Early advocates for the use of psychedelic mushrooms as part of a spiritual quest; Gordon wrote an article for *Life* magazine in 1957 that introduced many to the use of mushrooms.

Watts, Alan (1915–1973). Author of *The Joyous Cosmology* (1962) and early promoter of Zen Buddhism and psychedelic drugs.

Wenner, Jann (b. 1946). Berkeley student-journalist who went on to cofound *Rolling Stone* magazine.

Wilson, Wes (1937–2020). Pioneer of the psychedelic rock poster.

Sites

Avalon Ballroom. One of the major performance spaces for area rock bands during the '60s managed by Chet Helms.

City Lights Bookstore. Publisher, bookseller, and center for Beat writers founded by poet Lawrence Ferlinghetti.

Dead House (710 Ashbury Street). Home of the Grateful Dead and various hangers-on and associates during the height of the Haight-Ashbury period.

Fillmore Auditorium. Major home for rock concerts under the direction of promoter Bill Graham.

La Honda. A log cabin on six rural acres in the redwood hills that Ken Kesey purchased to be a center for his drug experimentation and his acid tests.

Matrix, The. San Francisco's second rock night club, located at the foot of Fillmore in the Marina district, where Jefferson Airplane made its debut performance.

Millbrook. Sixty-four-room mansion in Dutchess County, New York, owned by the Hitchcock family that became a center for Timothy Leary's drug and sexual experimentation from 1963 to 1968.

Open Theater. Performance space located on Berkeley's College Avenue that featured experimental multimedia productions.

Perry Lane. The bohemian neighborhood at Stanford where Ken Kesey settled in 1958; his home attracted the neighborhood arts crowd, when he began experimenting with LSD.

Psychedelic Shop. The first Haight-Ashbury head shop, opened by brothers Ron and Jay Thelin.

Red Dog Saloon (Virginia City, Nevada). Hippie hangout that flourished during the summer of 1965, founded by Don Works; it was the first significant center of psychedelic experimentation outside of Leary or Kesey's communities.

San Francisco State University (SFSU). Breeding grounds for the Haight-Ashbury community, the university was an early center for the arts counterculture; many future hippie artists, activists, and leaders studied there in the late '50s and early to mid-'60s.

Organizations and Groups

Berkeley Free Speech Movement (FSM). Lead by Mario Savio, the FSM arose in the wake of a campus-wide protest against limitations on student activism in fall 1964.

Brotherhood of Eternal Love. Led by an ex-biker acid mystic named John Griggs, the Brotherhood promoted LSD use as a cure for social evils rather than as a profit-making enterprise.

Diggers, The. Psychedelic, anarchist, nonideological group famous for its spontaneous, unscripted, see-what-happens, invent-it-as-you-go street theater.

Family Dog. Arising out of the ashes of the Red Dog Saloon, an early promoter of psychedelic rock concerts and performances.

Hells Angels. Anarchist biker group that was invited by Ken Kesey to participate in his acid tests; later they gained notoriety when they were hired to be the "security" force at the Rolling Stones' free concert at Altamont.

International Federation for Internal Freedom (IFIF). Nonprofit group established by Timothy Leary in early 1963 to promote the principle that everyone should have unlimited freedom to use mind-altering chemicals as a tool for enhancing inner growth.

Merry Pranksters. Group led by Ken Kesey that began as a summer vacation lark in 1964, riding a converted school bus across the country while participating in various "pranks" to tweak "straight society."

San Francisco Mime Troupe. Early experimental theater troupe founded by Ronnie Davis and at one point managed and promoted by Bill Graham.

SLATE. Founded circa 1957 at UC Berkeley as a means for nonfraternity members to run for student government posts, it became a force for change on campus, leading to the Free Speech Movement.

Warlocks, The. Original name of the rock group that became the Grateful Dead.

Notes

Chapter 1

1. Isn't it essentially the purpose of ingesting alcohol—or of smoking marijuana—to induce a kind of holiday from workaday reality? Doesn't the near-universal popularity of alcohol throughout history in festive and leisure situations reside precisely in the "holiday" provided by its consciousness-altering propensity?

2. Rinkel would later work closely with the CIA in his drug studies and experiments.

Chapter 3

1. Another fortuitous connection: When in 1968, the Yippies made plans to "bomb" the Pentagon with 10,000 daisies concurrent with the "exorcism" of the Pentagon masterminded by the New York–based band the Fugs, it was Peggy Hitchcock who fronted the money for it. The plan, though, fizzled because the FBI spotted an ad in the *East Village Other* soliciting a pilot to do the "bombing," answered it themselves, got the gig, and then never showed up at the airport. The Yippies were left flat-footed pranked, so Michael Bowen piled as many daisies as he could into his car, hauled them back to DC, and distributed them to demonstrators. It was these daisies that you see in the photographs of demonstrators putting flowers into the bayoneted rifle barrels of soldiers guarding the Pentagon.

Chapter 4

1. *One Flew over the Cuckoo's Nest* was Kesey's fourth novel. The first three, none of which were ever published, were *The End of Autumn, The First Sunday of September,* and *Zoo.*

2. In the nineteenth-century gold rush days, Central City—a mining town in the same vein as Virginia City in Nevada—started an opera house, and it had been revived in the twentieth century, bringing in members of the Metropolitan Opera to perform full-blown operas each summer. It was one of the major social events of the metropolitan Denver area at the time. One of the big events in *On the Road* involved a trip to Central City to see the opera, Beethoven's *Fidelio,* do the bars, and throw a party in an abandoned shack.

3. Footage of this trip is available through a video offered by KZ Productions in Pleasant Hill, Oregon (85282 Nestle Way; 541-484-4315). KZ Productions also sells books, records, videos, CDs, tapes, posters, and various other memorabilia that involve Merry Prankster and Haight-Ashbury activities, lore, and iconography.

4. McMurtry and Kesey were classmates at the Stanford Writing Program, and McMurtry's western novel *Horseman, Pass By* (1961) was the basis for the movie *Hud* (1963), which was playing in movie theaters at the time of this trip.

5. Kesey coined the term *acid,* which the Leary circle initially abhorred as sacrilegious and trivializing.

Chapter 5

1. It is fascinating to note that a large percentage of both SLATE and the FSM leadership were secular Jews. They contributed a certain style and flair to the more political wing of the counterculture—including the civil rights and antiwar movements—that was irreverent, playful, satirical, confronting, aggressive, and disdainful of authority. Jerry Rubin and Abbie Hoffman were perfect examples, and it was this style that characterized the Diggers and Yippies.

Chapter 7

1. *Chronicle* columnist Herb Caen coined the term *beatnik* in a piece that appeared in the *San Francisco Chronicle* on April 2, 1958. He used it to describe the bohemian coterie of artists, painters, musicians, and poets congregating in North Beach's coffeehouses, bars, jazz dives, and spaghetti dens. They were beatniks, à la Caen, because they took their cues from the Beats and were as "far out" as the recent Russian satellite, Sputnik. Caen held that things had degenerated in North Beach to the sorry state where the odor of wafting marijuana was overpowering the usual stench of garlic.

Chapter 8

1. Offstage would later be site of one of the acid tests. Both the venue and this acid test are described at some length in the "Cassady Issue" of Kesey's literary journal, *Spit in the Ocean,* no. 6, January 1, 1981, 224.

2. Among Wilson's finest work are the Grateful Dead, November 18–19 at the Fillmore; the "Purple Lady," the Grateful Dead and Big Mama Thornton at the Fillmore West, December 9–11; the Grateful Dead, Junior Wells, the Doors at the Fillmore, January 13–14; and the Jefferson Airplane and Big Brother "Tribal Stomp" show, February 19 at the Avalon.

3. Among the premier Mouse/Kelly collaborations are the Zig Zag emblem promoting a Big Brother/Quicksilver concert and the Grateful Dead skull and roses poster.

4. Among Griffin's best work is the "surfing eyeball" advertising Jimi Hendrix/John Mayall/Albert King; the Grateful Dead Aoxomoxoa album cover; Iron Butterfly/Buddy Miles at Winterland, August 10–12; the oversized "Bloom" poster for the Fillmore West, August 16–18 and 22–25; and Quicksilver Messenger Service/Kaleidoscope at the Avalon, January 13–15.

Bibliography

Amburn, Ellis. *Subterranean Kerouac: The Hidden Life of Jack Kerouac*. New York: St. Martin's Press, 1998.

Anderson, Chester. "The Seed," posted on Babcock, Jay. " 'The Revolution is the highest kind of fun': Chester Anderson on the Diggers and the communication company." Diggers Doc website, posted 6/12/2020. https://diggersdocshome. files.wordpress.com/2020/06/chesterseed1.pdf.

Anthony, Gene. *The Summer of Love: Haight Ashbury at Its Highest*. Millbrae. CA: Celestial Arts, 1980.

Anthony, Gene. *Magic of the Sixties*. New York: Gibbs Smith, 2004.

Babcock, Jay. "A Guiding Vision: A Conversation with Peter Berg of the San Francisco Diggers." *Digger Docs*, September 16, 2020. https://diggersdocs.home. blog/2020/09/16/peter-berg-of-the-san-francisco-diggers/.

Babcock, Jay. " 'I Lucked Out So Many Times, Man': Claude Hayward on His Life before, during and after His Time with the San Francisco Diggers." *Diggers Docs*, October 2, 2021. https://diggersdocs.home.blog/tag/claude-hayward/.

Bai, Nina. "Born in Summer of Love: The Haight Ashbury Free Clinic Transformed Drug Addiction Treatment." *UCSF News*, June 7, 2017. https://summerof. love/born-summer-love-haight-ashbury-free-clinic-transformed-drug-addiction-treatment/.

Burleigh, Nina. "A Tropical Retreat with a Psychedelic History." *New York Times*, May 9, 2022, B5.

Burroughs, William, and Allen Ginsberg. *The Yage Letters*. San Francisco: City Lights Books, 1963.

Charters, Ann. *Kerouac: A Biography*. New York: St. Martin's Press, 2015.

Campbell, Robert. "The Chemistry of Madness." *Life*, November 26, 1971.

Daloz, Kate. "The Hippies Who Hated the Summer of Love." *Longreads*, August 2017. https://longreads.com/2017/08/07/the-hippies-who-hated-the-summer-of-love/.

DeCurtis, Anthony. "The Musing Never Stops." *Rolling Stone*, September 2, 1993, 45.

Derogatis, Jim. *Turn On Your Mind: Four Decades of Great Psychedelic Rock*. Milwaukee. WI: Hal Leonard, 2003.

"A Digger Manifesto." *Berkeley Barb*, August 18, 1967. Posted July 14, 2020. https://www.diggers.org/mutants.html.

Drucker, Joel. "It's Only Rock & Roll, But I'll Buy It: Rock Posters from the Psychedelic '60s." *Cigar Aficionado*, July/August 1997. https://www.cigaraficionado.com/article/its-only-rock-roll-but-ill-buy-it-7519.

Eberhart, Richard. "West Coast Rhythms." *New York Times Book Review*, September 2, 1956.

Echols, Alice. *Scars of Sweet Paradise: The Life and Times of Janis Joplin*. New York: Metropolitan Books, 1999.

Ellis, Henry Havelock. "Mescal: A New Artificial Paradise." *Contemporary Review* 73 (January 1898): 130–141.

Fahey, Todd. "Al Hubbard: The Original Captain Trips," *High Times*, November 1991. Reprinted in https://www.trippingly.net/lsd-studies/2018/5/20/al-hubbard-the-original-captain-trips.

Flanagan, S. "The Untold Truth of the Merry Pranksters." July 30, 2021. http://www.grunge.com/53425/untold-truth-project-mkultra/.

Genzlinger, Neil. "Robert Hunter, Grateful Dead Lyricist with a Long, Strange Career, Dies at 78." *New York Times*, September 25, 2019, A23.

Gleason, Ralph. "On the Town." *San Francisco Chronicle*, January 24, 1966. http://deadsources.blogspot.com/2013/02/january-1966-san-francisco-acid-tests.html.

Gleason, Ralph. *The Jefferson Airplane and the San Francisco Sound*. New York: Ballantine Books, 1969.

Goines, David Lance. *The Free Speech Movement: Coming of Age in the 1960s*. Berkeley, CA: Ten Speed Press, 1993.

Goldberg, Michael. "The San Francisco Sound." *Rolling Stone*, August 23, 1989, 95.

Graham, Bill. *Bill Graham Presents: My Life Inside Rock and Out*. New York: Doubleday, 1992.

Greenfield, Robert. *Dark Star: An Oral Biography of Jerry Garcia*. New York: Broadway Books, 1997.

Groth, Gary. "An Interview with Victor Moscoso." *The Comics Journal*, February 9, 2011. https://www.tcj.com/an-interview-with-victor-moscoso/.

Grushkin, Paul. *The Art of Rock: Posters from Presley to Punk*. New York: Abbeville Press, 1987.

Gustatis, Rasa. *Turning On*. New York: Signet Books, 1969.

Harrison, Hank. *The Dead Book: A Social History of the Haight-Ashbury Experience*. San Francisco: Archives Press, 1986.

Hartogsohn, Ido. *American Trip: Set, Setting and the Psychedelic Experience*. Cambridge, MA: MIT Press, 2020.

Hawes, Hampton. *Raise Up Off Me: A Portrait of Hampton Hawes*. New York: Coward, McCann & Geoghegan, 1974.

Henke, James, ed. *I Want to Take You Higher: The Psychedelic Era, 1965–1969*. San Francisco: Chronicle Books, 1997.

Hofmann, Albert. *LSD: My Problem Child*. New York: McGraw Hill, 1980.

Hollingshead, Michael. *The Man Who Turned On the World*. New York: Abelard-Schuman, 1973.

Hoskyns, Barney. *Beneath the Diamond Sky: Haight-Asbury, 1965–1970*. New York: Simon & Schuster, 1997.

Huxley, Aldous. *The Doors of Perception*. London: Chatto & Windus, 1954.

"The Invisible Circus." Digger Archives, February 24–27, 1967. https://www.diggers.org/diggers/incircus.html.

James, William. *Varieties of Religious Experience: A Study in Human Nature*. London: Longman, Green, 1902.

James, William. *Pragmatism*. London: Longmans, Green, 1907.

James, William. "On a Certain Blindness in Human Beings." In *On Some of Life's Ideals: On a Certain Blindness in Human Beings, What Makes a Life Significant*. New York: Henry Holt, 1913.

Kerouac, Jack. *On the Road*. New York: Viking Press, 1957.

Kerouac, Jack. *Visions of Cody*. New York: McGraw Hill, 1972.

Kesey, Ken. *Kesey's Garage Sale*. New York: Viking Press, 1973.

Kesey, Ken. *Ken Kesey: The Further Inquiry*. New York: Viking Press, 1990.

Krieger, Susan. *Hip Capitalism*. Beverly Hills, CA: Sage, 1979.

Leary, Timothy. *High Priest*. New York: World, 1968.

Leary, Timothy. *Flashbacks: A Personal and Cultural History of an Era*. Los Angeles: J. P. Tarcher, 1990.

Leary, Timothy. *The Politics of Self-Determination*. Berkeley, CA: Ronin, 2000.

Lee, Martin, and Bruce Shlain. *Acid Dreams: The Complete Social History of LSD*. New York: Grove, 1994.

Myers, Marc. "She Went Chasing Rabbits: Interview with Grace Slick." *Wall Street Journal*, April 29, 2011. https://www.wsj.com/articles/SB10001424052748703778104576287303493094530.

Newman, Jason. "The Untold and Deeply Stoned Story of the First U.S. Rock Festival." *Rolling Stone*, June 17, 2014. https://www.rollingstone.com/feature/the-untold-and-deeply-stoned-story-of-the-first-u-s-rock-festival-124437/.

Ortega, Tony. "Ken Kesey Reappears, Is Busted," *Village Voice*, October 27, 1966, n.p.

Pearlman, David. "Haight-Ashbury Free Clinic." *San Francisco Chronicle*, March 10, 2017. https://www.sfchronicle.com/entertainment/article/Haight-Ashbury-Free-Clinic-as-it-was-described-10987562.php.

Perry, Charles. "What a Long Strange Trip It's Been." *Rolling Stone*, February 26, 1976.

Perry, Charles. *The Haight-Ashbury: A History*. New York: Random House, 1984.

"Ralph 'Sonny' Barger" Confronts the VDC/ Press Conference." *Bay Area Television Archives*. https://diva.sfsu.edu/collections/sfbatv/bundles/225552.

Reynolds, Frank, with Michael McClure. *Freewheelin' Frank: Secretary of the Angels*. New York: Grove Press, 1967.

Schumacher, Michael. *Dharma Lion: A Biography of Allen Ginsberg*. New York: St. Martin's Press, 1992.

Schwartz, Deborah. "David Freiberg Interview." Mill Valley Oral History Program, Mill Valley Public Library, 2019. http://ppolinks.com/mvpl39241/2019_013_001_FreibergDavid_OralHistoryTranscript.pdf.

Scully, Rock, and David Dalton. *Living with the Dead: Twenty Years on the Bus with Garcia and the Grateful Dead.* Boston: Little, Brown, 1996.

Silos, Jill Katherine. " 'Everybody Get Together': The Sixties Counterculture and Public Space, 1964–1967." May 2003. Ph.D. dissertation, University of New Hampshire.

Slick, Grace, with Andrea Cagan. *Somebody to Love?: A Rock-and-Roll Memoir.* New York: Warner Books, 1998.

Spider Magazine. "William Mandel vs HUAC, San Francisco 1960." https://oac.cdlib.org/view?docId=kt8489n9b1&chunk.id=d0e196&brand=calisphere&doc.view=entire_text.

Stevens, Jay. *Storming Heaven: LSD and the American Dream.* New York: Atlantic Monthly Press, 1987.

Stevenson, Robert Louis. "The Lantern Bearers." In *The Lantern Bearers and Other Essays,* sel. with an intro. by Jeremy Treglown. New York: Farrar Straus Giroux, 1988.

Swanston, David. "Angels Join Hippies for a Party." *San Francisco Chronicle*, January 2, 1967, 1.

Szatmary, David. *Rockin' in Time: A Social History of Rock 'n' Roll.* Hoboken, NJ: Pearson, 2019.

Thompson, Hunter S. *Hell's Angels: The Strange and Terrible Saga of the Outlaw Motorcycle Gangs.* New York: Random House, 1967.

Thompson, Hunter S. "The Hippies" (May 1967), +DISTRITO47+, February 3, 2014. https://distrito47.wordpress.com/2014/02/03/the-hippies-by-hunter-s-thompson.

Thompson, Hunter S. *Proud Highway: Saga of a Desperate Southern Gentleman, 1955–1967.* New York: Villard, 1997.

Troy, Sandy. *One More Saturday Night: Reflections with the Grateful Dead, Dead Family, and Dead Heads.* New York: St. Martin's Press, 1991.

Troy, Sandy. *Captain Trips: A Biography of Jerry Garcia.* New York: Thunder's Mouth Press, 1994.

Turner, Steve. *Angelheaded Hipster: A Biography of Jack Kerouac.* New York: Viking Press, 1996.

Unterberger, Richie, transcript interview of Chris Darrow. April 13, 1999. http://www.richieunterberger.com/darrow.html.

Unterberger, Richie. *Eight Miles High: Folk-Rock's Flight from Haight-Ashbury to Woodstock.* San Francisco: Backbeat Books, 2003.

Vassi, Marco. *The Stoned Apocalypse.* New York: Trident Press, 1972.

Vila, Benito. "Merry Prankster George Walker's Tales of Dropping Acid with Kesey and Traveling with Neal Cassady on Further." May 9, 2018. https://pleasekillsme.com/George-walker-merry-prankster.

Wasson, R. Gordon. "Seeking the Magic Mushroom." *Life*, May 13, 1957, 107–120.

Watrous, Peter. "Touch of Gray Matter." *Musician*, December 1989, 42.

Watts, Alan. *The Joyous Cosmology: Adventures in the Chemistry of Consciousness*. New York: Pantheon Books, 1962.

Wenner, Jann. *Rolling Stone*, November 9, 1967, 2.

Whitmer, Peter. *Aquarius Revisited: Seven Who Created the Sixties Counterculture*. New York: Citadel Press, 1987.

Winter, Jerrold. *Our Love Affair with Drugs: The History, the Science and the Politics*. New York: Oxford University Press, 2019.

Wolfe, Burton. *The Hippies*. New York: New American Library, 1968.

Wolfe, Tom. *The Electric Kool-Aid Acid Test*. New York: Farrar, Straus and Giroux, 1968.

"Words of Freedom." *Berkeley News*, September 30, 2014. https://news.berkeley.edu/2014/09/30/words-of-freedom-video-made-from-mario-savios-1964-machine-speech/#:~:text=%E2%80%9CThere%20is%20a%20time%20when,got%20to%20make%20it%20stop.

Index

Helms, Chet, 101, 120, 128, 134, 135, 141–43, 144, 158–64, 166–67, 169, 170, 185–86, 200–201, 211, 215
Hendrix, Jimi, 186, 188, 201
Hesse, Hermann, 10, 23, 45, 70
Hicks, Dan, 99
Hilyard, Roger, 166
Hippie Hill, 201–202
Hitchcock, Billy, 49, 50, 81, 82–83, 215
Hitchcock, Peggy, 44, 49, 215, 221
Hofmann, Albert, 3–5, 215
Hoffman, Abbie, 222
Hollingshead, Michael, 42, 50
Hollingsworth, Ambrose, 146
Holmes, Oliver Wendell, 8
Hoover, J. Edgar, 87, 191
Hubbard, Captain Al, 23–25, 35, 40, 46, 48, 215
Hubbard, L. Ron, 181
Hugo, Victor, 7
Hulme, T. E., 207
Human Be-In, 170, 180–81
Hunter, George, 98–99, 157, 215
Hunter, Robert, 35, 65, 187
Huxley, Aldous, 8, 9, 11, 13, 15, 17–22, 24–25, 27, 28, 39, 40, 42, 45, 47, 48, 55, 195, 210, 215
Hyde, Robert, 16

International Federation for Internal Freedom, 47, 220
Inaba, Darryl, 197
Isherwood, Christopher, 27, 28
Iturbi, José, 145

Jacopetti, Ben, 116, 131, 203
Jacopetti, Rain, 116, 203
James, William, 6, 7, 8, 12, 14, 207–208, 209

Jazz Mice, 116
Jefferson Airplane, 81, 108, 124, 125, 126, 128, 135, 139, 142, 148–52, 156, 157, 158, 182, 183, 186, 187, 188, 201, 213, 219
Johnson, President Lyndon, 124, 148
Jook Savages, 170
Joplin, Janis, 89, 100, 120, 141–42, 144–45, 148, 153, 160, 162, 184, 186, 189, 200, 206, 215

Kaleidoscope, 155, 165
Kandel, Lenore, 181, 182
Kantner, Paul, 89, 145, 150, 152, 153, 163, 167
Kaukonen, Jorma, 65, 89, 141, 150–51, 153, 163, 184
Kaufman, Denise "Mary Microgram," 73
Kelly, Alton, 100, 120, 121, 134, 156, 169–70, 223
Kerouac, Jack, 12, 42, 51, 53, 54, 56, 66, 67–68, 72, 122, 123
Kerr, Clark, 87, 95
Kesey, Ken, 3, 15, 21, 41, 57, 61–69, 70–77, 85, 89, 101, 102, 104–107, 110, 112, 116, 117, 127, 130, 132, 135, 161–62, 180, 191–93, 205, 214, 218, 219, 220, 221, 222
King, Martin Luther, Jr., 95
Klein, Franz, 56
Klein, Herbert, 32
Kleps, Art, 50, 82
KMPX, 189–90, 200, 217
Knight Riders, 103
Korzybski, Alfred, 6
Krassner, Paul, 50
Kreutzmann, Bill, 153–54
Krug, Peter, 203

Laing, R. D., 50
Lamantia, Philip, 89, 122